THE Only TEXAS ★ COOKBOOK

THE Only TEXAS ★ COOKBOOK

by
Linda West Eckhardt

Texas Monthly Press

Information concerning sourdough, chicken-fried steak, and son-of-a-bitch stew is from *Come an' Get It: The Story of the Old Cowboy Cook* by Ramon F. Adams. Copyright © 1952 by The University of Oklahoma Press.

The poem "Bob Sears' Chili Joint" is from *That Spotted Sow and Other Texas Hill Country Ballads* published by Shoal Creek Publishers, Inc. Copyright © 1975 by Carlos Ashley, Sr. Reprinted by permission.

Portions of recipes from game birds are from "Waterfowler's Woman" and "Wild Turkey and How to Cook It" by Linda West Eckhardt and originally appeared in *Field & Stream*. Copyright © 1973 and 1977.

The recipe "Bass Acuna" by Linda West Eckhardt is from *Ford Times*. Copyright © 1976. Reprinted by permission.

The recipes "Sourdough Starter," "Sourdough Biscuits," and "Sourdough Bread" are from the *Fort Worth Star-Telegram*. Copyright © 1968.

The recipes "Fig Conserve" by Marion Orgain and "Breaux Bridge Secret Gumbo" by David Whittaker originally appeared in a column by Ann Criswell in *The Houston Chronicle. Copyright* © 1968. Reprinted by permission.

The recipe "Fresh Mushroom Salad" by Julia Wallace is from the *Houston Junior League Cookbook*. Copyright © 1975 by the Houston Junior League. Reprinted by permission.

The recipe "Lela's Special Cobbler" is from *100 Years of Jowell Cookery*. Copyright © 1975 by Carmine Jowell Neely. Reprinted by permission.

The recipe "Sopa De Flor De Calabaza (Squash Flower Soup)" is from *Fiesta*. Copyright © 1973 by the Corpus Christi Junior League. Reprinted by permission.

Texas Monthly Press, Inc.
P.O. Box 1569
Austin, Texas 78767

A B C D E F G H

The Only Texas cookbook.

Includes index.
1. Cookery, American—Texas. I. Eckhardt, Linda West, 1939–
TX715.0534   641.59764   81-8814
ISBN 0-932012-19-1   AACR2

Book Design by Janice Ashford
Production by The Composing Stick
Typesetting by G & S Typesetters

Dedicated to Joe, Katherine,
Mark and Jay
who ate up the research

CONTENTS

FOREWORD

A book like this is not written from front to back but rather is pieced together like a quilt. The first words you read represent the very last piece sewn in to complete the design.

And what you have before you is a giant Lone Star. I can run my hand over it now and see that all the tiny pieces finally fit together into this patchwork that is Texas. There are bits of homespun and scraps of silk. There are rich scraps of hand-woven tapestries and ragged squares from old flour sacks. There are brilliant velvets and faded chintz. Rough textures and smooth ones. Some of the pieces have the scent of old trunks and others the smell of new sizing. The book, whose great swirling pattern seems all of a piece, could never have been completed without the addition of each small, important piece.

This cookbook can be your source for recipes that have pre-viously been held in flour-dusted tin boxes. There are German cakes and Texas tamales. Barbecue and chili. There are Texas Czech wild berry pies and Cajun sauces *piquantes*. Game reci-pes and sausages. The Texas food heritage is broad and it is deep. This book attempts to tap its sources. Some of the recipes are easy, and require only a spare moment and the simplest of ingredients. Others are complicated and demand patience, and even a special trip to the grocery store.

It has been a great adventure trying to fit all the pieces into a sensible ordered whole. I have gathered the recipes from all over the state, from young cooks and old cooks, from professionals and dedicated amateurs. I wish I had time to spin out the story behind each recipe, the fragment of history that goes without saying.

As the quiltmaker, I run my hand over the finished surface and pause here and there and remember the source for each piece. I remember how my heart pumped when I got the little precious scrap the neighbors said she'd never share. And I can remember how I felt when the old lady gave me a shoebox full, saying she was too old to need it so I might as well have the whole box. I wish you could know each piece as intimately as I know it.

I have come to see recipes as a window through which one can learn something about a people. You can learn who is generous and who is parsimonious. You can learn who has patience and who has little time. I'd swear you can almost tell who is skinny and who is fat—just by looking through a personal recipe box.

I have learned something about Texans that I already knew, but it has been reinforced during the long period of research for this book. Texans, whether they be of Scotch-Irish descent, or German, or Mexican, or Cajun, have melded into a generous open-handed people who always have room for one more at the table.

And to return to the analogy of the quilt one last time, the pieces have just passed through my hands. A great deal of trial-and-error work went into every piece before I got it, and even more work followed.

I thought you might be interested in how the process worked. I collected these recipes over several years when I was writing magazine pieces for *Texas Monthly* and other national magazines. After a final month-long sweep through the state, I came home and began sorting and stacking the recipes by category. I tried always for the best representation of the art as I found it.

For months the pots and pans flew. My daughter made numberless trips to the grocery store. My sons washed a million dishes. My husband had to have the button on his pants set over. We cooked and ate and criticized.

Some recipes were musts. Some just wouldn't work at all. But as we in the family accepted a piece, I typed it up; and, every Friday, I sent a batch to the *Texas Monthly* office, where some blessed volunteers rifled through the pages, took the recipes home, and tried them once again. Barbara Reavis, my editor, devised an evaluation sheet, and every recipe received written comments from the testers in Austin as well as the people who ate the results.

Again, some of the recipes got rave reviews, some were seen as pedestrian, and a few just wouldn't translate. We winnowed and refined the choices again.

So what you have before you is an effort by a large group of cooks to show you what is Texas. Sources for recipes are indicated; where no name appears, the recipe is my own.

But this doesn't necessarily mean that the person who gave me the recipe invented it. There really is no ownership to recipes. Each one of us starts from something; our own heritage, our habits, the limitations of the larder. We build on a base and come up with a concoction that we hope will work.

The variations on a theme are endless and that's what makes the art fascinating. I hope that you'll begin to make these recipes your own in the way that every good cook does. Open the book and lay a pen in the fold. As you cook and taste and criticize, mark your comments and changes right in the book. And write who came to dinner and the funny things the kids said and who washed the dishes.

And after a few years it won't be my book anymore, or the *Texas Monthly* staff's book; but it will be your book written by you and so valuable your grandchildren will fight over it. You can pass on a piece of your own history to those who follow in your own family. ¡Salud!

Linda West Eckhardt
Menlo Park, California
January, 1981

ACKNOWLEDGEMENTS

I would like to thank all the cooks in Texas who shared their knowledge of Texas cuisine and Texas culture. I could never have written the book without them.

In particular I wish to thank Shirley Barr, Peggy Vineyard, and Anna Kay Brewer for steering me to sources I could never have found on my own.

I also learned a lot about Texas cuisine from certain professional food purveyors. John Casey, Bobbie Covey, Martha Johnson, Martha Kavanaugh, and Patricia Slate all shared with me their experience as Texas restaurant operators. Thanks also to the Texas Restaurant Association for its kind cooperation.

I owe a huge debt to the *Texas Monthly* staff members who cross-tested the recipes. And of course to my editor, Barbara Reavis (second only to Ezra Pound in editing expertise) and my typist, Loretta Olson: there would be no book without them. I especially thank my mother, Bessie Lee Wood, who did such a good job on the index that she should go into the business.

Thanks to expert readers Marsha Berkman and Bob Casey, who helped clean up fuzzy prose and fuzzy thinking. Thanks to Susan Dondershine for help with the title. She knew what was essential.

Last I thank my husband and children. They didn't throw me out during the long months when I ran the kitchen like a chemistry lab, refused to speak to anyone, and waved a butcher knife at any poor hapless soul who asked for help with his homework. My family became my severest critics. (I'm thinking of farming out the oldest ones to do restaurant reviews.)

Writing a cookbook is a job that requires many people. It is horrible. It is wonderful. I loved every minute of it. Thank you for reading *The Only Texas Cookbook*.

Hot Black-eyed Pea Dip
Parched Pecans
Fried Camembert
Jalapeño Pie
Hot Artichoke Dip
Spiced Pecans
Pepitas
Bar Stool Black Olives
Shrimp Spread
Tomato and Green Chile Spread
Favorite Sandwich
Texas Sandwich
French Taco
Si's Delt Bloody Mary
Champurrado
Margaritas
Tequila Mockingbird
Tequila Sunrise Punch

I suppose this chapter might ordinarily be called "Hors d'oeuvres," except that the term has a whiff of meaning that I don't intend. In the American Heritage dictionary it is defined as an appetizer or canapé served with cocktails or before a meal. A literal translation from the French means "outside of work." Anyone who has ever prepared canapés knows full well that they can involve more work per bite than almost any other category of food. And the idea that this outside-of-work tidbit (or "titbit," as Elizabeth David says) should be served before a main meal bothers me immensely.

If I have really turned to and cooked a good meal for friends, I don't want to take the edge off their appetites by having them consume hors d'oeuvres in the living room. If I am having friends in for dinner, the focus of the party is the table. I intend for guests to spend most of the time in my house around that table. I want the magic to take place. You know the magic I mean: the wonder of a circle of 6 or so people who may or may not know each other, who sit together over candlelight and excruciatingly good food and wine and, for a moment, experience communion.

The magic is a delicate thing. If people wolf down too much pâté in the living room or drink too many martinis, I can never get the magic to work. So I try to keep them edgy and hungry in the living room. I never mind letting them wait a good half hour. I tantalize them with good smells and perhaps only a sliver of some fine cheese.

When I call them to table, everything is in place: hot smoking dishes that smell so good you would die for them, always candles, lots of dishes and glasses (none of which match), a well-starched tablecloth and napkins, cold water and the right wine, hot bread and real butter. The main impression is one of abundance. After all, it is a celebration, a feast if you will. I want my dinner guests to be overwhelmed. If I have conjured properly and all the elements are right, the spell will work. They'll come away from the table knowing they've had a mystical experience. Food can do that.

But there is another kind of magic one can work with food, and that magic depends on food one can eat out of hand. Mystifying 6 people around a table is like pulling a rabbit out of a hat. Mystifying 40 people is more like getting the Astrodome to levitate. But it can be done. And again food is at the heart of it.

I think one of the secrets to working magic with a large group of people is—again—abundance. Just cover about every square inch of your dining room table with various and sundry out-of-hand foods. Some hot and some cold. Some crunchy and some soft. Spicy and mild. Shoot for variety, an endless supply, flavors that complement, and you will probably work your magic on a whole group.

You can keep a party moving by placing the foods in several locations and keeping the liquor separate from all the food spots. Invite enough people so they are almost shoulder to shoulder. They move around. They are excited by the food and drink and close quarters. All the elements are right. The magic works.

Here are some recipes that you can try for parties. But don't forget other categories when planning a party table. For example, smoked venison—cut wafer-thin and served with hot sweet mustard and whole wheat bread—is wonderful and very Texas. If it's a holiday, have small slivers of pecan pie or **Fruitcake for People Who Hate Fruitcake.**

HOT BLACK-EYED PEA DIP
Paula Griffey

Every budding cook has a cookbook that serves as a bible. For me it was Helen Corbitt's first one. When I was studying home economics at the University of Texas, Corbitt's name was always mentioned in the most reverent tones. After I had lived with her book awhile, I decided my profs were right. You can't beat her meatless spaghetti sauce or her hollandaise. I've had people almost fall to their knees over Prairie Fire (basically mashed pinto beans with cheese), and in Texas she was the originator of Poppyseed Dressing as well as Canadian Cheese Soup. I always thought her pickled black-eyed peas were as necessary to a celebration of New Year's Day as a turkey for Christmas dinner. But I do believe Paula Griffey has almost matched her. Here is a delicious way to assure good luck all year by eating black-eyed peas on New Year's Day.

½ bell pepper, chopped fine
2 stalks celery, chopped fine
1 onion, chopped fine
1 tsp. black pepper
2 tbsp. Tabasco sauce (This amount makes a very hot product—start out with 1 tablespoon and taste)
½ cup catsup
1 tbsp. salt
3 chicken bouillon cubes

¼ tsp. nutmeg
½ tsp. cinnamon
2 15-oz. cans black-eyed peas (one of these cans must be Trappey's with jalapeño)
1 15-oz. can Ro-Tel tomatoes
1 clove garlic, pressed
1 tsp. sugar
½ cup bacon drippings
3 tbsp. flour

In a medium saucepan combine the bell pepper, celery, onion, black pepper, Tabasco, catsup, salt, bouillon cubes, nutmeg, and cinnamon. Over low heat cook and stir until it reaches a boil and the cubes have completely dissolved. Now add peas and tomatoes, garlic and sugar. Simmer for 30 minutes. Combine bacon drippings with flour and stir into peas. Cook 10 minutes more. Stir well and serve hot with plenty of corn chips for dips.

PARCHED PECANS
Nona Morriss

1 lb. pecan halves
½ lb. melted butter

Salt

Preheat oven to 250°. Place pecans one layer deep on a cookie sheet with sides. Salt pecans to taste and pour on melted butter. Bake until evenly browned (about 20–30 minutes). Stir every 3 or 4 minutes because they burn easily. Store in a tin.

FRIED CAMEMBERT

Peggy Karren

Only a Texan would fry French cheese.

1 6-inch round Camembert, medium soft, not too ripe	1 cup fresh bread crumbs
1 egg, beaten	4 tbsp. unsalted butter
	½ cup chopped green onion tops

Dip the unskinned cheese round in egg and then coat both sides with bread crumbs. Heat 2 tablespoons of butter until it starts to brown. Over high heat brown cheese round on both sides. Remove to a heated serving plate and keep warm. Add remaining butter to skillet. When foamy, sauté the onions for 2 minutes. Pour over top of cheese and serve immediately with water biscuits.

JALAPEÑO PIE

I have known people to go hog-wild for a little piece of Jalapeño Pie.

2 cups sharp Cheddar cheese, grated (about 6 oz.)	Jalapeños, seeded and cut in strips (preferably fresh, but you may use canned)
6 eggs, beaten until slightly frothy	

Lightly oil a pie tin. Place cheese in tin. Arrange jalapeños to taste over the cheese. Beat eggs and pour over cheese. Bake 45 minutes at 275°. Serve in pie wedges while warm.

HOT ARTICHOKE DIP

1 14-oz. can artichoke hearts, drained	2 jalapeños, seeded
¼ cup mayonnaise	3 dashes Tabasco sauce
Dash salt	Juice of ¼ lemon
	1 tbsp. olive oil

Combine all ingredients in blender or processor and blend until smooth. This is best served in a cooked and trimmed artichoke: place a clear glass bowl down in the middle of the vegetable, spread apart the leaves, and fill the bowl with dip.

SPICED PECANS

1 egg white
1 tbsp. water
3 cups Texas pecan halves
½ cup sugar

½ tsp. salt
1 tsp. cinnamon
¼ tsp. cloves
¼ tsp. nutmeg

Combine egg white and water. Stir in pecans and coat all surfaces. Combine remaining ingredients and sprinkle over pecans. Spread on well-buttered cookie sheet and bake at 300° for 30 minutes, stirring 2 or 3 times.

PEPITAS

Long before we knew *pepitas* as a Mexican delicacy, we were toasting leftover pumpkin seeds in the oven the day after Halloween. I think we figured it out from one of my second grader's friends. Our way of making this snack is a perversion of the Mexican way. In Mexico the raw unhulled pumpkin seeds are placed on a *comal* (those expanded metal rectangles with a handle that you can buy in border shops) and heated over a direct flame, being turned constantly to prevent burning. Our way is easier because we're not as expert as the Mexican cooks. *Pepitas* made the Texas way can be accomplished by grade school children who like to cook and eat them.

After scooping seeds from a pumpkin—as in making jack-o'-lanterns—spread the seeds out on a dry cookie sheet. Pick out as much of the white membrane as possible and spread the seeds so that they are only a single layer deep. They will be slightly damp. If you wish you can sprinkle them with salt, plain or seasoned. You can also brush them with a little melted butter. Bake the seeds in a 300° oven, turning and stirring every 5 minutes until they become a nice chestnut color. It will take the seeds 15 or 20 minutes to brown depending on how wet they are when you put them in the oven.

BAR STOOL BLACK OLIVES
Anna Kay Brewer

Black olives
Tabasco sauce

Drain a large can of unpitted black olives. Place olives in small glasses—something attractive and easy to get your hand into, like a champagne glass. Shake Tabasco over olives. Marinate at room temperature at least 1 hour before serving. Serve with **Parched Pecans** for the cocktail hour or buffet.

SHRIMP SPREAD

1 cup cooked chopped shrimp
2 cups grated sharp Cheddar cheese
6 small green onions and tops, chopped

½ cup *Homemade Mayonnaise*
1 clove garlic, pressed
Hungarian paprika to taste

Finely chop shrimp, cheese, and onions. Combine with remaining ingredients, sprinkle with paprika, and cover. Refrigerate at least 2 hours. Remove from refrigerator at least 30 minutes before you plan to serve it to allow flavors to ripen. Serve with fine crackers.

TOMATO AND GREEN CHILE SPREAD
Margaret Peavy Heisig

1 can Ro-Tel tomatoes and chiles
1 3-oz. package cream cheese, at room temperature

1 tbsp. grated white onion
Very thin sandwich bread
Mayonnaise

Drain thoroughly the can of tomatoes and finely dice any large pieces of tomato. Combine thoroughly with the softened cream cheese. Remove crusts from bread, dab on a thin layer of mayonnaise, then place a dollop of spread on each piece of bread.

FAVORITE SANDWICH
Betty Hunt

Serves 8

Here's a sandwich that comes out of the oven looking something like a pizza. Kids love it.

1 lb. Cheddar cheese	1 bell pepper, seeded
½ lb. uncooked bacon	Good bread
1 yellow onion, peeled	

Grind all ingredients except bread and mix together thoroughly. Using good bread for sandwiches (English muffin, sourdough, French, a hamburger bun in a pinch, or whatever is your own particular favorite—9-grain maybe), spread a thin layer of the cheese and bacon mixture on the bread. Run it under the broiler until cheese bubbles and browns. Serve open-faced.

This sandwich spread keeps in the refrigerator for 3 or 4 days and will freeze well for a couple of months.

TEXAS SANDWICH
El Metate Restaurant

Large flour tortillas	Guacamole
Mashed pinto beans (*refritos*), heated	Finely chopped onion
Thin slices of cooked brisket, heated	*Salsa Cruda*

Heat tortillas on a *comal* or griddle, then spread with thin layer of beans. Lay several slices of paper-thin brisket on one side of the tortilla, spread the meat slices with a layer of guacamole, top with chopped onion, and sprinkle with *salsa*. Fold tortilla and you have a true Texas Sandwich.

Here's the way Bobbie Covey at El Metate cooks a brisket. Rub an 8- or 10-pound lean brisket with a paste made from ½ teaspoon black pepper, ¼ teaspoon cumin, ¼ teaspoon salt, 3 tablespoons vinegar, and 1 teaspoon chile powder. (In Spanish, this is called *adobo*.) Wrap meat tightly in foil and bake in a 300° oven until fork-tender—about 3 hours. Cool and slice paper-thin.

FRENCH TACO

At The Store in Hunt, there used to be something you could order that wasn't on the menu. The cook called it a French Taco. She said her son invented and named it. Very simply, it is ¼ pound of hamburger meat shaped into a thick patty, seasoned with salt and pepper and grilled. Heat a large flour tortilla on a dry grill, then smear with a generous amount of mayonnaise, place the cooked meat patty on half of the tortilla and add the usual hamburger accoutrements—lettuce, thin-sliced tomato, and onion. Fold the flour tortilla over and you have a Texas hamburger better than McDonald's ever dreamed of. A French Taco. I think the cook finally relented and put it on the menu. But you can make it at home.

SI'S DELT BLOODY MARY

Silas B. Ragsdale

Serves about 24

1 48-oz. can V-8 juice	1 fistful of prepared horseradish
4 limes, squeezed	(squeeze out vinegar)
1 pint gin	Tabasco sauce to taste
1 heaping tsp. powdered sugar	Jalapeño slices
½ tsp. salt	Black pepper to sprinkle on top
1 tbsp. Worcestershire sauce	

Mix well and serve in 6–8-oz. glasses. Stick a fresh jalapeño slice on glass rim. Note: put ice in glasses, not in mix.

CHAMPURRADO

Serves 6

Christmas in San Antonio is a cultural mix drawing from Mexican, German, and Southern traditions. For many Texas Mexicans, no Christmas would be complete without *champurrado*, a hot drink that originated with the Indians of the Mexican peninsula. It is grainy, an acquired taste, but a vital part of a San Antonio-style holiday.

1 cup cornmeal or masa harina
1 cup water
1 cinnamon stick
6 cups milk
½ tsp. vanilla

1 cup sugar
Pinch salt
3 1-oz. squares unsweetened
    chocolate

Mix cornmeal and cold water until there are no lumps. Add cinnamon stick and bring to a boil over low heat, stirring frequently. Remove from heat. In another pan heat milk, vanilla, sugar, salt, and chocolate. Cook and stir until chocolate melts and the milk is just to the boiling point. Now combine with cornmeal mixture, stirring vigorously. Remove cinnamon stick and serve hot in cups.

MARGARITAS

Serves 10

Coarse or kosher salt
10 slices lime
Ice cubes

¾ cup fresh lime juice
¾ to 1 cup tequila
¾ cup Triple Sec liqueur

Chill 10 4-oz. cocktail glasses. Pour a generous amount of salt onto a saucer. Rub rim of glass with lime slice, then dip rim in salt. Combine remaining ingredients in a large cocktail shaker or pitcher with additional ice cubes. Shake or stir vigorously until well chilled. Strain into prepared glasses.

TEQUILA MOCKINGBIRD

If you are having a Tex Mex party and don't want your guests to get rip-roaring drunk, you can make this bastard Margarita punch.

1 part tequila
1 part freshly squeezed lime juice
1 part ginger ale

½ part Triple Sec
Coarse or kosher salt

Serve in a punch bowl with one large ice chunk. Using footed glasses, wipe rim with lime juice, then dip rim in salt (get that special margarita salt from the liquor store), and fill. Delicious.

TEQUILA SUNRISE PUNCH

Serves 16

8 cups orange juice
1½–2 cups tequila
½ cup grenadine syrup
Ice cubes
Orange slices

In a chilled 3- to 4-quart pitcher or small punch bowl mix the orange juice, tequila, and grenadine. Add ice and orange slices.

Fuzzy's Fantastic South Texas Road Meat Chili
Seven Pepper Chili
Rabbit Chili
Simple Avocado Soup
Tomato and Beef Broth
Black Bean Soup
Chicken Divine Soup
Essence of Mushroom Soup
Port Aransas Shrimp Bisque
Gulf Coast Fish Chowder
Texas Corn Chowder
Simple Beef Stew
Shrimp Stew
Son-of-a-Bitch Stew

BOB SEARS' CHILI JOINT

Carlos Ashley, Sr., Texas Poet Laureate, 1949–1951

There's a smell about good chili
That no poet can portray;
   It wafts a rare aroma
Where the gentle breezes play;
   And of all exotic odors
That the wings-of-time anoint,
   There's none can match description
With Bob Sears' Chili Joint.

Now it wasn't much to look at,
Just a hole there in the wall,
   No sign above the entrance
And no fancy front atall.
   A stranger couldn't find it
'Less the wind was blowin' right;
   Then he couldn't hardly miss it,
Even on the darkest night.

A dime would buy a bowl full
Of that wondrous bill-of-fare;
   A quarter got a milk shake
And another bowl to spare.
   It wasn't always fresh and clean
By sanitation's letter,
   But somehow it improved with age
And day by day got better.

I've eaten Antoine's Crepe Suzettes,
A joy beyond compare;
   I've dined at old Delmonico's,
Where famed gourmets repair;
   But no Chef has ever challenged
The high gastronomic point
   That was mine in early childhood
In Bob Sears' Chili Joint.

Chilies, Soups, and Stews

When I was growing up my daddy did most of the doctoring, and he had his own remedies. There was tomato soup for anything that put you to bed. There was Jello for the sore throat. There were milk shakes from the creamery for poxes. But the remedy I remember most—and which I still consider curative beyond measure—was a bowl of chili for the common cold.

Daddy and I would bundle up against the freezing weather of a Panhandle winter. He would wind a long wool scarf around my head and face until only my eyes showed—so the winter wind wouldn't stab me, he said—and we would set off for the Green Hedge Cafe.

It was in a shotgun-shaped building downtown with a long counter and chrome swivel stools cushioned with green plastic. Before the waitress would even get to us, Daddy would start snapping paper napkins out of the holder and open one out into a sort of place mat in front of me. The order was always the same. One bowl of chili, please.

Once I asked for a glass of milk. He shot me a look of incredulity and whispered, didn't I know that was a deadly poisonous combination? It was water in a short barrel glass for me.

He never paid any attention to me while we were in the cafe, but talked instead to the cook. They were both officers in the VFW and had important business to discuss. The chili came in a white bowl and had about a half inch of red grease floating on top. Without asking me, Daddy would take a handful of soda crackers and crumble them over the grease, talking all the while to the cook about the advisability of moving domino night at the VFW from Thursday to Wednesday to give the boys something to do while the women and children went to prayer meeting.

I would sit there quietly eating, gulping glasses of tepid water against the brown prairie fire of the chili, and hoping he would buy me a Mars bar when it was all over. Sometimes he would. Sometimes he wouldn't. But he always rewound the scarf around my head as we left and asked gruffly, "Now, don't you feel better?" Miraculously, I always did. Just as we would reach the door he always turned to the cook and said the same thing, "Nothing like chili to open up your head."

Since Frank X. Tolbert and cronies concocted the first chili cookoff at Terlingua, chili has known a renaissance. Now there are chili cookoffs all over the country and most any weekend of the year. The chili-heads even have their own newsletter called the *Goat Gap Gazette*. Chili captures the whimsical nature of Texans. They love to eat something hotter than hell. They love to serve chili to outlanders and watch their eyes water. They love to argue about the ingredients and origin of the state dish of Texas. As a result, recipes for the fiery dish have proliferated faster than a family of rabbits.

FUZZY'S FANTASTIC SOUTH TEXAS ROAD MEAT CHILI
Forrest Goodhue

Serves 20

Forrest Goodhue won a minor prize in a minor cookoff with what seems to me a typical version. Forrest's recipe is good. It is easy to make and freezes well. You can cut it in half without losing any delicate balance of flavors. And Forrest, known to his friends as Fuzzy, demonstrates not only a facility for cooking, but the Texan's gift for tall-tale telling. When the judges came by to taste his chili he claimed it was made from mostly armadillo and rabbit with some 'possum and 'coon, all cooked in stump water. In his own words:

3 green peppers, chopped medium
3 yellow onions, chopped medium
2 fresh jalapeños, seeded and
  chopped fine
4 cloves garlic, chopped fine
1 stalk celery, chopped medium fine
¼ cup cooking oil
4 lbs. chuck, coarsely ground
5 lbs. venison, coarsely ground
  (can use all beef)

3 oz. Gebhardt's chile powder
1½ tsp. cumin seeds
6 dashes Tabasco sauce
1 7-oz. can green chiles, diced
2 14-oz. cans stewed tomatoes
1 15-oz. can tomato sauce
1 can beer
Water
Salt and pepper

Chop vegetables. Heat oil in a well-seasoned iron pot. Sizzle vegetables in the oil a little, then add meat and brown. Stir in the remaining ingredients and cover with about 1 inch of water. Season to taste with salt and pepper. Let it bubble slowly 3–4 hours. Skim off the grease after it's cooked 2 hours and taste again to see if you need to add more salt and pepper.

When Forrest Goodhue gave me this recipe, he commented that a recipe is never more than a guide. The last time I made Fuzzy's chili was Halloween. I had signed up to cook a pot of chili for the school carnival. I didn't have time to go to the store. I ground up a chuck roast and was tossing the meat into the pot as I went. Once I had it ground and browning, I read through the directions closely. Whoops. Supposed to sauté the vegetables. Oh well. I turned the grinder on again and ran the vegetables through, then pitched them on top of the meat. Went to the cupboard. Crisis. No canned tomatoes. Nothing but a few green ones in the refrigerator. Estimated a pound. Ground them up. Tossed them in. Now I added the rest of the ingredients. Tasted it. Thought about it. Just for good measure, I gave the chili a shot of **Argyle Chile Sauce**. Simmered it about 3 hours. Adjusted the seasonings. Kitchen smelled so good. You know the funny thing was, the chili tasted better than ever. Forrest Goodhue was right. A recipe is just a guide.

SEVEN PEPPER CHILI

Serves 16

One legend about chili credits San Antonio as the birthplace. The so-called Chili Queens worked the downtown area, selling mouth-watering chili from big black pots until a German fellow named Gebhardt figured out a way to take chili making out of the *molcajete* and into the home. He ground several varieties of chile peppers together, combined them with other suitable spices, and Gebhardt's chile powder was born. Just a few spoonfuls added to meat and voilà—instant chili.

Only one problem with this. When blended and ground, peppers begin to lose their distinction. So my friends Ginny and Bob started monkeying around with a prize-winning recipe for chili developed by Allegani Jani Schofield called Hot Pants Chili. Ginny and Bob substituted some chile pods for the chile powder called for in Schofield's recipe. By the time I got the recipe the margins were completely filled in with Ginny's backbending script. I couldn't leave it alone, either. I plugged in fresh tomatoes for canned, real chocolate for the *mole* paste and even more varieties of honest-to-goodness chiles. Who knows whether the Chili Queens of old San Antonio would recognize this version which belongs to Allegani Jani, Ginny, and me—but at least it starts from scratch. This recipe is a lot of trouble and is recommended only for genuine chili fanatics.

3 lbs. lean stew meat—beef, venison, or other dark red meat (elk? bear? moose?), ground coarse or in ½-inch cubes	2 tsp. salt
	5 jalapeños, fresh, seeded
	1 lb. tomatoes, dead-ripe (or canned if you must)
1 lb. pork loin, ground coarse or cubed	7 dried *chiles anchos* (big black ones)
2 tbsp. pure lard or shortening	1 dried chile New Mexico (big red one)
3 large yellow onions, chopped fine	2 dried Jap chiles (little skinny red ones)
2 tsp. cumin seeds	1 tsp. sugar
1 tsp. ground cumin	1 can Tecate beer
7 cloves garlic	1-oz. square unsweetened chocolate
1 tbsp. ground *chiles pasillas*	1 quart water
1 tsp. crushed *chiles quebrados* (*pequíns*)	½ cup masa harina
1 tsp. Tabasco sauce	

Brown meat in lard until gray. Add onions and cook until clear. Combine in food processor or blender the cumin, garlic, *chiles pasillas*, *chiles quebrados*, Tabasco, salt, jalapeños, and tomatoes. Blend and set aside to steep. Remove stems, membranes, and seeds from dried *anchos*, red chiles, and Jap peppers. Place these last three peppers in a small saucepan and barely cover with warm water. Bring to a boil over medium heat and then simmer about 15 minutes. Next place softened peppers in the processor or blender. Save the water in which you boiled the peppers. You can use this water to hotten up the chili later. Now blend the peppers with the tomato mixture until smooth and add all this to the cooking meat and onions. Add sugar, beer, and chocolate to chili. Turn fire down real low and simmer without covering—at least 2 hours. Stir occasionally to keep it from sticking. Keep quart of water nearby. Add as needed to keep a soupy consistency. Thirty minutes before you are ready to serve chili combine masa with enough water to make a thin paste and, stirring vigorously, add to the chili. This will bind the chili and thicken it up. Stir chili frequently during the last half hour so that it doesn't stick. You can taste it at this point, and if it isn't hot enough to suit you, pour in a little of the seasoned water in which you cooked the chiles. This is liquid fire, so go easy. Pour a little and taste. Also adjust the salt during this last half hour.

If the meat you have used is lean, you will probably have no fat to skim off, but if there is fat floating on the top, skim. Once the chili has cooled, you can remove any congealed fat.

If you cook a pot of beans on the side to serve with this chili, you'll have enough to feed a spring branding outfit, a bunch of Shriners from out of town, or a film crew hunting for the Real Texas. You know, this chili is better the second day. And the third day it's perfect. Freezes well.

Remember that chili just doesn't taste right if you don't cook it in an iron pot. I suppose a little of the iron leaches out in the chili and provides that little extra push it needs. Ginny got her pot at San Jacinto Sales, the biggest size they had—about 14 inches across and 7 inches deep; but even this pot doesn't brown enough meat to suit her, so she browns the meat in two separate cast-iron skillets over a hot fire, then puts the meat in the iron pot.

You may be put off by all the different kinds of peppers. Chances are they aren't as hard to find as you think. In most grocery stores near the produce section, there will be a rack of various cellophane-wrapped ground and whole peppers along with whole garlic, oregano, and a lot of other kinds of Mexican spices. If this fails, then you may have to seek out a Mexican grocery store which will have all these peppers and several other varieties—fresh, dried, and ground. Every variety of pepper has its own special taste. You might enjoy just buying up a variety of peppers and fooling around with them. You'll get subtle differences in the food product by substituting different kinds of peppers.

RABBIT CHILI

Serves 10–12

Actually this could be called road meat chili. In place of the rabbit, or in addition to the rabbit, you could toss in neck meat from venison or a skinny little squirrel. Shoot. You might even like it with a 'coon.

1 lb. dried pinto beans, soaked overnight in water	6 dried red peppers, crushed
1 onion, chopped fine	3 *chiles pequín*, crushed
1 3-lb. rabbit, cut up	2 tsp. cumin seed
1 large onion, chopped	½ oz. unsweetened cooking chocolate
1 12-oz. can tomato paste	3 tbsp. chile powder
2 garlic cloves, pressed	Salt to taste

Cook beans in soaking water with chopped onion. At the same time stew rabbit with second onion in another pot of water until the meat falls off the bone. When the rabbit is cooked remove from stew. Reserve juice. Debone and place meat in a cast-iron stew pot. Now combine all ingredients except the beans. Add 5 cups of the rabbit stewing liquid to the mixture and salt to taste. Don't be shocked by the taste. It will improve. Stir thoroughly. Simmer over low heat for 2 hours. After 1 hour you may need to add a couple of cups of water (or rabbit juice if you have the nerve). At the end of 2 hours the basic chili should be quite thick and dark in color. Add beans and bean juice and cook another hour. Add salt to taste. The chili should be thick enough so that you can lay a spoon on top of it and it won't sink. If it's too thin, turn up the fire and boil it down a little. Be careful not to burn it. Those beans fall like sinkers, and you will ruin the whole pot if they burn.

When I took a whiff from my stew pot bubbling over with cottontail, it suddenly came to me how chili may have been invented. Think of it. They've got the cattle driven halfway to Dodge. The meat has run out. The cattle are restless because there's a full moon. The cowboys are hot and sweaty and edgy. So Cookie takes off and shoots a couple of rabbits. Settle the boys down a little tonight. He skins the rabbits, throws in his last onion along with what little water he has left in the bottom of the barrel. A couple of hours go by. He takes the lid off the pot and draws in his breath. Great God. Them cowboys will string me up alive. So he runs out into the hot desert, frantically plucking hot peppers off the wild bushes. Throws them into the pot, whistles to reassure himself. Heaves in a can of the ubiquitous tomato. A little garlic. He swipes some cumin and *ancho* from the saddlebag of a Mexican. Hell. Even some chocolate. Anything to kill the stench of that stewing rabbit. Time passes. Sun sets in glorious

West. Boys, come and get it. Howdy podner. What's for grub? Grunt, says Cookie, trying to be his most difficult self to fend off complaints. Glug, says Cowboy. Pretty good. What is it? Playing for time, Cookie answers, chili. Gimme some more, says Cowboy. Cookie sags against chuck wagon. Staying cool, he simply bellows, beans?

SIMPLE AVOCADO SOUP

Serves 4

1 very ripe avocado, peeled and pitted
½ pint whipping cream

2 cups hot chicken broth
Salt and white pepper to taste
4 tbsp. dry sherry

In a food processor or blender, puree avocado, add cream slowly, then pour in hot broth. Mix just until blended. Taste and season with salt and white pepper. Into the bottom of each soup bowl place 1 tablespoon dry sherry, then ladle soup over and serve. This soup takes about 2 minutes from the time you first notice that the avocado is going to go bad if you don't use it today. This is also delicious cold, but you can't add cold chicken broth, because the chicken fat will not properly blend. So you will have to heat the broth, then cool the soup. It is so good, I defy you to get people to wait until it cools off.

TOMATO AND BEEF BROTH

Serves 2–3

1½ cups beef consommé
2 large ripe firm tomatoes
Salt and pepper

2 tbsp. chopped parsley
1 tbsp. chopped chives
2 tbsp. port wine

A clear red soup with green parsley accents, this makes a quick lunch or a super appetizer. Bring consommé to a simmer in a saucepan. Drop tomatoes into boiling water 20 seconds, then slip the skins off. Add skins to consommé. Halve tomatoes and squeeze seeds and juice into consommé. Mince pulp very fine and set aside. After consommé has simmered 5 minutes, strain it into another pan and add minced tomato pulp. Heat 2 minutes. Add salt and pepper to taste, stir in herbs and wine. Serve it hot over Parmesan toast. It's good chilled, too.

BLACK BEAN SOUP
Melinda Schmidt

Serves 6–8

This soup looks like eggplant skin without the shine.

1 lb. dried black turtle beans	¾ tsp. ground cumin
Water	2 tsp. ground coriander
Salt	2 cloves garlic, pressed
3 pieces of bacon (optional)	½ tsp. coarsely ground pepper
1 yellow onion	3 whole cloves

Wash beans and cook with bacon in salted water. When the water in the pot is about 3 inches above the beans—taste it. The beans will be as salty as the water is. Adjust to suit you now and you won't have to resalt later. Cook until beans are *just* tender (2 or 3 hours). Now add onion, cumin, coriander, garlic, pepper, and cloves. Simmer about 2 hours. Stir occasionally. This should be like a very thick stew. Add more water only if you think the beans risk burning on the bottom.

Serve in soup bowls filled only about two-thirds full of soup. After the fashion of a curry dinner, set out containers of the following condiments and let the diners heap on whatever combination suits their fancy.

TOPPINGS

Chopped green onions	Sausage links or chorizo, fried and
Mashed very ripe avocado	skinned
Grated Swiss or Monterrey Jack	Corn tortillas
cheese	*Picante* sauce
Chopped tomatoes	Sour cream

This soup looks for all the world like a natural vegetable dye. Guard against purple-black stains on your table linens and clothes.

CHICKEN DIVINE SOUP
Peggy Vineyard

Serves 6

1 onion, peeled and chopped	1 quart chicken stock
1 stalk celery, chopped	2 tbsp. flour
1 carrot, scraped and chopped	2 tbsp. butter
1 clove garlic, crushed	3 eggs yolks
1 whole chicken	1 cup heavy cream
Water to cover	Salt and pepper
Salt and pepper to taste	Juice of 1 lemon
Pinch marjoram	Chopped chives or asparagus tips

Place chopped vegetables in soup pot, add chicken and water just to cover. Salt and pepper to taste, add marjoram. Boil gently until meat falls off the bone (about 2 hours).

Take chicken from stock, remove meat; discard bones, skin, fat, and gristle. Strain stock into bowl through fine-meshed sieve. Wash out soup pan. Cut white meat into julienne strips and set aside. Put dark meat into blender or processor with 1 cup of stock and puree. Brown flour in butter in a small heavy skillet, then combine with chicken puree in the soup pot. Stir in remaining 3 cups of stock. Bring to a boil, stirring constantly, and cook about 5 minutes. Lower heat. Beat egg yolks until light and lemon-colored; then beat in cream. Slowly stir a few tablespoons of the hot soup into the egg yolks and cream, then add the whole mixture to soup pot very slowly, stirring constantly. Bring to simmer but don't boil. Add reserved white meat of chicken, salt and pepper to taste, and lemon juice. Heat through, then pour into soup bowls and garnish with chives or, for an unforgettable experience, add fresh asparagus tips that have been steamed separately and tossed in a little butter.

ESSENCE OF MUSHROOM SOUP

Hilltop Herb Farm
Madeline Hill

Serves 12

1 lb. fresh mushrooms, sliced	½ tsp. dried tarragon leaves
1 cup sliced, peeled carrots	1 tsp. dried thyme leaves
2 stalks celery, cut in pieces	2 13¾-oz. cans chicken broth
½ cup water	4 tbsp. Madeira wine
¼ cup chopped fresh parsley	1 cup sour cream

Put all ingredients except Madeira and sour cream into a medium-sized saucepan and bring to a boil over moderate heat. Cover and cook 15–20 minutes, until vegetables are very tender. Pour half the mixture into blender, cover and blend a few seconds until smooth. Pour into another container and repeat with remaining mixture. Return pureed mixture to pan, stir in Madeira, and heat just to boiling. Pour into heated cups or bowls and serve topped with a spoonful of sour cream. Soup may be made 1 or 2 days ahead and refrigerated in a tightly covered plastic container. To reheat, put soup in a saucepan and warm over low heat.

PORT ARANSAS SHRIMP BISQUE

Serves 4

1 lb. cleaned, boiled, chopped shrimp	¼ tsp. paprika
	Salt and pepper
½ cup fish stock	¼ cup dry sherry (optional)
1½ cups heavy cream	1 tbsp. minced parsley and chives

Don't cheat and use milk in this recipe. I've tried, and it won't work. Cream provides the texture worthy of the name *bisque*. Blend half the shrimp and all the fish stock in a blender until smooth. Pour mixture into the top of a double boiler, add cream and paprika, and season to taste with salt and pepper. Cook over hot water, stirring occasionally, until soup almost comes to a boil. Add sherry and serve immediately in individual cups garnished with remaining chopped shrimp, parsley, and chives.

To make a quick fish stock, place shrimp peelings and heads into 2 cups water, salt to taste, and boil 10–15 minutes. Taste and adjust salt. Strain.

GULF COAST FISH CHOWDER

Serves 4

3 tbsp. olive oil
½ cup onion, chopped coarse
½ cup celery, chopped coarse
1 tsp. chile powder
1 1-lb. can stewed tomatoes with
    juice
¾ cup water

1 tsp. salt
1 tsp. sugar
1 tbsp. Worcestershire sauce
1 1-lb. fish, filleted, or a 12-oz.
    package frozen fish fillets
Parsley or cilantro

Heat olive oil in a heavy saucepan. Add onion, celery, and chile powder. Sauté over medium heat until onions are clear. Stir in tomatoes, water, salt, sugar, and Worcestershire sauce; bring to a rolling boil. Cut fish fillets into bite-sized cubes and add to boiling mixture. Lower heat and simmer covered for 15 minutes. Sprinkle with parsley or cilantro and serve over fluffy rice.

TEXAS CORN CHOWDER

Serves 4–6

1 cup salt pork, cubed
1 onion, cut fine
1 cup potatoes, cubed
1 cup boiling water
1½ cups corn, cut from
    approximately 3 ears

1½ cups milk
3 tbsp. butter
¾ tsp. salt
½ tsp. finely ground white pepper

Cube salt pork, then render out fat in a frying pan over medium heat. Add onion and cook until clear. Parboil potato cubes in the soup pot for 5 minutes and drain. Pour clean boiling water over salt pork and onion, and strain this water into the potatoes. Discard salt pork and onion. Bring to a boil. Cut corn from cob. Add corn, milk, butter, and seasonings to potato water. Keeping the fire low, simmer until corn is done through (about 10 minutes). Taste and adjust salt and pepper. Serve hot.

SIMPLE BEEF STEW

Serves 6

I think that more good cooking has been ruined by the addition of water than by any other single factor. Chicken broth, beef bouillon, tomato juice, coffee, wine, quick broth made by boiling shrimp peelings—any liquid with a little flavor that blends with the basic ingredients of the concoction is usually better than water. You can almost always improve a recipe that calls for large volumes of water by thinking of an appropriate substitute.

This simple stew is fairly close to what Mother used to make except in its use of wine for the liquid. I am an avid fan of Gallo Hearty Burgundy myself and use it in heavy beef or dark red meat dishes of all kinds.

4- to 5-lb. beef chuck roast	2 bay leaves
Salt and coarsely ground pepper	¼ tsp. each: thyme, rosemary, and
4 strips bacon, cut in squares	summer savory
1 lb. small white boiling onions	3 cups dry red wine
(about 15 or 16), peeled	3 tbsp. cornstarch
6 medium carrots, scraped and cut	½ cup water
into medallions	

Trim excess fat from roast, bone it, then cut it into large 2-inch chunks. Salt and pepper generously. In a heavy 5-quart Dutch oven (cast-iron is the best), cook bacon over medium heat until most of the fat is extracted. Add onions and continue cooking until onions begin to brown. Add meat, carrots, bay leaves, thyme, rosemary, and summer savory. Cover and cook, stirring occasionally, until meat is browned on all sides. Add wine, reduce heat, cover and simmer for 2½–3 hours, or until meat is fork-tender. Remove bay leaves if you can find them.

With a slotted spoon, transfer meat and vegetables to a tureen. Skim excess fat from pan juices. Blend together cornstarch and water until you have a lumpless, thin paste. Stirring constantly, pour cornstarch mixture into juices and stir until gravy thickens and becomes translucent. Season to taste with salt and pepper. Pour over meat and vegetables. The sauce is wonderful with mashed potatoes.

SHRIMP STEW
Peggy Vineyard

Serves 6–8

Nothing that tastes this good should have such an ordinary name.

½ cup cooking oil
¼ cup flour
1 medium onion, chopped
1 cup chopped green onions and
    tops
2 cloves garlic, pressed
2 tbsp. tomato paste
3 cups warm water
1 tbsp. sugar

1 tsp. salt
½ tsp. black pepper (I usually add
    more)
1 bay leaf
Dash of Tabasco sauce
Juice of 1 lemon
3 lbs. raw, cleaned, and deveined
    medium shrimp
Chopped fresh parsley

Brown flour in oil. Add onions, garlic, and tomato paste until paste browns. Add water slowly, stirring constantly. Add sugar, salt, pepper, bay leaf, Tabasco sauce, and lemon juice. Simmer over low heat for 1 hour. Add shrimp and simmer just until shrimp are cooked (they turn from a translucent blue to a solid pink color)—about 20 minutes. Don't overcook shrimp or you'll toughen them. If the mixture seems too thick you can add a little more water. Toss in parsley. Serve over rice.

Peggy says if you want to really add resonance to the flavor of this stew you could go the extra mile in this manner: add shrimp hulls to the 3 cups of water. Simmer on the back of the stove while you begin the recipe. Then strain in this primitive broth rather than plain water.

SON-OF-A-BITCH STEW

Back in the early days, roundup was serious business to the cowboy. It was held in the springtime when cattle outfits pitched in together to sort out the stock that had gotten mixed up on the winter range. Calves were branded and cut (castrated), cattle were worked, cowboys signed on for the season. A period of long days' work and short nights' rest began. A good cook could attract good hands, so during roundup they worked to show their stuff. Son-of-a-Bitch was the customary meal served for the occasion, and camp cooks did their best to make a more delectable stew than their neighbors.

The origins of this famous cowboy stew are lost. Some say the stew originated with the Indians, who ate organ meats for both physical and spiritual sustenance. Perhaps the stew came from some Scottish range cook who hated to waste anything. However the stew was invented, it's a good bet that the first diner said, son-of-a-bitch but that's good, and the name stuck. Whenever a line preacher or a woman came to chuck, the name was sometimes softened to son-of-a-gun, but the stew remained the same.

According to Uncle Dick, my grandfather—who was a ranch foreman—carefully chose the first animal to be slaughtered at roundup. For a good Son-of-a-Bitch, a milk-fed calf was best because the marrow gut, which is actually the connecting tube between two stomachs, was filled with partially digested milk solids, the secret flavoring of a good Son-of-a-Bitch. After the calf was killed and bled, the meat was turned over to the cook.

Old Cookie dug a fire trench, built him up a good fire, then let it burn down to a nice even bed of coals. He hung his pots from iron rods. He placed a Dutch oven—half filled with water—over the coals and let it come to a good rolling boil. First he threw in diced pieces of skinned tongue and heart. After these had cooked and tenderized awhile, he added sweetbreads, kidneys, lungs (called "lights"), a little liver, and the essential marrow gut, carved into rings. Sometimes brains, precooked separately with a little flour until they became "beady," were added to the stew. Occasionally an onion—known to cowboys as a "skunk egg"—was tossed in.

Skunk eggs were the only concession to vegetables. No corn, limas, potatoes, or tomatoes ever found their way into a bona fide Son-of-a-Bitch. Uncle Dick says it was real good to smell this on the first day of roundup. One of the chief signals that spring had come at last.

The stew bubbled slowly all day. Cookie would cuss a blue streak at anyone who raised dust around the chuck wagon, the cowboys would cast an approving eye toward the pot swinging over the glowing coals, and at last, after a hard day's work, the boys would stand around the chuck wagon until Cookie hollered, come and get it, boys. Then each would take his turn dipping out a tin plate full of Son-of-a-Bitch, grabbing a sourdough biscuit, and hunting for a proper place to "set" while he ate his favorite meal.

Son-of-a-Bitch was always the first meal after a beef was killed. As the summer wore on and the boys moved the herd up the trail, the stew might be less carefully constructed, but on the day when several outfits pitched in together to sort the herds, it was usual for each outfit to claim that his cook made the best damn Son-of-a-Bitch on the high plains. When I asked Uncle Dick why people don't eat Son-of-a-Bitch anymore, he snorted, arched his eyebrows, flicked the ash off his cigarette with his little finger and said, hell. Nobody can pick 'em. Nobody can dress 'em and nobody can cook 'em.

Pecos Cantaloupe and Chicken Salad
Marinated Cauliflower Salad
Crabmeat or Shrimp Salad
Cucumbers in Sour Cream Dill Sauce
Gordon Barrett's Salad
Fresh Fruit Salad with Toasted Pecans
Garlic Grapes
Grapefruit Ambrosia
Fresh Mushroom Salad
Ensalada de Nopalitos (Cactus Salad)
Hot German Potato Salad
Zula's Potato Salad
Spinach Salad
Homemade Croutons
Salad Seeds
Homemade Mayonnaise
Old-fashioned Cooked Salad Dressing
Blender Salad Dressing
Coleslaw Dressing
Houston's English French Dressing
Seafood Salad Dressing
Seafood Sauce #2

Salads and Their Dressings

After my final month of scouring the state for its best recipes, I began sorting through the two or three thousand recipes that had been given me to consider for this book. The first thing I noticed was that the salad stack was the shortest. I began to wonder why.

Although Texas is reluctant to admit it, a good portion of the state is actually a desert. The only thing Texas had to start with in the way of salad greens was weeds. On the frontier, gardens were sparse and short-lived. Obviously, times have changed. Good fresh fruits and vegetables are available on a year-round basis in the smallest Texas hamlets. There is a revival of interest in home gardens. But the tradition of salad making is scant.

For that reason, there are still a lot of bad salads served in Texas. In the first place, sharpened steel should never touch lettuce. Lettuce *cut* for a salad looks mortally wounded, whereas lettuce *torn* looks lively and appetizing. The knife, when over-zealously applied to other salad ingredients, can prove fatal. There is nothing more unappetizing than a salad that looks as if it had been burped up by a cranky garbage disposal. The elements of a mixed salad should be identifiable. Pieces of tomato should look like tomato, not like pimiento.

The second element in a bad salad is usually a bottled dressing. It has always amazed me that an earnest cook would work to prepare a meal for company, then start them out with cut-up iceberg lettuce and bottled dressing. After the tongue is be-numbed by harsh vinegar and corn oil, who cares what comes after? A well-executed green salad topped with a subtle, carefully blended dressing is not only a joy to behold; it will make people so hungry they'll be willing to eat the legs off the table. That's what the cook should strive for.

You can invent good salads by reversing the usual presentation of certain vegetables. Raw squash is delicious. So is cooked lettuce. It can be interesting to transpose in the vegetable department. You should experiment. Just diddle around in your own kitchen and see what surprises and delights you.

Please note one glaring omission in the salad section. There are no congealed salads here. In that short stack of salad recipes given to me by Texas cooks, both professional and private, there were a goodly number of congealed salads. That is where I ran into a serious dilemma. I hate congealed salads. But they *do* represent Texas. I finally asked myself: whose book is this, anyway? There are no congealed salads here.

PECOS CANTALOUPE AND CHICKEN SALAD

Serves 2

1 cantaloupe, diced
1 cup cubed, cooked chicken
½ cup seedless green grapes,
    halved
1 stalk celery, chopped fine
½ cup slivered toasted almonds

¼ cup mayonnaise
¼ cup sour cream
2 tsp. soy sauce
1 tsp. curry powder
Pinch salt

Combine cantaloupe, chicken, grapes, celery, and almonds and set aside. Mix thoroughly mayonnaise, sour cream, soy sauce, curry powder, and salt. Combine with first mixture. For optimum results, cover and refrigerate at least 1 hour.

MARINATED CAULIFLOWER SALAD

1 head cauliflower, cored and
    sliced
1 cup chopped pitted green olives
1 green pepper, cut in thin
    julienne strips
¼ cup (1 2-oz. jar) pimiento
1 medium onion, chopped fine

DRESSING

½ cup mild salad oil
Juice of ½ lemon
3 tbsp. white wine vinegar

2 tsp. salt
½ tsp. sugar
¼ tsp. pepper

This is one of those salads that is better the second day. The way I do it is to mix the dressing in the bottom of a large crockery salad bowl, using a fork so that a sort of emulsion forms, then toss in the cut up vegetables, turn them several times, cover and refrigerate. Then whenever I think about it, I give it a stir. It should marinate a minimum of 1 hour. This salad has a very sour, tart flavor and would go well with some sort of heavy meat dish, such as a roast pork loin with gravy.

CRABMEAT OR SHRIMP SALAD

Serves 4

1 lb. fresh lump crabmeat, or
   medium-sized cooked and
   peeled shrimp
2 hard-boiled eggs, sliced

4 green onions, chopped
1 cup celery, chopped
Mayonnaise
Lettuce

Marinate the meat 1 hour in:

1 tbsp. Worcestershire sauce
6 dashes of Tabasco sauce
¼ tsp. salt

Black pepper to taste
1 tbsp. white wine vinegar
1 tbsp. peanut oil

Just before serving, add remaining ingredients and mix with mayonnaise to thoroughly moisten. Serve on bed of lettuce.

CUCUMBERS IN SOUR CREAM DILL SAUCE
B. K. Wagner

Serves 6–8

4 small, firm cucumbers
1 cup boiling water
¾ cup sour cream
2 tbsp. cider vinegar
3 tbsp. minced fresh dill *or* 1 tsp.
   dill seed *or* 1 tbsp. dried dill

1½ tsp. salt
⅛ tsp. white pepper
1 tsp. sugar

Peel cucumbers and slice very thin. Pour boiling water over them and count to 10. Drain and cover with ice water. Mix together sour cream, vinegar, dill, salt, pepper, and sugar. Drain cucumbers again and dry. Toss cucumbers with dressing. Chill for 30 minutes. Good with shrimp.

GORDON BARRETT'S SALAD

Gordon Barrett is one of those good old boys from East Texas with a silver pompadour, a spare tire from too much good food, a slight wheeze from cigarettes, and a certain flat look that comes from serving the public too long. He affects a kind of boredom that belies his real creativity. His basic premise toward food would serve any cook. Gordon says you gotta mess with it, play with it, taste it. Just sort of fool around with it. One good example of one of those things that he figured out for his ladies at the country club was this easy salad which changes every time you make it, dependin' on what you've got.

Salad greens—vary these. Use romaine, brown-tip, spinach, chicory. **Parmesan, grated** **Browned, slivered almonds**	**Tarragon vinegar and mild olive oil** **Herbs and spices of your choice. Taste it. Play with it.**

Gordon says to make this salad different every time. Vary the greens. Fool around with the herbs. Try a little dill. Next time some chervil or rosemary. Dust it with cayenne pepper once. The main thing is to use good cold greens, serve them on a cold plate, mix them up at the last minute, season to taste, and just barely toss. Use about twice as much olive oil as vinegar.

My son, Jay, says this salad reminds him of Seizure Salad like they served at the Rice Hotel.

FRESH FRUIT SALAD WITH TOASTED PECANS

Serves 8

1 grapefruit, peeled and sectioned 5 oranges, peeled, seeded, cut into half circles 2 cups strawberries, washed and hulled	2 bananas, cut in bite-sized pieces ¼ watermelon or cantaloupe, peeled and cut into sticks 1 cup pecan halves, toasted *Fresh Orange Dressing*

Group fruit on large serving platter. Serve with toasted pecans and **Fresh Orange Dressing**.

FRESH ORANGE DRESSING

½ cup fresh orange juice
2 tsp. sugar
½ tsp. salt

¼ cup white wine vinegar
½ cup mild salad oil

In jar, combine all ingredients; cover tightly and shake well. Chill. Shake well before serving.

To toast pecans: spread one layer deep on cookie sheet and bake in 300° oven, turning every 5 minutes until brown (15–20 minutes).

GARLIC GRAPES
Anna Kay Brewer

Serves 8

A good accompaniment to a piece of roast meat: lamb, beef, venison, and so on.

1 lb. white seedless Thompson
  grapes
6 cloves of garlic, peeled and left
  whole

1 8-oz. package cream cheese, at
  room temperature
1 tbsp. milk or cream

Wash grapes. Remove from stems and dry gently. Using 1 clove of garlic, rub bottom and sides of a wooden salad bowl thoroughly until most of the essence of the garlic has been extracted (try cutting the garlic into thin strips to do this). Discard garlic. Place grapes in bowl and shake the bowl gently so that they roll around against the garlic-impregnated wood. Combine softened cream cheese (one quick way to soften cream cheese is to zap it in the microwave for a few seconds) with milk or cream, and stir with a fork until it is smooth. Combine with grapes. Place remaining 5 cloves of peeled garlic in the top of the grape and cheese mixture. Cover. Refrigerate at least 2 hours. Before you are ready to serve, remove the 5 garlic cloves and discard. Serve grapes on lettuce leaf. You'll find the wooden bowl doesn't look too appetizing. I'd suggest individual servings or a glass bowl lined with lettuce leaves.

GRAPEFRUIT AMBROSIA

Serves 8

1 ripe pineapple	2 bananas
3 oranges	2 cups freshly grated coconut
3 grapefruit	¼ cup dry sherry

Peel and core pineapple, then cut into rounds. Peel and section oranges and grapefruit, removing membrane and seeds. Grate coconut. In an attractive glass bowl, layer the fruit, using coconut to separate the layers. When you have a layer of oranges, cut bananas into rounds directly onto the oranges, cover with coconut, and follow with layer of grapefruit. (The acid will prevent the bananas from turning brown.) Repeat the layers, using all the fruit, then pour sherry over all, cover and refrigerate at least 30 minutes before serving.

This is a very good salad to serve with roast pork or roast leg of lamb.

FRESH MUSHROOM SALAD
Julia Wallace

Serves 4

¼ lb. fresh mushrooms, sliced thin	Salt and pepper to taste
¼ cup red wine vinegar	Lettuce leaves
¾ cup olive oil	Chopped chives and fresh parsley
1 tsp. lemon juice	

Wash, dry, and slice mushrooms. Combine vinegar, oil, lemon juice, salt, and pepper. Beat until blended. Pour over mushrooms. Cover and marinate in refrigerator at least 1 hour. Serve on lettuce leaf and sprinkle with chives and parsley.

ENSALADA DE NOPALITOS
(Cactus Salad)
Bobbie Covey

Serves 6

1 16-oz. can *nopalitos*
3 tomatoes, peeled, seeded, and
   chopped

3 tbsp. white onion, finely chopped
1 tbsp. fresh cilantro, chopped
¾ cup oil and vinegar dressing

Carefully rinse and drain the cactus pieces. Mix with the tomatoes, onion, and cilantro, then toss in the dressing. Serve chilled.

HOT GERMAN POTATO SALAD

Serves 8–10

8 medium russet potatoes
½ lb. bacon
1 medium onion, chopped fine
½ cup cider vinegar

1½ tbsp. sugar
1 tsp. salt
Coarsely ground pepper to taste

Peel potatoes and cook in boiling salted water until just tender. Remove and drain, then dice coarse. While potatoes are boiling, fry bacon crisp in a 10–inch skillet, then remove from skillet and crumble. Pour bacon grease from skillet, then measure ¼ cup grease back into the skillet. Sauté onion in bacon grease until golden. While onion is sautéing, combine vinegar, sugar, salt, and pepper to taste. Once onion is golden, pour vinegar sauce over and heat to boiling. Add diced potatoes and bacon to skillet, toss gently until combined. Cover and heat to a good hot eating temperature. Serve at once.

    Germans like the leftovers kept in the refrigerator and eaten cold the next day.

ZULA'S POTATO SALAD
Zula Gilliam

Serves 6

When I confessed to my Aunt Zula that I couldn't make a decent potato salad, she gave me one of her water department looks. She collected for the water department in Hereford for thirty years, and she had a way of looking you dead in the eye to see if your story was plausible. She'd heard every excuse in the book for not paying water bills, and she was known to be a fine judge of character.

I can't believe it, she said. Then I asked, don't you have a recipe? Don't need a recipe, she snorted, in her water department tone. All I'm trying to do, I took on my patient tone, is to make potato salad as good as yours. I have tried everything: olives, green peppers, various and sundry seeds, parsley. Parsley, she interrupted. You mean like they put on the Friday Fish Plate at the Ranch Room? Yes, I answered in my smallest voice. Why honey, she heaved her ample breast, don't you know that God meant for potato salad to be plain?

She leaned back in her beige damask chair with the cabriole legs. She sighed. Go get us some of those Fuv crackers and a Co-cola and I'll try to remember. I dutifully marched to the kitchen and opened up the pantry. Then one of those miracles of memory happened. Aunt Zula didn't live in the same house she'd lived in when I was a child. She didn't even live in the same town. But the overwhelming scent of that pantry was exactly the same. I stood there and soaked in that pungent aroma. I was five years old again. And there on the floor were shiny clean bottles of Coca-Cola that she always washed with hot soapy water when she got them home from the store. The FF&V lemon thins were still on the middle shelf to the left. So I retraced our ancient routine and took the FF&Vs, Fuv crackers to her, and one Coke— she always said nobody could drink a whole one—arranged the cookies on a china plate, poured the Coke evenly into 2 glasses, added a cube of ice, and returned to her bedroom. Now she would tell me how to make potato salad.

Count out 1 potato for every person you plan to feed and throw in 1 for the pot, she explained. Boil the potatoes in their jackets in salted water to cover until just barely soft through (you don't want to overcook them or they'll go to mush). For every 3 potatoes you're cooking, count out 1 egg. Say you're boiling 6 potatoes, then you should hard-boil about 2 eggs. 'Course if you favor eggs, you can throw in 1 for the pot. Boil eggs separately.

For every 6 potatoes, choose 1 stalk of celery and a nice mild onion. You know the flatter an onion the milder, don't you? No, I answered, I didn't know it. She took a big bite from the lemon thin and held up the new-moon remains and nodded, well, now you know.

Peel and dice the onion fine. Dice the celery fine. Now you need to make your sauce. Start out with real mayonnaise—I always use homemade. Anyway, you thin your mayonnaise with a little high-quality white wine vinegar. How much? Say for 6 potatoes, about ⅓ cup of mayonnaise and 1 tablespoon of vinegar. Add a little whiff of dry mustard and 1 spoonful of sweet pickle relish. Slop a little pickle relish juice in for the sugar. Salt moderately and pepper generously. Stir it all up. Taste. It should taste good to you, but strong, because potatoes are bland. If it sort of shocks your tongue it's so good, you've probably got it just right.

When the potatoes are cooked and cool enough to handle, peel them, then break them up in the mixing bowl with a fork, leaving large and small lumps and some just sort of mashed. Peel and chop up the eggs irregularly and add to potatoes. Mix in onions and celery—you could put in a little jar of pimientos for color if you like—pour the mayonnaise sauce over, and mix lightly with a fork until it looks just right. Should be good and moist. You may have to adjust things a little here to suit you. Maybe a dash more vinegar. Another spoonful of mayonnaise. Salt? Just taste it until you like it. Cover and refrigerate. Get it good and cold before you serve it. And put it in a pretty bowl, Aunt Zula said, as if I surely didn't even have enough sense to know that.

6 potatoes, plus 1 for the pot,
    boiled, drained, peeled, and
    broken up
2 eggs, hard-boiled, peeled and
    chopped coarse

1 flat onion, diced fine
1 stalk celery, diced fine
1 2-oz. jar pimientos

DRESSING

⅓ cup real mayonnaise
1 tbsp. white wine vinegar
½ tsp. dry mustard

1 tbsp. sweet pickle relish
1 tsp. relish juice
Salt and pepper to taste

SPINACH SALAD
Linda Clarkson

Serves 8–10

1 lb. fresh spinach, washed, stemmed, and drained
2 bunches green onions and tops, chopped
½ lb. fresh mushrooms, sliced thin

8 slices of bacon, fried crisp, drained, and broken into bits
4 hard-boiled eggs, peeled and quartered

DRESSING

⅔ cup sugar
1 cup salad oil
½ tsp. dry mustard

½ tsp. salt
½ cup apple cider vinegar

Place all dressing ingredients except vinegar in a blender or processor and mix thoroughly. Pour a thin stream of vinegar into whirling mixture.

When you wash spinach remember that it is always grown in sandy soil, so to avoid grit salad you'll have to take it through about 3 washings. Once the spinach is washed, pinch off the stems, tear the spinach into bite-sized pieces, and place in a colander to drain while you are preparing other vegetables. Combine onions, mushrooms, and bacon bits with spinach in a salad bowl. Toss with dressing. Garnish with hard-boiled eggs. Serve very cold.

HOMEMADE CROUTONS

Slices of leftover bread (any good kind: sourdough, French, whole wheat, what have you)
Mild olive oil

Parmesan cheese
Clove garlic, minced
Dried parsley

Brush oil on both sides of bread. Combine cheese, garlic, and parsley, and spread over bread. Cut into small cubes. Bake on cookie sheet, one layer deep, at 225° for 30 minutes or until cubes turn golden brown, stirring once or twice.

SALAD SEEDS
Hilltop Herb Farm
Madeline Hill

Mix 3 or more of the following toasted seeds and nuts:

Sunflower seeds
Sesame seeds
Pumpkin seeds

Coarsely chopped cashews
Walnuts
Filberts

Set out in a bowl and let guests sprinkle on salads as desired.

HOMEMADE MAYONNAISE

Makes 1 pint

There are a lot of recipes around for homemade mayonnaise which are more complicated than this one, but this always works. It is so simple you can memorize the recipe. My only advice is to use a tasteless oil. Olive oil or any other strongly flavored oil will turn it into something more potent than mayonnaise is supposed to be.

1 egg, room temperature
2 cups oil
1 tsp. each: salt, sugar, and dry
    mustard
Juice of ½ lemon

Beat the egg in a mixer at high speed until good and stiff. Now add *very slowly* 1 cup of oil. It should look like mayonnaise at this point. Still mixing at high speed, add salt, sugar, dry mustard, and lemon juice. Now add the remaining oil *very slowly*. What you are doing when you make mayonnaise is creating an emulsion between the egg and oil. If you add the oil too fast, it won't bind to the egg and you will end up with a runny soup that can be used to dress a salad, but isn't really mayonnaise. According to Helen Corbitt, you can add 1 tablespoon of cream to a failed mayonnaise, but I find it always works if you are just patient enough to add the oil slowly. I use a 2-cup Pyrex measuring cup, hook the lip over the edge of the bowl, and just dribble the oil down the side of the bowl.

From this you can make any sort of fancy mayonnaise you wish. You can add dill, or chopped jalapeño, or parsley, or anything that strikes your fancy. Because this mayonnaise contains no preservatives it *must be* refrigerated, and don't let anyone stick a freshly licked spoon into it.

OLD-FASHIONED COOKED SALAD DRESSING
Mary Elizabeth Barnard

Makes 1 pint

4 eggs	3 tbsp. sugar
1 cup heavy cream	½ cup white wine vinegar
1 tbsp. dry mustard	¼ tsp. salt
1 tbsp. butter	Dash cayenne pepper

Combine eggs, cream, dry mustard, butter, and sugar in the top of a double boiler. Slowly add vinegar, stirring all the while. Season with salt and pepper. Cook and stir until the mixture coats a silver spoon. Store in covered jar in the refrigerator. Don't let the kids stick an already used spoon in the dressing.

BLENDER SALAD DRESSING

Makes 1 quart

You can vary this dressing with good results by playing with oils and vinegar. Try sesame or walnut oil for a change. Use champagne vinegar for the smoothest possible product.

1 medium onion, chopped fine	2 cups oil
3 cloves garlic, minced	¾ cup vinegar (not white distilled)
1 tbsp. salt	¼ cup water
¼ tsp. dry mustard	1 tsp. fresh parsley, cut fine with
¼ tsp. paprika	scissors
⅛ tsp. pepper	1 tsp. finely minced celery
3 tbsp. sugar	

Blend all ingredients in blender. Make ahead so that it can ripen. Store in covered jar in the refrigerator.

COLESLAW DRESSING

2 tbsp. *Blender Salad Dressing*	1 tsp. white wine vinegar
4 tbsp. *Homemade Mayonnaise*	1 tbsp. cream
2 egg yolks, beaten	¼ tsp. celery seed

Combine all ingredients. To make a Gulf Coast coleslaw, add small, cold, boiled shrimp to finely chopped cabbage and toss with dressing. Serve ice cold.

HOUSTON'S ENGLISH FRENCH DRESSING

Serves 2

This salad dressing comes to Texas in the same manner that Marco Polo brought spices to Europe. A man from London who lives in Houston says this is the way the English and especially the Houston English like their French dressing. Make sense?

Salt and pepper to taste	1 tsp. vinegar
1 tsp. Dijon mustard	5 tsp. olive oil
1 tsp. sugar	1 clove garlic, crushed
¼ tsp. mild curry powder	

Give the salt and pepper shakers a good shake into a small bowl. Now add mustard, sugar, curry powder, and mix. Add vinegar and oil. Squeeze in garlic and go at it with a wire whisk. Makes enough to dress ½ head of lettuce. Good with hard-boiled eggs.

You probably get tired of my saying salt and pepper to taste. But you have to taste things. Cooking is an art, not a science. For example, in this recipe, I'd be moderate with the salt and pepper, combine all ingredients, whisk it a little. Stick my left forefinger into it and taste it. Narrow my eyes like a wine taster. Think about it. Roll it around. If by some horrid accident I really overdid the salt, I'd do one of two things. Double the recipe or throw the whole thing out and start over.

SEAFOOD SALAD DRESSING

Makes 1½ pints

If you have made **Argyle Chile Sauce** and **Homemade Mayonnaise,** here's a salad dressing so good it'll make you hit your uncle. If you don't have the first two ingredients on hand, substitute commercial products.

1 cup *Homemade Mayonnaise*
¼ cup *Argyle Chile Sauce*
¼ **cup bell pepper, cut fine**
¼ **cup green onions and tops**

Juice of ½ lemon
¼ **cup whipping cream, whipped
    stiff**

Combine mayonnaise, chili sauce, pepper, onions, and lemon juice. Mix well. Fold in stiffly whipped cream. Refrigerate in covered jar. Mellows and improves if made at least 4 hours before you plan to use it. Very good with green salads as well as with seafood salads.

SEAFOOD SAUCE #2

A good, quick seafood sauce. Best if the basic ingredients are homemade, but still good made with commercial products.

1 cup *Homemade Mayonnaise*
1 **tbsp. catsup**
2 **tbsp.** *Argyle Chile Sauce*

1 **tbsp. wine vinegar**
Juice of 1 lemon
1 **tbsp. prepared horseradish**

Combine and allow to steep, covered, in the refrigerator 30 minutes before serving. Good for crabmeat or shrimp cocktail.

Aunt Helen's Memorial Beans
Kohl Kopf (Stuffed Cabbage Head)
Carrot Casserole
Corn Pudding
Celery Casserole
Glazed Cushaw
Eggplant Soufflé
Garlic Grits
Fried Okra
Black-eyed Peas and Okra
Baked Potatoes Jack
Ranch-fried Potatoes
What To Do with Rice
Green Rice
Tex Czech Spinach
Pretty Summer Squash
Yellow Squash Casserole
Tomato Okra Pilau
Sautéed Green Tomatoes
Zucchini Casserole
Texas Pecan Butter

Vegetables

When I think of vegetables, I don't think of home gardens or expansive produce sections in supermarkets. I think of the time vegetables came to the Texas Panhandle.

When my grandfather came to the Panhandle with his Oklahoma bride, the Great Plains was a sea of grass, unmarred by trees, or many people, or even water. All the way to the ranch my grandmother wept at the vastness of it all. Following the cattlemen were the dryland farmers, who turned the earth and made a hard-scrabble living from grain.

But after World War II the Panhandle experienced a great boom, and people who had been struggling subsistence farmers grew prosperous. Much of this prosperity was due to the discovery of water, a great ocean of water under the ground which was there for the taking. I remember the first big well I ever saw.

My parents' friends, Jess and Ellen, were part of the boom. One Sunday they came by in their new Cadillac convertible and we all went for a ride. Leaning back onto the leather seats and blinking against the white hot sun of a Panhandle summer, we felt a little shy in the face of all that opulence. Jess drove the car as if it were a great beast, but totally under his subjugation.

We whipped along a country road kicking up a furious plume of dust, when suddenly we came into a throbbing, pulsing sound; it overwhelmed the purr of the automobile's engine. We looked around and there it was. A water well.

We jumped out of the car and stared in wonder at a chugging gasoline engine shooting out an enormous stream of water that surged horizontally for a distance longer than the Cadillac before it fell into the freshly dug irrigation trench. The water even smelled good.

Daddy and Jess stood off to one side and talked in low tones, pointing and looking at the difference in the two fields of wheat. The watered wheat was as high as my head and as lush as the car. The dryland wheat looked pitiful and apologetic. The watered wheat undulated in the wind, almost in time with the throbbing of the engine, as if all were a part of a great machine.

Ellen, who was full of life and laughing at the sun, took me by the hand and ran with me through the tall golden wheat. The wheat beards were as rough as files and slapped me on the cheeks. We came back to the well, out of breath and dizzy with it all. We stooped and drank the cold clear water, the best water in the whole wide world, we said. Then Ellen lifted up her skirts and jumped into the ditch, pulling me in with her. The water was freezing, so cold it numbed our feet instantly. We screamed in delight and scrambled for the warmth of the bank.

Jess sat down on the raw fresh earth and dabbed his hands in the water. You know what this means, he said. We're all free, and he jerked his thumb toward the heavens. We won't have to pray for rain anymore.

Vegetables

And then out of the golden sky came the sound of another engine. An airplane landed right on the dirt road facing the Cadillac, taxied a bit, and then stopped. I heard Jess say to Daddy that it was one of the vegetable men. He knew him.

The man bounded out of the plane, tan and tall and with a mouth full of white teeth. The grownups shook hands all around and shouted over the noise of the well pump until the vegetable man threw a switch and killed the motor. Sudden silence, and for an instant everyone was uncomfortable and had to draw in his breath and lower his voice. Only the wind remained, sighing through the wheat.

Jess and the man admired each other's new vehicles when suddenly Ellen grabbed the man by the hand. How about a ride, she asked. Sure, he said, and she took my hand and into the tiny plane we went. I saw my mother's mouth drop open, then close.

Up we went, the thrust of the plane both wonderful and terrifying. I clutched the jump seat with both hands and held my breath. Ellen and the man were laughing in the front seat. He banked the plane sharply and we could look out and see the checkerboard of the high plains, green and brown and golden squares all laced together with silver ribbons: glistening silver ribbons of precious water that held it all together.

The mysterious man pointed to various squares and told Ellen what he would plant and how the country was going to change. It wasn't going to be just wheat anymore, he said. And change it did. With the water came vegetables. Farmers no longer relied on rain. Farmers no longer relied on wheat. They planted onions and potatoes and sugar beets and carrots. People would point to a field and say, did you know Jack made eight thousand dollars from that one field, and the other people would shake their heads in disbelief.

The vegetable people became a common sight in Hereford. Mostly from the Valley, they came like affluent gypsies, purring through town in big cars, living in motels (just think of the expense, my mother would cluck), building giant sheds to process the harvest. They were like people from another planet.

You could spot a vegetable man in a group of local farmers as easily as you could spot a sheik at a barbecue. He would be more smooth and tan, and his clothes would be shiny with laundry starch. Local farmers had red faces and necks, and they wore home-washed denims and carried themselves with the humility that comes from a lifetime of dealing with the vagaries of nature. But the vegetable men wore arrogance and pride like they wore their high shiny boots. They could speak Spanish, and they carried pistols in their glove compartments.

Sometimes their women would come along, too. And we shy small-town girls would look on them with awe. They were elegant, worldly, sleepy-eyed women and girls. A fifteen-year-old once had a sale in a motel room of all her last year's clothes: clothes from Neiman-Marcus and Sakowitz and even some from Saks Fifth Avenue. The girls went to boarding schools and had been to Mexico and New York and some even to Europe. They never stayed in Hereford long, but drifted on with the harvest, I never knew where.

The very air we breathed changed with the vegetables. When the onions were "on," the whole county smelled like an enchilada. And when the beets were being made into sugar at the great Holly plant, the entire town smelled like freshly baked sugar cookies. And the night skies were no longer inky velvet, spangled with stars, but were brown instead, choked with particles belched up from the mill.

With the vegetable people and their new enormous sheds and mills came another thing we hadn't had before. Alien labor. There were stoop workers for the fields. There were line workers for the sheds. Workers who followed the harvest. The summer found our town crawling with enormous trucks bearing Mexican license plates and blaring mariachi music. Sometimes the insides of the truck cabs would be sensuously decorated with silver fringes and red velvet roses. Sometimes the drivers' names would be written in gold on the doors. But in the backs of those trucks, packed tighter than jars full of olives, were Mexican laborers and their wives and children, looking considerably less gay than the truck's driver and front seat riders.

There had been a prisoner of war camp outside of Hereford during World War II; and now that the German prisoners had been shipped across the water, this site became known as the labor camp. High school home-economics classes and Methodist youth groups went to the camp, stepping over the slops and turning away from the rows of outdoor toilets, feeling virtuous and Christian as they painted gentian violet on the sores of the workers and handed out used clothing. Once I remember looking into a small cave-like room, hot and musty, and discovering at least fifteen pairs of eyes staring back at me. There was a baby in a tiny white hammock.

And all of us local people looked on this new industry with a cautious optimism. We feared and embraced change simultaneously. We were glad for the money. Now there could be a new school. Soon we would plant trees downtown. The REA worked furiously to lace up the county with wires to power the wells. My friend Barbara remembers driving home with her parents from the Saturday night movie and seeing her house ablaze with electric lights—for the very first time.

The lives of the farmers changed with the water, with the vegetables. But once in awhile, at a public gathering, if you stood quietly and looked closely, you might see a shadow of anxiety pass across some farmer's eye. Just a glimmer, and quickly covered over, because the water and the vegetables and the money, both borrowed and earned, took Hereford into a place it had never been, and no one knew for sure what it all meant or how it would all turn out.

AUNT HELEN'S MEMORIAL BEANS
Melinda Schmidt

Serves 6

When I began the research for this book, I swore to include no processed foods. But I ran up against a conflict almost immediately. If I was to remain true to the state of the art in Texas, there had to be some processed foods included. No self-respecting cowboy would use anything except tinned milk. Anybody who grew up on the frontier absolutely swore by canned tomatoes and tomato sauce and catsup. And more canned pork and beans have been served to Texans than any Boston Baked Beans made from scratch. My mother always made some sort of baked bean dish from the can when I was growing up. I always thought it was awful. I also thought the versions made by my friends' mothers were awful. But here is a version that destroyed my prejudice against canned beans. Aunt Helen's reputation was made with this recipe.

1 large can (1 lb., 12 oz.) pork and beans (pick a good brand— this is no time to go for the cheap stuff)	1 small onion, chopped
	1 tbsp. brown sugar
	1 tsp. chile powder
	½ cup catsup
2 slices bacon, chopped	½ cup water
1 green pepper, chopped	1 small jalapeño, chopped fine

Mix and bake in a 1½-quart casserole dish, uncovered, in a slow oven (325°) for 3 hours. *Stir often.* Did you ever hear of anything easier?

Once you provide these beans for a party, they'll never ask you to bring anything else. For a large group:

2 large cans (1 lb., 12 oz.) pork and beans	3 tbsp. brown sugar
1 1-lb. can pork and beans	3 tsp. chile powder
6 slices bacon, chopped	1½ cup tomato catsup
1½ large green peppers, chopped	1½ cup water
2 large onions, chopped	2 jalapeños, chopped fine

Mix well. Cook in large casserole dish, uncovered, for 4½–5 hours, stirring frequently.

KOHL KOPF
(Stuffed Cabbage Head)
Emily Mickler

Serves 8

The Germans in South Texas used to serve a stuffed cabbage at Christmas and Thanksgiving. The whole green head was presented on a silver salver, and when uncovered, all the dinner guests would gasp in appreciation. One of the secrets to this dish is the browned butter. When I first tried the recipe, I thought the butter was supposed to be melted, but when I served it, my German husband leaped up from the table screaming no—no—no and took the butter back to the stove. Turning the fire up high, he boiled the butter until the milk solids began to separate out and turn brown. That, he said, looking awfully triumphant for a man who claims he can only boil water, is browned butter. This butter smells like caramel, and I guess it is—minus the sugar. It tastes so good, I think you could pour it over tennis shoes and they'd taste wonderful. Try the butter with any steamed vegetable. The cabbage head must have been time-consuming when the poor cook had to grate everything by hand, but with a food processor it goes together in 5 minutes.

1 large head cabbage	1 medium onion, grated
2 cups bread crumbs	Cheesecloth and clean cotton
2 cups cooked ham or bacon,	string
chopped	½ lb. butter, browned and served
3 well-beaten eggs	on the side
Salt and pepper to taste	

Carefully remove 6 outer leaves of the cabbage. Grate the remaining cabbage and combine with all ingredients except butter. Place 5 of the cabbage leaves in a cheesecloth-lined colander. Add stuffing loosely. Place the sixth leaf on the top and draw the cheesecloth up into a ball and tie with a clean cotton string. Choose a pot large enough so that this ball can float without touching the bottom and yet be completely submerged in water. Fill the pot with water and bring to a boil. Place the cabbage head in the boiling water. Using a wooden spoon forced through the cheesecloth, you can suspend the top so that the ball won't bob around. Boil it for 1 hour. Drain in a colander. Carefully remove the cheesecloth and place on a flat platter. Brown the butter in a small skillet and pour into a gravy boat. Serve small pie-shaped wedges with butter.

CARROT CASSEROLE
Nona Morriss

Serves 12

2 lbs. carrots	2 cups grated Cheddar cheese
¼ lb. butter	Salt and pepper to taste
4 cups yellow onions	Bread crumbs to cover
2 tbsp. oil	

Preheat oven to 350°. Scrape and cut carrots into chunks. Steam until tender. Mash with butter and set aside. Peel and slice onions into thin rounds. Sauté in oil until they begin to brown and soften. Add to carrots. Blend in cheese, salt, and pepper to taste. Place in a 2-quart casserole and top with bread crumbs. Bake at 350° until top begins to brown (20–30 minutes). Freezes well (freeze before baking).

Whenever a recipe calls for bread crumbs, I always use some sort of good bread. Leftover French bread. Dried-out English muffins. Bagels. Real whole wheat. Anything but plain white enriched bread, which as far as I can tell, is only good for one thing, and that I learned from a friend in Dallas. You can use white fish-food bread for picking up broken glass off the floor.

To make bread crumbs, I simply freeze whatever bread ends I have and then pop them into the food processor frozen. Takes about 10 seconds.

CORN PUDDING

Serves 6

1 pint scraped corn (about 12 large ears)	Salt and pepper to taste
	2 cups cream
4 well-beaten eggs	1 tbsp. butter

To scrape corn, shuck the ear and hold it vertically in a large dish. Using the dull side of a heavy knife, scrape firmly so that you get lots of milk and the heart of the corn, but not whole kernels. Corn spurts when scraped, so be careful not to get it on the walls. It sticks. Add remaining ingredients to the scraped corn and place in a buttered baking dish. Put the dish in a pan of hot water and bake 30 minutes in a 350° oven.

CELERY CASSEROLE

Martha Johnson

Serves 8

1 heaping tsp. butter	½ cup grated American cheese
1 heaping tsp. flour	¼ tsp. salt
1½ cups milk	¼ tsp. white pepper
1 bunch celery	¾ cup fine bread crumbs
½ cup blanched, slivered almonds	

Place butter in pan and melt over medium heat. Add flour and stir until completely blended—turns from butter yellow to a deep golden color. Add milk, cook, and stir to make a thin white sauce. Set aside.

Wash and dry celery and cut at an angle into ½-inch pieces. Place in a buttered 9″ × 12″ dish. Cover evenly with almonds and grated cheese. Add salt and pepper to prepared white sauce and pour over celery and cheese. Top with bread crumbs. Refrigerate at least 3 hours; overnight is better. (Refrigeration is the secret which guarantees the desired results.) Bake in a 375° oven for 20–30 minutes until top browns and casserole is bubbly hot. Do not cook celery before combining it with other ingredients. The finished casserole is crunchy and wonderful.

GLAZED CUSHAW

Elysee Peavy

Serves 4

The cushaw is an old Southern squash that is close kin to a gourd. The main trouble in choosing one is to get one small enough. You may find that one cushaw makes too many cubes to fit in the bottom of a skillet. Don't crowd the skillet. Cook the remains the next day as you would any other squash.

1 cushaw	Cinnamon, cloves, and nutmeg,
1 cup sugar	ground
1 cup water	2 tbsp. butter

Peel, seed, and cube the cushaw. Combine sugar and water. Boil syrup over high heat until it's thick (about 260°). Place cushaw in a 10-inch iron skillet, one layer deep, with the pieces not touching. Pour hot syrup over the squash, turn heat to low, and cook slowly.

Turn pieces occasionally with a spatula. When the cushaw is fork-tender and glazed to a luscious caramel color, dust lightly with cinnamon, cloves, and nutmeg. Just before removing cushaw from the pan, add butter. Good with poultry, roast turkey, or chicken.

EGGPLANT SOUFFLÉ

Elysee Peavy

Serves 6

1 eggplant	2 tsp. grated onion
2 tbsp. butter	1 tbsp. catsup
2 tbsp. flour	1 tsp. salt
1 cup warm milk	1 cup grated Cheddar cheese
¾ cup bread crumbs	2 eggs, separated

Peel and cut eggplant into chunks. Place in saucepan with just enough water to cover and cook until soft. Drain and mash eggplant. Set aside. Make a light roux with butter and flour by melting butter in small pan, then adding flour and stirring until golden. Add milk and cook and stir until you have a nice white sauce. Now add mashed eggplant, bread, onion, catsup, salt, cheese, and egg yolks. Beat whites until they hold firm peaks, then fold into first mixture. Turn into a well-greased baking dish. Put dish into a pan of water and bake at 375° for 45 minutes—or until the soufflé has set (it shouldn't jiggle when you tap the side).

In making this or any other soufflé choose a 1½-quart round casserole dish and make a sort of lip around it with a long piece of aluminum foil, folded over lengthwise and fitted around the edge of the dish to extend the sides a good 2 inches. This seems to guide the soufflé in the right direction and makes any soufflé picture-perfect.

GARLIC GRITS

Serves 4

1 cup grits	½ lb. Swiss cheese, grated
4 cups water	3 eggs
2 cloves garlic, pressed	Salt and pepper to taste
1 tsp. salt	Parmesan cheese
¼ lb. butter	Hungarian paprika

Preheat oven to 300°. Cook grits in water seasoned with garlic and salt according to package directions. Remove from heat. Add butter and stir to dissolve. Add Swiss cheese, holding back a good handful to go on the top—and stir again. Now add eggs and mix completely. Add salt and pepper to taste. Place in a buttered 2-quart baking dish. Sprinkle remaining Swiss cheese on top. Sprinkle top with a generous amount of Parmesan, dust with paprika, and bake uncovered in a 300° oven for 45 minutes.

FRIED OKRA

For years I tried to fry okra. The cornmeal would never stay on. It always fell to the bottom of the skillet and quickly burned, ruining the okra as well as the pot. Somebody finally told me how to do it. First, you have to use young okra. The best way to test okra for tenderness is to try to stick your thumbnail into the skin up close to the stem. If you get resistance, the okra is too stringy and won't work. Okra is another of those vegetables that is best picked early and cooked quickly. Pick small, bright green pods that have a tender skin.

Okra	Small brown bag
Cornmeal	Skillet full of very hot oil

Place young okra into a pan full of cold water. Take the okra out one piece at a time, cut into medallions, and drop them in a bag of cornmeal (without shaking off water). Shake the sack vigorously to coat the okra. When you remove the okra, use your hands to shake off any excess cornmeal (so it won't come off in the oil), and drop into very hot oil. Cook quickly, a little at a time; scoop it out and drain on paper towels. Now that's fried okra. Some people add salt and pepper to the cornmeal.

    Last night that crazy fool husband of mine came up with a new invention. Using equal parts of each, he fried okra, onion rings, and (you'll never believe this) jalapeño. He simply cut the peppers in half, seeded them, then dipped them in a little beaten egg before coating them with the cornmeal. To tell you the truth it was delicious. Nobody but a Texan would try it.

BLACK-EYED PEAS AND OKRA

Serves 6–8

Real Texans always cooked a "mess" of black-eyed peas in the summertime. If tender young okra was available it was added to the mature shelled peas and "snaps," combined with a chunk of salt pork, and cooked at least 2 hours in boiling water so that the resulting dish was a kind of soup—usually served with corn bread and, at our house, for some reason, always with spiced peaches and a glass of buttermilk.

If you want to cook up a mess of peas and snaps, here's a close approximation of the old country dish.

4 lbs. fresh black-eyed peas	**Salt**
1 lb. tender young okra pods	**Water**
¼ lb. salt pork	

The peas will range from almost dried yellow pods to tender thin shoots. Shell mature peas into a pan. (Get someone to help you. This is a wonderful companionable task but pretty miserable alone.) Snap the young, bright green pods into the pan. If the pod is hard to snap, it's too mature and should be shelled. Wash the peas and snaps in cool running water. Drain. Make sure okra is tender by trying to stick your thumbnail up under the stem cap. If your nail meets resistance, the pods are too stringy and shouldn't be used. Wash okra pods (don't remove caps) and set aside.

Place peas in kettle, make slashes in the salt pork, and add it to peas. Cover peas with at least 1 inch of water. Raise to a boil over medium heat. Taste. If salt pork is sufficiently salty, you won't need to add salt, but if you do, taste and salt now. Simmer gently, uncovered, for at least 2 hours. Add okra and cook at least 45 minutes more, or until vegetables are cooked through.

Good salt pork is hard to find these days. Uncured raw pork can become rancid in a hurry, and today's salt pork is sometimes undercured. Choose salt pork that has a fine coating of salt on the surface. The fat should be very white and the stripe should be brown (this means the pork is well cured). Knock off any excess salt, but don't wash the pork. Be careful that you don't oversalt the food. Taste the water. If it isn't salty enough you can add a little salt, but remember that some salt will leach out of the pork as the cooking proceeds.

BAKED POTATOES JACK

Serves 6–8

Easy to make ahead for company.

6 medium russet potatoes, baked
    and cooled
½ cup butter, melted
1 cup sour cream
1½ cup grated Monterrey Jack
    cheese

¼ cup fresh parsley, chopped
1½ cup green onions and tops,
    chopped
Salt and pepper to taste

Preheat oven to 325°. Peel baked potatoes and mash with a fork, leaving lumps. Place potatoes in a Pyrex utility pan (13½″ × 8¾″). Combine sour cream, butter, and cheese (this will be a smooth paste if made in processor). Sprinkle potatoes with parsley and green onions, salt and pepper to taste. Spoon cheese sauce over. Don't try to smooth it out. Leave hills and valleys. (You can do this ahead and refrigerate covered until 40 minutes before serving time.) Bake uncovered in a preheated oven until slightly browned on top—about 30 minutes.

RANCH-FRIED POTATOES

John Charles Casey

Serves 4

3 russet potatoes
1 onion
Salt and pepper, coarsely ground

3–4 tbsp. peanut oil, or fresh
    bacon drippings
Cast-iron 10-inch skillet with lid

Peel potatoes and slice into varying thicknesses from ¹⁄₁₆ inch to ³⁄₁₆ inch. Slice onion into ⅛-inch thicknesses. Heat grease in skillet and add potatoes and onions. Salt and pepper to taste. Cover. Using a spatula, turn every 3 minutes. The thin slices will begin to crisp and brown. The thick slices will begin to stick together. Let 'em stick. Cover skillet between turnings to permit some steaming. When a fork goes in the thick slices easily, the potatoes are done (20–25 minutes). Remove from heat and serve immediately.

For optimum results don't cook more than 3 potatoes and 1 onion at a time in a 10-inch skillet. If you double the recipe, make separate batches. Otherwise the potatoes will turn to mush. Also tasty but a different result.

WHAT TO DO WITH RICE
Patricia Slate

Serves 6

1 onion, chopped fine
1 stalk celery, chopped fine
1 carrot, chopped fine
3 tbsp. oil

1 cup rice
Salt and white pepper to taste
2½ cups water

In a skillet sauté onion, celery, and carrot in oil. Add rice and sauté until rice becomes golden brown, stirring constantly. Add water and season to taste with salt and pepper. The water will be as salty as the finished rice will be, so salt and taste until it suits you. It's better not to salt it after cooking, or you'll just have crystals bleeding out onto the rice. Cover skillet, lower heat, and cook rice until tender and all water is absorbed—about 15–20 minutes.

Another good thing to do with rice is to add finely shredded raw carrots to cooked rice.

For looks, you can press freshly cooked rice into an oiled ring mold. It will knock out into a pretty ring. Pile parsley in the middle of the ring and serve. You can mold rice into almost any shape. An individual mold is desirable if you want to serve rice with a shapeless entree and don't want two formless items on a plate.

GREEN RICE
Katherine Thurber

Serves 6

1 cup cooked rice (½ cup raw rice
   cooked in 1¼ cups water)
2 eggs, beaten
½ cup cooking oil
½ lb. grated sharp Cheddar
   cheese

1 cup fresh parsley
1 small onion, chopped
1 clove garlic, pressed
1 large can evaporated milk
Salt and pepper to taste

Preheat oven to 300°. Cook rice in water in a covered pan until tender (about 15 minutes), then combine with all ingredients. Place in well-greased baking dish, set dish in a pan containing about 1 inch of water, and bake in a preheated oven for 1½ hours or until it sets.

TEX CZECH SPINACH

Serves 6

1 10-oz. package fresh spinach	½ tsp. salt
4 slices bacon	2 tbsp. flour
1 clove garlic, pressed	1 cup milk

Wash spinach thoroughly and discard stems. Place wet spinach in a skillet, cover, and cook over medium heat until just tender. Drain spinach in a colander, then finely chop. In a 10-inch skillet, cook bacon until crisp, then remove and crush into bits. Place pressed garlic clove in a small dish and mash with the salt. Add garlic to the bacon fat and cook for 1 minute. Stir in flour and cook a couple of minutes to make a light roux. Add milk and stir until it thickens. Stir in chopped spinach and crushed bacon bits. Salt and pepper to taste. Good with **Tex Czech Pork Chops**.

PRETTY SUMMER SQUASH
Patricia Slate

Serves 4

2 cups squash, yellow crookneck and zucchini	Fresh squeezed garlic clove
2 tbsp. clarified butter or peanut oil	Hot 10-inch skillet

Hand-grate squash into longest possible strips. Put a thin coating of butter or oil into skillet and heat until the oil becomes thin and runs to the edges. Add a touch of freshly squeezed garlic. Now add grated squash and toss quickly in the hot skillet for 2 minutes. Pretend you work in a fancy restaurant, and try to jump the squash over itself. I hope it doesn't wind up on the floor. Try it again. Fun, huh? Serve immediately.

Don't cook more than 2 cups at a time in a 10-inch skillet. Keep skillet very hot. If you only want 1 cup of squash, you can use an 8-inch skillet or sauté pan.

If you don't have clarified butter, use a little peanut oil. Plain butter will burn before it gets hot enough to sauté.

YELLOW SQUASH CASSEROLE

Linda Clarkson

Serves 6

1 lb. yellow squash, cut in rings
¼ lb. pork or venison sausage,
    crumbled
Salt and pepper
1 onion, chopped fine
1 cup celery, chopped fine

1 cup pecan halves
1 egg
¼ cup milk
½ cup grated Cheddar cheese
Bread crumbs

Parboil squash until tender. Fry sausage. Remove sausage from skillet and place onion, celery, and pecan halves in grease and fry until onion turns clear. Drain squash and place in a 2-quart casserole dish. Season to taste with salt and pepper. Cover with fried and crumbled sausage. Add a layer of sautéed vegetables. Mix egg with milk and pour this over. Now sprinkle grated cheese and bread crumbs on top. Cook in 350° oven until top browns (about 25 minutes). Serve as a main course for supper.

TOMATO OKRA PILAU

Serves 8

3 slices bacon
1 small onion, chopped
2 cups stewed tomatoes
2 cups thinly sliced okra

Salt and pepper to taste
1 cup rice
2 cups water
1 tsp. salt

Cook chopped bacon in a deep frying pan until brown; add the onion and cook until brown. Add tomatoes and okra and cook, covered, stirring occasionally; add salt and pepper. Cook rice, covered, in water with 1 teaspoon salt; after 12 minutes mix with tomato and okra mixture and let simmer for 15 or 20 minutes.

SAUTÉED GREEN TOMATOES

Linda Clarkson

Green tomatoes	Butter, 2 tbsp. per tomato
Flour	Brown sugar, 1 tsp. per tomato
Salt and pepper	Heavy cream, 1 tbsp. per tomato

Core tomatoes but don't peel them. Slice each tomato into ½-inch slices, dredge in flour seasoned with salt and pepper. Fry slowly in a little butter. When the first side is golden, sprinkle the floured side with a pinch of brown sugar and turn the slices. Sprinkle the golden side with a tiny bit of brown sugar as well. When second side has browned, add a little heavy cream, put the lid on the skillet and steam for 1 minute.

ZUCCHINI CASSEROLE

Serves 6

Did you ever notice the way zucchini grows? One day it's a few inches long, the next day it's a foot and a half. Here's what you can do with one of the monsters (or several small ones).

1 3–4 lb. zucchini, washed and sliced thin	Oregano
	Cilantro
Salt	Coarsely ground pepper
¼ cup butter or olive oil	4 ripe tomatoes, sliced thin
2 cloves garlic, pressed	2 cups grated Swiss cheese
2 onions, chopped	

Slice zucchini very thin, salt generously, and place in a colander. Let stand for about 30 minutes to express water. Rinse salt off, then pat zucchini dry.

Cover the bottom of a 10″ × 13″ Pyrex utility pan with half of sliced zucchini. Sauté the garlic and onion in butter or olive oil. Sprinkle zucchini with moderate amounts of oregano, cilantro, and pepper. Place thin tomato slices over zucchini. Then add half of the sautéed onion, garlic, and olive oil (or butter). Repeat layers. Top with cheese. Bake uncovered at 350° for 30–45 minutes, until the top is glazed and golden brown.

TEXAS PECAN BUTTER

Katherine Thurber

½ cup melted butter
2 tbsp. chopped chives
½ tsp. salt
¼ tsp. coarsely ground black
    pepper

¼ tsp. dried marjoram
3 tbsp. lemon juice
½ cup chopped pecans

Combine all ingredients and heat just enough to blend flavors.
Serve over cooked vegetables.

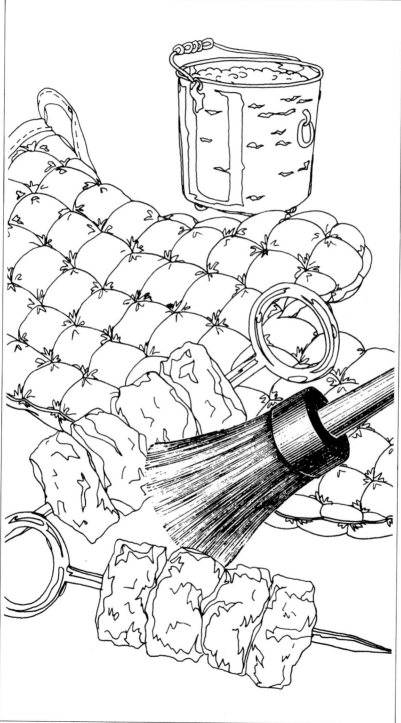

How to Build a Barbecue Pit
Malcolm DeShields' Barbecued Brisket
Basic Dry Rub for Barbecue
Barbecue Mop
Texas Table Sauce for Barbecue
Charcoaled Steak from Casey's John Charles Restaurant
Wesley's Ribs
Roast Beef Al Pastor
Baked Beef Head
Calf and Turkey Fries
J. Frank Dobie's Beans
Refritos
Hot Cowboy Beans
Cabrito Al Pastor

HOW TO BUILD A BARBECUE PIT

The directions for cooking barbecue are designed primarily for Texans who, through no fault of their own, are forced to live outside the state. If you have ever ordered barbecue in such outrageous places as New York or Los Angeles, you will understand from experience the murderous rage that lives in us all. You may even break down and cry in a public place. There is nothing like Texas barbecue. It is one of those things that simply doesn't export.

I spent a lot of time talking to the pros, eating barbecue, and trying to devise some way that barbecue could be cooked at home. It takes some doing. Frankly, if I lived within fifty miles of a decent barbecue place, I'd never be so presumptuous as to try and compete with a professional. But I don't live near a barbecue place, and from time to time I am overwhelmed with a primordial urge for barbecue. So I give myself a day and make the real thing.

But before I tell you how to do it, I want to speak to those readers who may have just moved to Texas. You might know how to define a fine French restaurant, but can you tell a good barbecue joint?

1. They serve only barbecue. You go there at noon.
2. A stack of wood is outside, and smoke is curling up from a large smokestack somewhere.
3. When you walk in the door, you may see a sign that says "Snickers in the Cooler."
4. More than likely there will be picnic tables with loaves of bread still in the plastic wrappers, gallon jars of jalapeños, and sliced onions. Maybe a pot of pinto beans.
5. Look carefully at the other diners. They should be just-folks. They should be hunched over squares of butcher paper, chewing thoughtfully. Ideally, there will be no conversation other than murmurs of approval and considered belches.
6. There are toothpicks beside the cash register. You buy the meat by the pound. The carver cuts it to order.
7. You are probably in a small town west of a line running from Columbus and northward to Dallas-Fort Worth.
8. You are eating Central Texas Barbecue—you lucky son-of-a-gun.

But can you cook it at home? With some effort, yes. In the first place, don't confuse barbecuing with grilling. Grilling over charcoal will produce a marvelous steak or lamb chop or even chicken, but that is not barbecue.

Barbecue is smoke, and not too much heat, and plenty of time. You can barbecue less-than-choice cuts. You cannot grill them. It takes low heat to tenderize a brisket. Remember that old physics rule. Water boils at 212°. Boil the water out of a tough piece of meat and what have you got? New sandals.

Commercial barbecue pits in Texas are usually brick, 10 to 20 feet long, about waist high, and with a sheet-metal lid so heavy it is suspended on pulleys. They build a fire in one end, put the meat at the other end, draw the smoke up over it, swab the meat and turn it for up to 24 hours. That's the process you are trying to imitate.

Wes Gulley does a good job of home barbecuing using his modified oil-drum barbecue pit. Wes is from Uvalde and knows the real thing. He had a rectangular sheet-metal baffle cut that just fits inside the oil drum between the grill and the firebox. Wes creased the baffle like a rooftop so that juices from the meat would run down the sides and back into the fire. He rigged up some sort of little legs that keep the baffle just about halfway between the fire and the meat. He didn't want the baffle to be lying on the fire—it would put it out. Nor did he want it so close to the meat that it would send up too much radiant heat.

He was trying to prevent the meat juices from dripping into the fire and flaming up. It works. When the juices and grease hit the baffle, they simply smoke. Just what you want. He builds a parsimonious little fire in one end of the drum, puts the meat at the other end, closes the lid, and barbecues away. Wes seasons the meat dry, then mops the meat with a sauce (recipe follows) about every half hour; he cooks his barbecue at least 4 hours no matter what the meat (see recipe for **Wesley's Ribs**). When he mops the meat, he dabs it on, since dragging the mop across the meat would knock off the dry seasonings.

I made a pretty fair imitation of Wes's baffle by sacrificing an old cookie sheet to the cause. I just propped the sheet up on bricks inside our oil-drum cooker. It was fairly successful although the bricks took up a lot of room in the firebox.

We have had good luck barbecuing in a metal cooker called Smoke 'n Pit. This cooker is designed with a bottom pan filled with charcoal and hickory chips, then a pan of water sitting on top of that, then the grill where you put the meat, and finally a dome lid.

You gain a lot of control with this type of barbecue. It never seems to get too hot. In truth, it produces meats that might better be described as smoked. As the meat cooks, juices drip down into the water, which boils and sends steam up to help the cooking procedure. Although you have to check the draft from time to time and may have to add more fuel or water, you can produce a good barbecue without much risk in this sort of cooker.

I also have used this waterpan cooker for game with very good results. Smoked haunch of venison is wonderful. Smoked game birds work equally well. One of the greatest things about this piece of equipment is that the cooking time is printed right on the lid. You don't have to think much, just read.

When I use this cooker, I usually just use a dry rub on the meat. Don't baste it because every time you open the lid, heat escapes and slows down the already slow process.

If all of these methods seem too complicated, you can try barbecuing in an open grill by building a modest charcoal fire at least 8 inches below the grill and placing a log at one end of the charcoal for smoke. As the fat drips out of the meat it will fall on the charcoal, creating more smoke. But that old demon, flame, will be a problem. Keep water nearby and quench any flameup immediately. The water will create steam, which will help your barbecue along. You should cover the entire top surface of the grill with meat. Every hole in the grill permits heat to escape and increases the draft which will, in turn, raise the temperature. You want the temperature as low as possible. You will have to mop and turn the meat about every 30 minutes. Since there are very few of us who can make the fire and the meat come out even, this can work to your advantage. You can cook meat for several meals in one sitting, freeze what you don't eat today, and reheat later. If you use this open method of barbecuing, you'll have to watch it every minute and judge the doneness by sight. It should take at least 2 hours.

Just remember that ribs and chicken should be limber when they are cooked through. Real barbecued beef is never rare, so the meat should be moist and gray when it is done. My only concern with this type of barbecuing is that it is so hard to get people to keep the heat down. I remember well when we were young poor graduate students and some eager soul would invite us over to a barbecue wherein the cook had marinated a chuck roast for hours and hours in some magic secret sauce, then attempted to grill it like a fine T-bone steak. Tastes just like steak, the hopeful cook would say. We could usually only nod politely because the tough meat seemed to be growing in our mouths. It's just one of the most elementary laws for cooking protein. You must have moisture and a low heat source to tenderize a tough piece of meat.

MALCOLM DeSHIELDS' BARBECUED BRISKET

Malcolm DeShields is a wiry little chap from Corpus Christi who calls himself the Barbecue Man. He is the sort of fellow who calls women under fifty "girl" and those over fifty "lady." He makes his points by giving you a jab to the shoulder for emphasis. Malcolm belongs to the school that says wet sauces are bad for barbecue. He says, and I agree, that *any sauce with tomato or sugar will burn.* Barbecue cooked dry—over a very low heat and in a covered barbecue pit—will produce a marvelous real Texas barbecue.

This is what Malcolm says about cooking a brisket:

Choose about a 9-pound brisket. One with some fat on it. You don't want it too lean. Make you up a dry rub of equal parts of salt, fine pepper, and paprika—say about ⅛ cup of each—and rub this all over the meat real good. Don't ever pierce it with a fork. Turn it with them tongs.

Build you up a good fire in your barbecue pit—at one end—using mesquite, hickory, or oak. If you have to you can use hickory chips soaked in water with charcoal. Now let your fire burn down real good. If you have a pan of water to put in—all the better. You'll have to figure out how to get it in dependin' on your own pit, but the water should be somewhere kinder in the middle. Your fire cain't be too hot. But you cain't let it go out either. You may have to kinder nurse it along, addin' little logs from time to time, 'bout as big around as yore wrist. Remember to keep the fire off from the meat.

Well, anyway, when you got your fire just so, put the brisket on and cover it up. You'll need some sort of draw so the smoke just sucks right over the meat. I'd say a 9-pound brisket 'ud cook about 18 hours. Now, girl, don't think you can just go off and forget it. You got to turn it once in awhile with them tongs, add wood or add water, but um-um, that barbecue will be just right.

You can do the same thing with pork ribs, steak, or chicken. Use the same seasoning. Cook ribs about 3 hours, chicken about 2. Steak just 20 minutes.

BASIC DRY RUB FOR BARBECUE

3 tbsp. salt
3 tbsp. black pepper
3 tbsp. paprika

For ribs you may add:

1 tbsp. lemon powder
6 tbsp. sugar (Remember to watch
    for flameups if you choose to
    add sugar—it burns)

For chicken you may add to the basic rub:

2 tbsp. garlic powder
2 tbsp. dry mustard
1 tsp. crumbled bay leaf

BARBECUE MOP
Wes Gulley

Makes 1 quart

1½ tsp. salt	1 tsp. Louisiana Hot Sauce
1½ tsp. dry mustard	⅔ cup Worcestershire sauce
1 tsp. garlic powder	⅓ cup apple cider vinegar
½ tsp. ground bay leaf	2⅔ cup beef stock
1 tsp. chile powder	⅓ cup cooking oil
1½ tsp. paprika	

Combine all ingredients and use to mop meats that are barbecu-ing. You can go to the dime store and buy a dish mop or you can rig one up at home by using a long-handled wooden spoon and some clean rags which you tie to the end of the spoon with string. I always use the rag version, then simply throw the rags away. It seems easier to me than keeping the mop clean between bar-becues. Leftover sauce will keep well in the refrigerator. You will notice that as you stick the mop in the sauce the color darkens and becomes more chocolate brown because meat juices are blending with the sauce. This enhances the flavor of the sauce and will make it better the second time you use it. You can use this mop for beef, pork, or chicken with equally good results.

As you can see, this sauce has no tomato and no sugar. Any so-called barbecue sauce with tomato or sugar should be served on the side and not rubbed on cooking meat because sugar or tomato will burn and char the meat surface. Read labels on commercial products and apply the same rule.

TEXAS TABLE SAUCE FOR BARBECUE

Sauce for 6 pounds of meat

If you are barbecuing with a dry seasoning and/or with the mop sauce you may still wish to serve a sauce at the table. The way I get that good smokey flavor in the table sauce is to cook it on the edge of the grill for an hour or so while the barbecue is going. I have a personal aversion to bottled smoke, but do like the table sauce smokey. Cooking the sauce outside will produce the desired effect. You may notice a few ashes floating up into the sauce. So what? Stir them in. If you wish to make this sauce inside, add a little artificial smoke if you like, but don't compare it to that cooked outside.

This sauce will keep well in the refrigerator. You can use it for oven barbecuing if you keep the temperature low, say about 275°, and cover the meat, but never use this sauce for outside barbecuing. It will char meat because it contains both sugar and tomatoes.

¾ cup cider vinegar	3 tbsp. dry mustard
¾ cup warm water	½ cup catsup
1 tbsp. salt	¼ cup chile sauce
1 tsp. coarsely ground pepper	3 tbsp. Worcestershire sauce
1 tsp. Hungarian paprika	1 clove garlic, pressed
2 tbsp. dark brown sugar	2 tbsp. onion, minced very fine
1 tbsp. dark molasses	1 cup butter

In a 2-cup measure, combine vinegar and water. Stir in salt, pepper, paprika, brown sugar, molasses, and dry mustard. Set aside to steep. Combine catsup, chili sauce, Worcestershire sauce, garlic, onion, and butter in medium-sized saucepan. Raise to a boil over medium-low heat. Stir in vinegar water. Transfer to outside cooker and simmer uncovered for 1 hour or so, stirring from time to time. (If cooked indoors, simmer about 30 minutes.) Store covered in refrigerator. Serve hot with barbecue.

CHARCOALED STEAK FROM CASEY'S
JOHN CHARLES RESTAURANT

John Casey, who owns a San Antonio steak house and has taught plenty of maverick cooks how to turn out the perfect steak, gives these hints for grilling over a charcoal fire. Buy steaks 2 inches thick—either strip or T-bone. Salt and pepper them. Put the steak over a hot fire. Cover with a roaster lid. Don't let the cover touch the meat. Leave for 5 minutes. Flip the steak. Cover again. Cook 5 minutes more. Now you have a beautiful medium-rare steak.

WESLEY'S RIBS
Wes Gulley

Everybody wants Wes to bring his ribs to a barbecue. He even knocks off from work early to give them enough time to cook.

After building a cool fire in his oil-drum pit, with a baffle over the coals, Wes puts on a side of pork ribs to cook and begins mopping each side with his mop sauce. He sits out in the backyard and reads or talks to his wife or plays with his little boy—whom he calls Honey—and about every 20 minutes, he goes back to the barbecue pit, mops the ribs, and turns them. He doesn't necessarily cover the pit, but he might, just depends. After *4 hours*, the ribs are done enough to suit Wes. The way he can tell is this: he takes a pair of kitchen tongs and lifts up one end of the ribs. The meat should be real flexible and bend almost double without threatening to break.

When I first started cooking ribs by this method, everybody told me I was crazy. It couldn't possibly take 4 hours to cook little skinny ribs. They quit arguing after they ate them.

Need I mention that if the fire is too hot you will burn them to a crisp. Take Wes's advice. Be parsimonious with the fire. Just a little heat, a lot of smoke, mop and turn the ribs regularly, and by nighttime you'll have the best damn barbecued ribs you ever ate.

ROAST BEEF AL PASTOR

John Casey has spent a lot of time in South Texas and has watched the Mexican cowboys cook over an open fire. Here is the way he says to make a perfect *al pastor* roast beef. First of all go to the best butcher you know and buy a good quality roast beef, a rump roast, that weighs between 6 and 8 pounds.

Next, you go to the hardware store. Get a steel rod 4–5 feet long and ½ inch in diameter. Have one end of the rod sharpened so you can drive it into the ground. Drill 4 holes 6 inches apart— at 2 feet, 2½ feet, 3 feet, and so on. Each hole must accommodate a good-sized cotter pin, which is inserted through the hole at right angles to the rod. Thread a big flat washer onto the rod and let it rest on the cotter pin. These pins and washers keep the meat from sliding down the rod. The various holes allow you to adjust the distance between the meat and heat source, as necessary. Salt and pepper the roast, then impale the meat on the rod. Fix the washers below and above the meat, drive the rod into the ground at a 60° angle, and you have an alfresco spit.

Now here is the way Casey says to build the perfect outdoor fire. Get the kids to find 2 logs that are well seasoned but not rotten. They should be about 3 feet long and at least 4 to 6 inches in diameter. Butt these logs into a right angle. Build a hardwood fire—oak, hickory, or pecan—in the crotch or the joint of the logs. Keep the meat on the rod which is hanging out over this fire about 3 feet above the heat. Turn the meat from time to time. Casey says the fire will smoulder in the logs and that if you have everything positioned just so, you can go away at dawn and by 2 o'clock in the afternoon have a good dinner waiting.

BAKED BEEF HEAD

John Casey tells me the South Texas ranchers had some help from Mexicans when it came time to butcher. The Mexicans taught them how to make use of all the animal. They would take a steer or heifer head, skin it, salt and pepper it, wrap it in several sacks of wet burlap. Dig a deep hole. Line the hole with rocks made hot by a roaring camp fire. Put the head in. Cover it with a thin layer of dirt. Then pour on more hot rocks and dirt until the whole thing was covered. They would come back 18 or 20 hours later, dig the head up, unwind the burlap, pull out the tongue, hit the skull with an ax, and eat the brains, the tongue, everything. Casey says it's a real treat.

This meat-in-a-hole method is an old trick. Sometimes it doesn't work out. They were having a huge barbecue in the Panhandle recently—one of those public celebrations where they killed 7 or 8 animals and meant to barbecue them all. Well, you can imagine how this story went. The Caterpillars were driven in to dig a huge pit. The barbecue man laid his fire, got it just right, put in all this meat, covered it up. Came back in 24 hours with 20,000 hungry people behind him, dug it up, and discovered the fire had gone out. He had lots of beans, lots of cole slaw, and lots of rotting meat in a hole. No wonder some cooks turn to drink.

CALF AND TURKEY FRIES

Castration and branding were done in the spring at roundup. Uncle Dick says when they castrated the calves they simply threw the testicles onto the branding fire and when the skin popped, the cowboys would fish them out of the fire and eat them. He swears they were delicious.

The frontier version of Victorian sensibility demanded that this delicacy be called Mountain Oysters. Out behind the barn the good old boys just called them bull nuts. But calf fries pretty well describes them. Now where can you get them? Feed lots and beef packing plants usually can advise you as to availability. Specialty grocers sometimes have frozen calf fries. When we bought them last, they came in a 1-gallon jar, skinned and packed in salt water, looking for all the world like pickled bratwurst. They were easy to cook. If you like sweetbreads, you'll like calf fries.

As for turkey fries, they're just the same, only smaller. No larger than a crouton. I once knew a poor devil who worked his way through law school castrating turkeys in one of those enormous Central Texas poultry houses. Needless to say, he ate nothing but red meat.

HOW TO COOK CALF AND TURKEY FRIES

First you have to get them. Second, if they didn't come to you skinned, you have to skin them. Now all you do is heat fat to 350°, cut the testicles into medallions, dredge them in seasoned flour, and deep-fry. If you prepare these outside on a Coleman stove your guests will eat them as fast as you can get them cooked.

BEANS

People sometimes say to me, I'll bet you spend a lot of money for groceries, cooking all the time the way you do. They generally go on to say, I can't afford to cook well. Our budget just won't stand it.

And I am reminded of the word that Hollywood uses for art. The word is *treatment*. In the L. A. jargon they speak of the treatment of material. It's all in the treatment. What the image makers know is that there are only 32 plots anyway, so it's how you treat the material that counts. The same goes for cooking. How you approach the materials at hand is what determines the results. When my father came home from World War II, money was in short supply. Sunday dinner in Texas has always been an *event*, and many of our events during those postwar years centered around a pot of pinto beans, corn bread, and canned spinach.

My father would eat with great relish. He would reach over and pat my mother on the arm, or if she got up to refill the bowl, on the fanny. He must have said a million times during that period, I'll bet President Truman isn't eating this good today. My mother would blush and beam and spread butter on a hot piece of corn bread for him. When he took it from her he would inhale deeply. I could see the steam rising. I could see the butter melt.

My mother used a starched tablecloth. She insisted that one come to table with hair combed and clothes clean. There was never any question that we would all sit down together at the same time. After the meal we sat telling about our day. My father praised Mother's homemade jellies—and he helped her with the dishes.

My mother took a lot of care for that all-important Sunday dinner. On Saturday night she would sit and sort the beans, one at a time, rejecting broken beans, rocks, and twigs. She soaked the beans until morning. She watched the pot carefully, tasted it from time to time, commented on the quality of salt pork she had purchased from the butcher that week. Sunday dinner was a celebration, and it started with a humble pot of beans.

J. FRANK DOBIE'S BEANS

There is no way to improve on the recipe given by a real *frijoles* man. Dobie says to wash a pound of pinto beans, soak them overnight. Add water to cover beans generously. Also add a cube of salt pork. Cook until tender, adding water as necessary and salt to taste. The end result is bean soup.

REFRITOS

Lift beans out of the soup with a slotted spoon and place them in a hot cast-iron skillet with a little lard. Mash them with a potato masher. Cook and stir until the beans are dry and thick.

Living at sea level, I find it's never necessary to soak beans overnight. I believe that idea must have come from the higher elevations where water boils at a lower temperature and beans are harder to cook.

An old hand told me never to pour cold water in the boiling bean pot because that's what causes the beans to split. If you need to add water, make it warm water.

HOT COWBOY BEANS
Jabe Wills

Enough for Coxey's Army

2 lbs. dried pinto beans
½ lb. salt pork, slashed into a fan shape
½–1 lb. leftover ham, hamhock, or bacon
2 medium yellow onions, chopped coarse
2–3 finely chopped jalapeños (canned or fresh-seeded)

1–3 fresh green chiles, seeded and chopped fine (adjust the peppers to your own taste)
1 tbsp. Tabasco sauce
1 tbsp. Worcestershire sauce
½ of a 3-oz. bottle of Gebhardt's chile powder
Salt to taste

Pick over beans for rocks, wash and soak overnight. Next morning, cook in soaking water. Add remaining ingredients and enough fresh water to cover the beans about 2 inches. Bring to boil, then reduce heat and simmer. For 3 days stir and inhale the marvelous aroma from time to time. Turn fire off at night. Keep covered at all times. Watch water. You may have to add a little as you go along. Of course you can eat these beans the first day, but here's the way the cowboys did it. They ate a few the first day. Let them cool at night. Cooked them the next day and ate them again. By the third day they were rubbing their bellies and saying they sure as hell wished they'd waited, 'cause the beans was just gettin' good.

CABRITO AL PASTOR

In another time and another place, the getting of meat was cause for celebration. In Texas last summer, getting together was cause for the getting of meat. Through a happy coincidence, a group of us who were raised together in Hereford happened to be back there at the same time. There was a twenty-fifth class reunion of the high school. There was the "wetting-down" of a naval commander who happened to be from that sea of grass. There was a cookbook to be researched. For these and other reasons, an inordinate number of survivors of the fifties in a Panhandle town met and agreed to kill the fatted calf, or milk-fed goat as it were.

We decided to have a barbecue. After all, I had this recipe for Cabrito Al Pastor to try out. We all wanted to see each other. Everyone could bring something. We could, for a moment, recapture a piece of our shared history—the covered-dish supper. Here's how it went.

I hadn't been home 20 minutes before my friend from the cradle, John Gililland, stopped by. John always knows when I get home—even if nobody tells him. Part of the reason is that his parents' house and business is one block from my mother's house. Part of it is ESP.

Are we going to test recipes? John asked. You bet your boots, I answered. How'd you like to cook a goat outdoors? Great, he answered. Like his father and grandfather before him, John is the local mortician. He is by turns either swamped with work or idle, depending on whether he "has a body." Fortunately for the recipe testing, John was not busy when I got there. He had gone down to Close's Drug Store to drink an interminable cup of coffee when he ran into Wes Gulley, the district judge and an old South Texas ranch boy. He told Wes our plans, and Wes said he'd help. Wes has dressed out a lot of deer. Good. Now along comes another old boy in town for the class reunion, Jabe Wills, an underwater rescue teacher who lives in Southern California, wearing one of those big waterproof watches still set on California time. He'll help, too. So these three crowd into a telephone booth and call around. They find a goat.

John and Jabe pick me up. Judge goes back to court. The three of us head for the country. John's brought along Tecate, and he shows me how to hold the lemon in the crook of my hand, put the salt on top of the can, mix, and drink. We head for the house of the fellow with goats. His name is Pasqual Delgado, and he said he lives in the big house on the south side of the draw. We can tell we're getting close when we spot the big herd of goats.

On the way out John says he had asked Pasqual how big his goats were, and Pasqual had answered, thirty dollars. John sighs. Anything for research.

Here we are at Delgado's. Flat plain as far as you can see; barbed wire, a lean-to with shoats and a sow, little garden, water hose going, and everywhere children in white, barefoot and twirling on the dusty road, flapping their wings, playing a game and smiling.

We shake hands all around. And where is the goat? Delgado gives an expansive wave of the arm. *Alla*. We give over our thirty dollars and we all head for the herd of goats. We leave the rope in the truck. I have on walking shorts and Birkenstocks. Jabe has on Adidas. John has thought to bring along his mortician's apron. He knows how to keep stuff off his clothes.

Over a plowed field. Heat shimmering. Step up, step down, step up, step down. Knock the sand out of your shoe. Pick the sticker out of your toe. Don't touch the fence—it's hot. Okay. Over the single strand of wire—gingerly. And now we see the goats— maybe two hundred of them.

Delgado speaks. You can have your choice. He has one goat that he hadn't thought he'd sell because it is "castrate," but may- be—for forty dollars—he will let it go. No, we say firmly. We'll take the thirty-dollar goat. Delgado's nine-year-old girl is bare- foot among all these clods and stickers. He motions to her, then waves his arm in our direction, and we begin to move in on the black kid that he has pointed out. The goats trot along, tense and wary but not really worried. Delgado wants them to go through this trap that leads to the shed, but the lead goat is too smart for him and always veers just at the last moment. By now they are milling around; we are fanned out in a semicircle. We have trotted and run some ourselves, hearts pounding and pumping. This time we get them headed right for the trap. I'm positioned just past the gate to scare them from fading in the stretch, but wily old Billy takes one glance at me with that human-looking yellow eye of his, ducks his head, and runs right past me. They all sweep by, and I am scared to death they'll step on my bare toes. Run, you suckers, I holler, and take off after them. It's hell to be a goat roper with no rope.

This sort of milling and trotting goes on until we are all heav- ing and blowing. Then the lead goat gets real smart and finds a hole in Delgado's fence and leads the entire herd into a pasture holding seven cows and a range bull. Delgado shouts and we all follow. We chase the goats up into these cows who also begin to trot; at one point I see the bull just brush past me. At last Del- gado speaks to his nine-year-old. She lunges under one old cow and grabs out chosen goat by the hind foot. Goat obliges her by kicking her right in the teeth. No worry, says Delgado, as he hands us the goat. Back at the truck, we tie up the black kid, throw her in the back, and head for the vet's. Good God, get out the beer.

Need I tell you that the vet says that we were all very cruel to run the poor animal down. We put her in a pen for a few hours so that she will be composed for her last moments.

John and Jabe and I drive around Hereford for a couple of hours in this pickup, drinking Tecate, looking at the rows of elm trees the founding fathers put here to break up the treeless landscape.

Barbecue and Beans

We are forever shooing flies. Feed lots ring the town now, and the air is perfumed with the smell of cow manure and the air is polka-dotted with flies. It's been a long time since we dragged Main.

Just as the burning sun is about to drop—there is a vapor trail and a bank of clouds in the west all shimmery and magenta, I'd forgotten what a real sunset looks like—we all gather back at the office of the large-animal veterinarian.

The judge is here now, wearing his three-hundred-dollar, some rare-kind-of-creature boots and good pants and volunteering to dress the goat.

After we bleed the goat, the judge steps up and pulls out his little two-inch, razor-sharp silver penknife; and with his well-manicured lawyer's hands he begins to skin and gut the goat. He has the mild manner of a man sure of his power. He never spills a drop of blood on himself. He never gets hair on the meat. He never says a word. It strikes me as funny that the vet and the mortician are hanging back while the lawyer does the job. Standing there holding the offal bag, I am having trouble refraining from laughter. I can see that this is a serious moment, however; so I keep a straight face.

Now John and I take the goat back to his house. In the back-yard we hose it down for a good half hour to cool the meat. John's wife, Amy, coordinates everything. She goes to the funeral home for folding chairs. She makes suggestions to the twenty invited guests, and pretty soon the menu looks complete. We have calf fries coming, and hot cowboy beans, and corn bread, and even a champagne mousse made by the most popular cheerleader from my high school class.

Just as John and I are wrapping the goat in white paper to put it in the refrigerator, his daughter Suzy interrupts, insistent. Day after tomorrow she'll be sixteen, and she wants permission to drive a carload of friends to Amarillo. My God, girl, John says. I just killed a goat. What else do you want? That should be a birthday party fit for a princess. She searches his face. Is he serious? She wavers between laughing and crying.

The next morning John calls me to come over to the funeral home. I arrive, marveling at the overwhelming aroma of roses. John straightens up from an ancient ledger in which he is entering figures with an Esterbrook pen. He hands me a long grocery list. He will be done with the books by noon, he says, and will go home to build the fire.

John and I have both seen goats cooked outdoors, on a stake. We know how it's supposed to be done. About two o'clock he and I talk it over. He pokes around his workshed and comes up with a 5-foot steel stake that we ram through the goat, placing sticks between the forelegs and between the hind legs, breaking open the breastbone with an ax so that the carcass lays nice and flat—the way you see them in the Mexican markets. We rub the kid down with salt, finely milled black pepper, and crushed cloves of garlic. We lard it lightly. The meat is so fresh and young that it is completely odorless. It is a lovely pale veal color.

Barbecue and Beans

Now we hit a problem. We can't build a fire in John's backyard and ruin the carefully nurtured grass. Then Jabe comes along with a solution. His father, an avid fisherman, had a blacksmith build him this strange steel contraption that looks like a big black fruit box on legs and stands about waist-high. As best we can tell he'd fill this thing with water, and clean all the mountain trout he'd caught near Pagosa Springs in it. Jabe and John use it to cool beer and have named it the Doctor Wills Memorial-Fish-Cleaner-and-Beer-Cooler. It must weigh two hundred pounds. Anyway, we clean it out, put a little sand on the bottom, make a good fire of mesquite and oak, throwing in some charcoal for good measure. We let the fire burn down, lay the staked goat a good 8 inches over the hot coals, and begin. We turn the meat every 30 minutes, holding on to the rod—kind of a giant shish kebab. We make a foil tent over the top to encourage smoke and to discourage the ubiquitous flies. When we notice that the thin ribs are beginning to char, we make little foil booties for them. At the end of 2 hours, we take it off. We know it is done because when we press the flesh, it gives nicely. Now it is a splendid glistening caramel color. It smells so good you could faint.

Soon the guests arrive, each bearing a platter of food. John is cooking calf fries on the Coleman stove. Amy has to run for more card tables to hold it all. Our own children are here, mostly strangers to each other, bouncing on the trampoline, their strong young bodies glistening in the twilight. They eye each other warily. Most of us have children as old as we all were when we were together last. I look around. The failing light is merciful. None of us looks any different than we did at sixteen.

Our parents are here, too, seeming smaller and less powerful than I can imagine. We queue up, pile our plates high with food, and sit down on the funeral home chairs to eat. Every bite of food tastes better than the last. There is as little talking as there used to be around a chuck wagon. We were all raised in cattle country and we knew the rules: eat first, talk later.

After the meal, when miraculously all the food is gone, we sit back in the dry night air and talk of many things. Someone says, did we know our favorite high school teacher just died. The vet's wife announces that she has accepted an appointment at eight o'clock the next morning for Aaron to remove the stink glands from a litter of baby skunks. Aaron turns red in the face and tells her she can do it herself. He's not taking any more damned skunks. Another man bemoans the gas mileage of his vintage T-bird. If only our friend Barbara were here, we say. We discuss the bed length of the new Ford van and how it ruins the ride.

We talk some more about the food. How we would do this or that differently, but how it sure was good this way. The conversation is unimportant. In truth, we are practically strangers now. But the shared meal is what counts. It is getting late. The children, tired, bored, and not getting sufficient attention, begin to knock each other around. We know this is the signal to get on with it, so we begin to fold chairs, scrape plates, and wash dishes. We are all reluctant to leave. Oh. There is one more thing. We'll wait until midnight, just five minutes away, and wish Suzy a happy birthday.

Amy digs around in the kitchen and comes up with a birthday candle. Jabe sticks it into a melting mousse. On the stroke of twelve, we burst into her room singing happy birthday.

She sits up almost before she can get her eyes open. She has been dead asleep. I am struck by the resemblance to John when he was just her age. I love this child that I scarcely know. I love her with the certainty of blood and tribe. We give her a kiss and retreat.

We quietly close the bedroom door and walk back to the den. The energy in the room has gone, like a puff of summer wind that blows open the curtains, washing over with a quick soft warmness, then retreats. There is nothing left to do. We begin loading into cars and go our separate ways.

Jabe, the motherless boy who, at twelve, got his own life back in the Hereford Municipal Swimming Pool after polio had withered a leg will go back to Southern California where he will teach underwater safety to divers. John, my very first friend, with whom I used to play in and around the caskets, sometimes getting up the nerve to poke the stone-hard cheek of a man laid out before the wake, will go back to the funeral home and take the place his father and his father before him held. Wes, the South Texas import, will go back to getting people in and out of jails and in and out of marriages. Aaron will go back to the office and face the litter of skunks his wife has arranged for him to deperfume. Suzy will go to Amarillo with her friends after all. I will go away to write this book.

But for a day, we have dropped our current lives. We have worked and cooked and eaten together. We have been—for a moment—a family again.

Chile Con Queso
Nachos
Picante Compueste
Tostadas
Fried Jalapeños
Jalapeño En Escabeche
Jícama En Escabeche
Quesadillas (Cheese Turnovers)
Guacamole
Posole
El Metate Menudo
Elotes (Roasting Ears)
El Metate Black Beans
Sopa De Arroz (Mexican Rice)
Vegetable Chalupa
Green Enchiladas with Chicken
Tomatillo Sauce
Texas Cheese Enchiladas
Salsa Cruda (Mexican Hot Sauce)
Salsa Colorado (Red Chile Sauce)
Enchiladas Colorado
Acapulco Enchiladas
Instant Chile Verde Sauce
Hot Tamales
Chiles Rellenos
Mexican Ranchero Sauce
Tamale Pie
Cabrito Con Salsa (Baby Goat with Sauce)
Cabrito Asado (Braised Baby Goat)
Tex Mex Beef Tacos
Oaxaca Eggs with Nopales
Huevos Rancheros (Ranch Eggs)
Sopa De Flor De Calabaza (Squash Flower Soup)

Pollo Flauta (Chicken Flute)
Tex Mex Chicken or Turkey Mole
Camarones Y Arroz El Paso (Shrimp and Rice)
Homemade Corn Tortillas
Flour Tortillas
Buñuelos
Flan Almendra (Almond Flan)
Capritoda (Mexican Bread Pudding)
Pastel De Camote (Sweet Potato Pie)
Postre De Mango (Mango-topped Cream Pie)
Emily's Mexican Candy
Nogada (Mexican Pralines)

Tex Mex from A to Z

Trying to define Tex Mex cuisine is something like trying to define love. It's hard to say what it is; but you sure know it when you see it. I must have asked fifty people in Texas to put into words what Tex Mex food was and how it differed from plain Mexican cuisine. One fellow would say, well, it's hotter for one thing. No sooner would he get the words out of his mouth than he'd be interrupted by his companion who'd say, naw it isn't. What about guacamole?

Then someone would pipe up and say, it's the Texas beef cow and Gebhardt's chile powder. Hell no, he'd be shouted down. It's jalapeños and lard and beans and lots of eggs. How did it get here, I'd ask. Wetbacks, they'd say. Was not. It was the families who came to San Antonio. High-class families.

And what about Austin-style Mexican food, I'd say? What's that? Well you know, they'd say. It's Austin-style. And I'd have to answer, yes, I did know that it was different, but I'd be hard pressed to say quite how.

So I kind of got carried away with this section of the book. Bobbie Covey, an Austin Tex Mex restaurateur, was the most help. She's made it her lifework to try and understand and produce genuine Tex Mex food. She makes trips to Mexico. She knows ranch families in South Texas. She responds to the ever-shifting currents in Austin's palate. You can't go wrong with her recipes.

Of all the types of food in Texas, Tex Mex is the one that everyone in Texas has an opinion about. It's not the same as what you find in New Mexico. It's not the same as what you find in California. It's not the same as what you find in Mexico. It's—well, you know—it's Tex Mex.

CHILE CON QUESO
Bobbie Covey

Makes 4 cups

2 tbsp. oil
1 cup chopped onions
2 small cloves garlic, pressed
1 4-oz. can chopped green chiles
1–2 jalapeño peppers, chopped
    (seed them if you don't want
    them too hot)

1 8-oz. can stewed tomatoes
8 oz. Monterrey Jack cheese,
    shredded (2 cups)
8 oz. Longhorn cheese, shredded
    (2 cups)
1 cup sour cream

Heat oil in a 10-inch skillet and add onions and garlic. Cook until clear. Add chiles, peppers, and tomatoes, breaking up the tomatoes with a spoon. Lower heat and add cheeses. Cook and stir until cheeses melt. Stir in sour cream; cook until heated, but do *not* boil. Serve with tortilla chips in a chafing dish or in a dish that has a candle warmer.

NACHOS
Barbara Reavis

Serves 6

12 tortillas
Oil for frying

½ lb. grated Longhorn cheese
12 thin slices of canned jalapeño

Stack the tortillas on a cutting board and cut into 3 pie-shaped pieces, making 36 pieces. Heat ½ inch of oil in a heavy skillet to approximately 375°. Place the tortilla pieces in the skillet, 4 to 6 at a time. They will puff up at first, so just mash them down with your pancake turner and turn them and mash again till they get flat. Chips will cook in 45–60 seconds.

When crisp, drain the excess oil back into skillet and use tongs to lay tortillas on a paper towel.

Place crisp tortillas on a cookie sheet or an oven-proof platter. Cover the tops with grated cheese and a thin slice of jalapeño. Place in the broiler just long enough to melt the cheese. Serve hot.

PICANTE COMPUESTE

Cynthia Colvin

3 cups refried beans
1 avocado, chopped coarse and
   mashed into lumps
8 oz. sour cream

Shredded iceberg lettuce
2 finely chopped tomatoes
Picante sauce
Tortilla chips

In an attractive glass bowl layer the ingredients, beans on the bottom, then mashed avocado, then sour cream, then lettuce, then tomatoes topped with *picante* sauce. Serve with tortilla chips. As you dig in you will get some of all the layers. This can be made ahead, except for the addition of lettuce and tomatoes, and will hold, covered, for several hours in the refrigerator.

TOSTADAS

Barbara Reavis

Serves 4

4 whole corn tortillas, fried crisp
1 cup hot refried beans
½ cup shredded Monterrey Jack
   cheese
½ to ¾ cup shredded or thinly
   sliced cooked chicken, turkey,
   pork, or ground beef

2 cups shredded lettuce
Chicken or pork slices for garnish
   (optional)
Avocado slices or *Guacamole*
Salsa Cruda or fresh tomato slices
   and *Tomatillo Sauce*

For each *tostada*, spread a warm fried tortilla with about 3–4 tablespoons hot refried beans. Sprinkle with about 2 tablespoons cheese, cover with about 2–3 tablespoons hot meat, top with about ½ cup shredded lettuce, and garnish with a few pieces of meat and avocado slices or about 3 tablespoons **Guacamole**. Serve with sauce.

FRIED JALAPEÑOS

Serves at least 6

1 14-oz. can whole jalapeños
About ½ cup Longhorn cheese,
    grated fine
Flour

2 eggs
½ cup milk
Oil for deep-frying

Cut caps off jalapeños and carefully scoop out seeds and membrane without tearing the peppers. Stuff each jalapeño with about
½ teaspoon grated cheese, pressing it down into the pepper with
your little finger. Mix eggs and milk. Roll pepper in flour, then in
egg mixture, and again in flour. Set aside to allow the coating to
set while you raise the temperature of the oil to 350°. Deep-fry the
peppers until they are browned (no more than 1 minute). Do not
serve to cowards or Yankees.

JALAPEÑO EN ESCABECHE

12 jalapeños, roasted, peeled, and
    seeded (see *Chiles Rellenos*
    for instructions)
1 large onion, sliced thin
5 large cloves garlic, pressed
½ cup olive oil

1 cup white wine vinegar
½ cup water
2 tsp. salt
1 tsp. oregano
4 bay leaves

Roast, peel, and seed jalapeños. Sauté onion and garlic in olive
oil until clear. Add vinegar, water, salt, oregano, and bay leaves.
Bring to a boil. Add peppers, simmer 10 minutes. Store in covered
jars in the refrigerator.

JÍCAMA EN ESCABECHE

Jícama is a Mexican tuber that looks like a rough brown turnip, and tastes like a cross between a radish and a Jerusalem artichoke. Sold in supermarkets in El Paso, San Antonio, and Hereford. Ask your produce manager to get you one.

1 *jícama*   1 clove garlic, pressed
¼ cup olive oil   Cilantro to taste

Peel and slice *jícama* in thin slices. Place in glass dish with olive oil, garlic, and cilantro. Cover and allow to marinate in refrigerator at least 2 hours. Serve cold. Add salt if you wish.

QUESADILLAS
(Cheese Turnovers)
Camille Jones

Serves 12

These mild turnovers can be made *picante* simply by adding chopped chiles.

Filling:
1½ cups grated Muenster cheese   1 large egg, beaten
1 tbsp. unsalted butter, softened

Grate the cheese, add butter and egg, and beat with an electric mixer until fluffy.

Masa:
2 cups unbleached flour   1½ sticks cold unsalted butter
1 tsp. baking powder   ¼ cup cold water
½ tsp. salt   1 large egg, beaten

Sift together flour, baking powder, and salt. Cut in the butter until the mixture is the consistency of coarse cornmeal. Add the water and mix quickly; do not overmix.

Roll out the dough to a ⅛-inch thickness on a lightly floured board. Using a cookie cutter, cut rounds 4 inches in diameter. Place 2 tablespoons of filling in each round. Dampen the edges of the dough rounds, fold over, and press together. Brush with the beaten egg and place on an oiled cookie sheet. Bake at 400° for 15 minutes or until well browned.

GUACAMOLE

Makes 3 cups

There are as many recipes for guacamole as there are counties in Texas. You will find every ingredient from mayonnaise to French dressing suggested as a binder. Do not be deceived. The real McCoy depends on a very ripe avocado and no extenders.

2 very ripe avocados
1 green peeled *chile pequin*,
    ground fine
Juice of ½ lemon or lime

2 medium tomatoes, peeled and
    chopped
1 small white onion, chopped fine
Salt to taste

Mash avocados with a fork, not too smooth, and add the other ingredients. Mash with a potato masher. If you can't serve it at once, put the seed back in, cover tightly and refrigerate to prevent darkening. Remove seed before serving.

POSOLE
Bobbie Covey

Serves 12

Posole is a Christmas Eve favorite in Mexico, and on the New Mexico side of Texas *posole* holds the position that chili holds in Texas. I actually prefer it to chili. The flavors are subtle and delicate. The textures of cooked meat, corn, and raw vegetables are fascinating.

4 fresh chile pods made into a
    paste
3 pig's feet (ask the butcher to cut
    them into quarters for you)
1 whole head garlic, separated
    into cloves and peeled but not
    pressed
1 large onion, chopped
1 3½- or 4-lb. chicken, cut into
    serving pieces
1 lb. lean boneless pork loin, cut
    into 2-inch cubes

2 cups canned hominy (or, if you're
    on the western edge of the
    state, an equal amount of
    fresh or frozen *posole*)
Salt and freshly milled pepper
Chicken broth
Chile pequins, crumbled
2 limes, cut into wedges
1 bunch radishes
1 head iceberg lettuce, shredded
1 Bermuda onion, minced

First, make chile paste. Open pods, remove stems and seeds, toast on a grill or *comal* for a few minutes until they begin to soften. Then soak in boiling water to cover for 10 minutes. Now puree into a paste. You can always use this chile paste in place of chile powder for more flavor in stews and chili. How hot the paste is depends on the kind of peppers you use.

In a soup pot, simmer pig's feet with garlic and onion in salted water to cover for about 3 hours. Add chicken and pork and chile paste and cook gently for 45 minutes; add hominy (or *posole*) and cook 15 more minutes—or until meats are fork-tender. Season to taste with salt and pepper. Skim off excess grease.

Since this is a soup as well as a meat dish, there should be plenty of broth. If your stock boils down, add chicken broth. Serve the meat and broth together in deep soup bowls. Pass bowls of crumbled chiles, limes, radishes, lettuce, and onion, and let everyone garnish soup according to individual tastes.

EL METATE MENUDO
Bobbie Covey

Serves 8–10

Joe's father called a hangover "having the hog's breath." Mexicans call *menudo* the world's greatest hangover remedy. So, think of *menudo* as the cure for the hog's breath. In fact, until you get used to *menudo*, one bowlful could cure you from ever drinking again.

6 lbs. tripe	2 medium onions, chopped
Water to cover	2 cloves garlic, minced
1 soup bone	1 tsp. cumin
1 pig hock	2 15½-oz. cans golden hominy
1 bay leaf	Salt and pepper to taste
1 dried *chile pequín*	1 tsp. oregano
¼ lb. red chile pods or ½ cup chile powder	

Cut tripe into bite-sized pieces, wash, place in a soup pot, and cover with water. Add soup bone, pig hock, bay leaf, red pepper, and simmer until tender.

While this is cooking, prepare chile pods by removing stems and seeds and washing pods; add water to cover and simmer in a small saucepan for about 10 minutes. Next, using a blender or processor, coarsely puree chiles.

When tripe is tender, add chile puree or chile powder, onions, garlic, and cumin and simmer for another 30 minutes. Add hominy and simmer until all ingredients are well blended, about 30 minutes more.

Fill soup bowl with *menudo*, sprinkle with chopped onion and oregano; serve lime on the side.

ELOTES
(Roasting Ears)
Patricia Slate

Serves 6

Although Mexican cooks make a paste of butter and lime juice by hand, it's hard for gringos. Use a blender or processor for sure-fire results.

Water to boil *or* **charcoal grill fire**   **Juice of 1 lime**
6 ears corn   **½ tsp. paprika**
¼ lb. butter, softened

While corn is cooking, make a paste from softened butter, lime juice, and paprika. Taste. If butter isn't salty enough, you can add a little salt. Once corn is cooked, smear the butter mixture on corn. This is the way corn is prepared on the border, and, boy, is it good. It is best to cook the corn outside on a grill. To do this simply wet the husks, place the whole ear on the grill, and cook 15–20 minutes, turning often. The husks will brown but the corn will be succulent. If you don't use a charcoal grill, boil or steam corn until tender, 6–12 minutes. Remove husks and silks before serving.

If there is any way humanly possible for you to cook corn within 4–6 hours after it was picked, you will be amazed. The natural sweetness of corn begins to break down into starch almost immediately from the time it is picked, so the sooner you cook it, the better it tastes.

EL METATE BLACK BEANS
Bobbie Covey

Serves 6–8

The vegetarian influence in Austin is gaining. Here is a popular side dish for a Mexican plate, or a main dish for vegetarian purists. It calls for *epazote*, an herb which is actually a weed that grows in Texas as well as in Mexico. When Bobbie Covey hung some up in her kitchen to dry, her kids thought she was curing marijuana. It grows everywhere, but you can buy it in an herb store or Mexican market. Diana Kennedy says it soothes the nerves and dispels intestinal parasites. Diana Kennedy says that to prepare a pot of black beans without *epazote* is unthinkable.

2 cups dried black beans
1 onion, chopped
2 cloves garlic, pressed
1 sprig *epazote*

2 *chiles serranos* (optional)
3 tbsp. lard or vegetable oil
Salt to taste

Wash beans, place in saucepan with enough cold water to cover. Add chopped onion, garlic, *epazote*, and chiles. Cover, bring to a boil, reduce heat and simmer gently, adding hot water as necessary to keep the beans just covered. When beans begin to wrinkle, add lard or oil and continue cooking until beans are soft (2–3 hours). Salt to taste and cook for another 30 minutes. (You can presoak beans overnight to hasten cooking time.) When you are through cooking, scoop out any water higher than level of beans.

Mash with potato masher until you have a thick lumpy consistency. Serve hot as a side or a main dish.

SOPA DE ARROZ
(Mexican Rice)
Bobbie Covey

Serves 6

This is the basic, traditional Mexican rice. For variation and color you may also sauté a chopped bell pepper with garlic and onion. For a more *picante* flavor, add a small amount of green chile pepper. For a richer flavor substitute chicken broth for water.

For a party dish add ½ cup cooked green peas and strips of pimiento at the end of the cooking time.

2 tbsp. lard or peanut oil
1 cup long-grain rice
2 cloves garlic, pressed
1 medium white onion, chopped
    fine

3 medium tomatoes, chopped fine
2 cups water
1 tsp. salt

In a 10-inch skillet, heat fat, add rice, and stir over medium high heat until rice grains are golden brown. Add pressed garlic and chopped onion and sauté until onion begins to brown slightly. Add tomatoes, water, and salt. Bring to a boil uncovered. Turn heat down very low; cover and cook for 15–20 minutes without peeking or stirring, until all water is absorbed. At the end of cooking time, toss lightly with a fork and leave rice uncovered. The grains should be separate and fluffy.

VEGETABLE CHALUPA
Cathy Abercrombie

Zucchini, sliced in rounds
Onion, chopped coarse
Mushrooms, cut lengthwise
Celery, cut crosswise
Olive oil
Corn tortillas

Sour cream
Fresh ripe tomatoes, chopped
Very ripe avocado, sliced
Cheddar cheese, grated
Picante **sauce**

Braise equal amounts zucchini, onion, mushrooms, and celery in small amount of olive oil until onion is clear. Brown tortillas in a dry skillet for about 15 seconds on a side. Put each tortilla on a dinner plate. Pile on the braised vegetables. Top with a dollop of sour cream, tomatoes, avocado, cheese. Run under the broiler until bubbly. Serve with *picante* sauce.

GREEN ENCHILADAS WITH CHICKEN

Serves 4

1 whole chicken breast, cooked (or canned chicken in a pinch)
¾ lb. Monterrey Jack cheese, grated
Tomatillo Sauce

8 corn tortillas
Hot oil
1 cup sour cream
1 ripe avocado
Pickled jalapeños for garnish

Cook chicken breast in a small saucepan with just enough salted water to cover until tender (about 45 minutes). Cool. Debone, remove skin, and then shred meat with a fork (this is what Mexican cooks do instead of dicing meat with a knife). Set meat aside. Grate cheese. While chicken cooks make **Tomatillo Sauce** in 7-inch saucepan. Preheat oven to 350°. Once sauce is ready, heat a small amount of oil in a 7-inch skillet. While this is heating, oil a baking dish and place it at hand next to the stove. You should have these things lined up: the skillet, the saucepan, and the casserole dish. Close to the casserole dish should be shredded chicken and grated cheese.

Using tongs, dip tortillas in hot fat for 15 seconds, let excess oil drip off, then dip into sauce for 30 seconds. Place coated tortilla in casserole dish, put a pinch of chicken breast and a hefty pinch of cheese on each tortilla. Roll. Leave flap side down. Repeat until you have used all the tortillas and meat. Pour additional sauce on top and finish off with remaining shredded cheese. Heat in 350° oven until cheese is bubbly—about 10 minutes.

To serve, place 2 enchiladas on a hot plate. Top with a dollop of sour cream, slice of avocado, and a pickled jalapeño on the side.

TOMATILLO SAUCE

Makes 1½ pints

The *tomatillo* is sometimes known as *tomato verde*, *fresadilla*, *tomate de cascara*, or *tomate de bolsa* ("tomato in a bag"). It is not an unripe tomato, but is a particular variety of tomato which grows in its own husk. Fresh *tomatillos* are increasingly easy to find in the grocery store, but if unavailable fresh you can either grow them or buy them canned. Diana Kennedy prefers Clemente Jacques brand.

If you are using fresh *tomatillos*, keep your fire very low and simmer the sauce long enough to thoroughly cook the *tomatillo*. If you use canned ones, drain them. You may need to add a little water to the sauce at the beginning, depending on the moisture content of these little tomatoes.

1 medium onion, minced	1 7-oz. can chopped green chiles
3 cloves garlic, minced	1 chopped jalapeño with or
2 tbsp. peanut oil	without seeds (depending on
1 14-oz. can *tomatillos* (green	how hot you like the sauce)
Mexican tomatoes) or 1½ cups	½ tsp. sugar
fresh *tomatillos*	Salt to taste

Sauté onion and garlic in oil until onion is clear. Combine with *tomatillos*, chopped chiles, and jalapeño. Run mixture through blender, food mill, or processor to make a coarse puree. Return to saucepan. Season with sugar and salt. If the sauce seems dry add a little water. Simmer over low heat until thick and thoroughly cooked, 20–30 minutes. Stores well in a jar in the refrigerator.

If you are making this sauce in the summer and have a garden, toss in a few ordinary hard green tomatoes. The sauce will be a more brilliant green, and the acidity of the green tomatoes will sharpen the flavor.

TEXAS CHEESE ENCHILADAS

Serves 4

12 corn tortillas
2 tbsp. cooking oil
2 large yellow onions, chopped
4 cups grated cheese—either
    Longhorn or **Asadero** but
    never **Monterrey Jack**
1 recipe of *Chili Gravy*

Allow 3 enchiladas per person. Use a Pyrex utility pan (13½" × 8¾") to cook them. Lightly grease the utility pan (for authenticity, use lard). Preheat oven to 400°.

Chop onions and grate cheese—either Longhorn or Asadero (a Mexican white cheese made from cow's milk, salty and wonderfully rubbery). Make **Chili Gravy**.

Heat oil in skillet. Using kitchen tongs, dip each tortilla in hot oil until well softened (about 15 seconds). Hold tortilla up and allow oil to drip back into the skillet.

Using kitchen tongs dip tortillas in hot **Chili Gravy**. Place the tortilla in the Pyrex pan, put a good-sized pinch of onions and cheese in the middle, and roll the tortilla, placing the flap side down. Continue filling and rolling tortillas until the pan is full. Pour more **Chili Gravy** on top of the enchiladas, sprinkle the top generously with more grated cheese, and pop into preheated oven. Cook only until the cheese begins to bubble (about 10 minutes). Serve immediately.

CHILI GRAVY

Makes 3 cups

2 tbsp. lard (or shortening)
2 tbsp. flour
2 tbsp. chile powder or ground
    chiles pasillas
3 cups warm water
Salt to taste

Melt lard in skillet. Stir in flour. Make light roux. Add ground chile, water, and salt. Cook until thick. The gravy will vary according to what kind of ground chile you use. Gebhardt's chile powder is best, but it isn't as good as pure ground *chiles pasillas* (found in Mexican market).

SALSA CRUDA
(Mexican Hot Sauce)
Bobbie Covey

Makes 1½ cups

Here is the table sauce you see in Tex Mex restaurants.

1 medium tomato	3 *chiles serranos* (**or any fresh, hot**
½ medium white onion	**green chiles**)
6 sprigs cilantro leaves	½ tsp. salt

Chop all ingredients very fine. You can do this with a sharp knife, or in a blender or food processor, so long as you don't turn the whole thing into a baby food puree. If the sauce seems too thick, add a little fresh tomato juice.

This sauce is good for about 3 hours. After that it begins to lose some of its pungency.

SALSA COLORADO
(Red Chile Sauce)

8 tbsp. powdered red chiles (not	1 tsp. salt
chile powder)	2 tbsp. lard
2 cups water (more or less)	1 tbsp. flour

Soak powdered chiles in 1½ cups of water; reserve ½ cup of water. Stir in salt. Heat lard in a heavy 7-inch saucepan. Add flour. Cook and stir until flour browns. Pour in chile paste. Cook and stir until thick as catsup. The consistency may vary according to moisture content of flour and powdered chiles. Add remaining ½ cup of water a little at a time until you achieve a catsup-like thickness.

ENCHILADAS COLORADO

Serves 4

Out in West Texas enchiladas are not always rolled. Sometimes they are layered. This 3-layer enchilada with egg reflects the New Mexico influence in Texas.

12 corn tortillas	2 cups red chile sauce
2 tbsp. cooking oil	4 eggs
2 cups grated Longhorn cheese	Shredded lettuce
½ cup chopped onions	

Preparing this dish is sort of like Chinese cooking. It's all in the organization. You will need a 7-inch skillet for the tortillas, a 7-inch saucepan to heat the chile sauce, and 4 dinner plates that can go into the oven.

Preheat oven to 185°. Grate cheese, chop onions, shred lettuce, and arrange these close at hand by the stove. Heat the chile sauce in the saucepan. Heat the oil in the skillet and, using tongs, dip each tortilla in hot fat for about 15 seconds, or just until well softened. Hold tortilla up out of fat and allow fat to drip back in skillet, then immerse the tortilla in the red chile sauce for a full 30 seconds. Place 1 tortilla on each of the 4 plates and sprinkle with generous amounts of cheese and onion. Make another layer, repeating the procedure and spooning on any additional sauce. Fry the 4 remaining tortillas *crisp* in the skillet. (You may have to add more fat to do this.) Place crisp tortilla on top of each serving and place the 4 plates in the prewarmed oven. Now fry to order 1 egg per person and place it on top of each stack of tortillas. Sprinkle lettuce around the edge and serve.

ACAPULCO ENCHILADAS
Cathy Abercrombie

Serves 6

Filling:

1½ lbs. ground round	Salt and pepper to taste (substitute
2 tbsp. Gebhardt's chile powder	1 package commercial taco
½ tsp. cumin	seasoning for dry seasonings
½ tsp. oregano	if you are in a hurry)

Preheat oven to 400°. Brown meat in skillet and season with chile powder, cumin, oregano, and salt and pepper to taste. If the meat is very dry, add a little water; if the meat extracts its own juices, simply push the meat filling to a back burner and simmer while you are preparing the sauce.

Sauce:

4 tbsp. peanut oil
4 large yellow onions, chopped
   coarse
1 15-oz. can tomato sauce
1 6-oz. can tomato sauce
1 large can and 1 small can of
   water (equal to amount of
   sauce)

Salt and pepper to taste
12 corn tortillas, very fresh
Oil for frying
8 oz. Longhorn or
   Cheddar cheese, grated

In a Dutch oven, heat peanut oil. Add onions and sauté over medium-low heat until onions are completely limp and transparent. Add tomato sauce and water. Season to taste with salt and pepper. Simmer over low heat until thickened to a catsup-like consistency (at least 10 minutes).

Meanwhile grate cheese. Grease a 10" × 13" Pyrex utility pan. Heat a little oil in a 7-inch skillet and with tongs, dip corn tortillas in hot oil for 15 seconds, then into hot tomato sauce for 30 seconds. Place in Pyrex pan. Stuff with meat and roll tightly, flap side down. Pour remaining sauce over, cover with grated cheese, and bake until cheese bubbles and browns (about 10 minutes). Serve with **Instant Chile Verde Sauce.**

INSTANT CHILE VERDE SAUCE
Cathy Abercrombie

4 whole fresh jalapeños, seeds
   and all
2 large cloves garlic, peeled

2 tbsp. white wine vinegar
Dash salt

Whirl all ingredients in processor or blender and serve on the side with **Acapulco Enchiladas.**

PORK FILLING FOR TAMALES

2 lbs. lean, boneless pork cut in 2-inch chunks
Water
Salt and pepper
½ cup raisins
⅔ cup chopped, peeled onion
2 large cloves garlic, peeled and chopped
1 lb. tomatoes, chopped (2 cups)

1 8-oz. can tomato sauce
1 tsp. oregano
1 4-oz. can green chiles, drained
Jalapeño peppers, roasted, skinned, and seeded (to taste)
2 tbsp. lard
1 large bay leaf
Pinch sugar

Place pork in a large, heavy saucepan or Dutch oven and add water just to the top of the meat. Add 2 teaspoons salt and ½ teaspoon pepper and raisins. Cover and bring to a boil over high heat. Reduce heat to moderately low and simmer about 2 hours, or until meat is very tender. Strain pork stock into a container for use in **Dough for Tamales** recipe. When meat is cool enough to handle, shred with a fork or fingers. Puree onion, garlic, tomatoes, tomato sauce, oregano, chiles and jalapeño in blender or processor. Heat lard in a skillet over moderate heat. Add puree, 1½ teaspoons salt, bay leaf, and sugar and cook for about 10 minutes, stirring constantly. Mix puree with the shredded meat and raisins. Taste and add additional salt, pepper, or jalapeños if desired. Makes about 4½–5 cups filling.

DOUGH FOR TAMALES

Make this recipe twice.

⅓ cup lard at room temperature
2 cups masa harina
1½ tsp. salt
1½ tsp. baking powder

About 1½ cups warm pork stock
(from *Pork Filling for Tamales* recipe)

In a small, straight-sided mixing bowl beat the lard with an electric mixer, processor, or fork until it is light and fluffy. On a piece of wax paper mix masa with salt and baking powder and beat into lard, adding about ¼ of mixture at a time. When well mixed, beat in stock ¼ cup at a time to make a slightly mushy, but not watery, dough. Make a second batch of dough. Use for tamales recipe.

Wet your hands. For each tamale spread about 2 tablespoons of the dough into a rectangle on the inside of a shuck; spread to within ¾ inch of the edges and leave about 3 inches at the pointed end and 1½ inches at the wide end of each shuck. Spread 1½–2 tablespoons filling lengthwise down the center of the dough. Fold over ends of shucks so that dough completely covers filling. Arrange tamales upright in steamer with folded wide ends down.

HOT TAMALES

Mary Alice Cisneros

Serves 10–12 (about 40 tamales)

Invite friends to help you fill and wrap the tamales.

48 dried corn shucks
Additional corn shucks for lining
   steamer (optional)

2 batches *Dough for Tamales*
Pork Filling for Tamales

Put shucks in a large bowl, cover with very hot water, and let soak for at least 1½–2 hours, until soft and pliable. If using packaged shucks, separate them after a few minutes of soaking to make sure each one is in contact with the water. Before using, shake excess water from the softened shucks. Fill and wrap tamales as described below.

To cook tamales, fill the bottom of a steamer with water to a depth of about 1 inch. If desired, line steamer basket with additional corn shucks. Pack wrapped tamales upright in basket with the broad ends of the shucks down. When steamer is full, cover tamales with additional shucks or a clean dish towel to prevent condensation from soaking them. Cover pot tightly and bring to a boil over high heat. Reduce heat to moderately low and steam 1–1½ hours. Add water as necessary. Unwrap a tamale, and if dough comes away from the shuck easily, tamales are cooked. Tightly covered, tamales may be kept several days in the refrigerator, or they may be frozen for several weeks. Reheat, covered, in a 300° oven.

A steamer may be improvised using a large pot and a large colander. Prepared dried corn shucks, also known as tamale wrappers, may be purchased in packages—or you may dry your own. Tamales may also be wrapped in rectangles of aluminum foil.

CHILES RELLENOS
Bobbie Covey

Serves 3–6

I will tell you straight out that this dish is hard to make. Every time I make one of the basic Mexican dishes I am struck by the skill of the Mexican cook—and the patience. Properly done, *chiles rellenos* are one of the best things about the Deluxe Dinner at your favorite Tex Mex restaurant. Trouble is, so many restaurants buy them predone, flash frozen, and just zap them in the microwave. It's enough to give the *relleno* a bad name. Next time you have someone you love a lot coming to table, and plenty of time, make these. Another thing about this recipe is that I end up covered from head to foot in flour; it makes a whale of a mess. You may also notice that the filling, peppers, and batter don't come out even. This is due to variation in the size of the peppers. If you have meat left over you can freeze the filling and save it for another day. Or you can eat it on an English muffin. You can also freeze the whole peppers once they are stuffed and cooked.

6 fresh *chiles poblanos* **(use bell or banana peppers in a pinch)**
1½ lbs. ground beef (or a mixture of ¾ lb. pork and ¾ lb. beef)
1 clove garlic, pressed
1 medium onion, chopped fine
1 tomato, peeled and chopped coarse
¼ cup chopped pecans
¼ cup raisins
Salt and freshly ground pepper
⅛ tsp. *each*: **cinnamon, cloves**
2 eggs separated (you may need to double this—I usually do)
Flour
Oil for frying

Skinning peppers is a devilishly difficult job. I have tried doing it in the oven. Doesn't work. It cooks the meat of the pepper. I have tried doing it under the broiler. I burned them up. I finally relented and did it the way the Mexican cooks do—one at a time—over an open fire. It works. It also takes a hell of a long time.

Stick peppers on a long-handled fork and hold over a gas flame or electric burner until the skins blister. They will turn an amber color. This is the way I do it. Hold the pepper just away from the actual flame and count to 10. Then turn the pepper a quarter and count again. I do this over and over, slowly turning the pepper until it is evenly blistered. Some parts of the skin will look charred. That's okay. It takes at least 3 minutes per pepper. Once you have blistered the skin, immediately wrap pepper in a damp towel and allow to steam for 30 minutes. Then holding the pepper stem up, begin peeling the skin off down to the tip.

Make a small slit in one side, open the pepper up, and remove the seeds and membrane. Now you are ready to stuff the peppers. Whew. What a job. If your peppers tear some, don't worry. The egg will seal them back up.

Sauté the ground meat, garlic, and onion until meat is cooked. Add tomato, pecans, raisins, and spices. Salt and pepper to taste. Stir. Simmer 5 minutes. Remove from heat and stuff peppers.

Beat egg yolks until lemony. Beat egg whites separately until very stiff, then fold in yolks. While you are beating the eggs, begin heating oil in a skillet to fry the peppers. You need about 1½ inches of good cooking oil (I like peanut oil); get it plenty hot.

Now dredge stuffed peppers in flour, then dip them in the egg, coating all surfaces. Be sure you put the slit side *up* in the skillet first (it will seal). Fry until golden on one side, then carefully turn and fry the other side. Serve with **Mexican Ranchero Sauce**. The peppers will hold in a 250° oven until ready to serve.

You can stuff the peppers with other things: Monterrey Jack cheese. *Frijoles* and cheese. Chicken prepared in the same manner as the meat, substituting thyme and oregano for cinnamon and cloves.

Once you've gotten the hang of making *chiles rellenos* and your kitchen is a wreck anyway, you may want to go ahead and stuff 20 or so. After frying you can freeze them, then reheat in a casserole by pouring **Mexican Ranchero Sauce** over the frozen stuffed peppers and placing in a moderate 325° oven until heated through— about 25 minutes. Or you can (sigh) zap them in the microwave for 45 seconds.

MEXICAN RANCHERO SAUCE
Bobbie Covey

Here is the basic sauce for **Huevos Rancheros** and **Chiles Rellenos**. Also good over chicken, meat, or cheese-filled enchiladas.

1 whole white onion, chopped	2 cloves garlic, pressed
2 bell peppers, chopped	2 lbs. fresh dead-ripe tomatoes
1 finely chopped small fresh *chile* serrano or jalapeño	3 tbsp. peanut oil or lard
	Salt and pepper to taste

Sauté onion, peppers, and garlic in hot oil until onions are clear. Run tomatoes through blender, processor, or food mill, but leave some texture—no baby food, please. Add tomatoes to onion, pepper, and garlic mixture and simmer until tomatoes are cooked and sauce is slightly thickened. Add salt and pepper to taste.

This sauce keeps well in a covered jar in the refrigerator, but should be heated before serving.

TAMALE PIE

Serves 6

1 medium onion, chopped	1 cup cornmeal
1 garlic clove, pressed	4 cups water
1 green pepper, chopped	1 tsp. salt
1 tbsp. cooking oil	1 tsp. chile powder
1 lb. hamburger meat	Ripe olives
3 medium tomatoes, chopped	
Salt, pepper, and chile powder to taste	

Brown the onion, garlic, and green pepper in cooking oil. Add hamburger and brown. Add tomatoes, salt, pepper, and chile powder to taste. Cook over moderate heat for 20 minutes. Stir occasionally. While this is cooking, prepare a cornmeal mush. Slowly add cornmeal to 1 cup *cold* water. Bring remaining 3 cups water to a boil. Add salt and chile powder. Stirring constantly, slowly add cornmeal and water mixture. Cook and stir 5 minutes. Cover and set aside. After meat is cooked line a buttered baking dish with half of the cornmeal mush. Fill with meat sauce. Dot the top with olives. Cover pie with the remaining cornmeal mush. Place in a 350° oven until browned, at least 20 minutes.

CABRITO CON SALSA
(Baby Goat with Sauce)
Bobbie Covey

Serves about 6

Cut ½ baby goat into serving pieces and brown (about 20 minutes) in small amount hot lard in a turkey roaster or big Dutch oven. Now add water to cover and add the following:

Salt to taste (remember to do this by tasting the water)	1 cup green peas
	3 cloves garlic, pressed
1 tsp. sugar	Pinch marjoram
3 tomatoes, chopped	10 cumin seeds
2 onions, chopped	3 whole cloves
2 chile peppers, green or dry (if dry, crumble well; if green, cut fine)	2 bay leaves

Cover and simmer until done, about 45 minutes. Serve in soup bowl.

CABRITO ASADO
(Braised Baby Goat)
Bobbie Covey

Serves 6–8

It isn't too likely that you'll be cooking *cabrito al pastor*, so I'll tell you a couple of other ways to cook *cabrito*. Generally *cabrito* means a milk-fed goat weighing no more than 18 pounds. If, however, you are using an older animal, you'll need to cook it longer—say from 45 minutes to 1½ hours.

Preheat oven to 400°. Clean and wash goat well. Rub all surfaces with soft butter or cooking oil, then salt and pepper generously. Put goat in an open roaster and place in preheated oven until it browns (about 20 minutes). Pour over the juice of 1 orange or 1 cup of dry white wine, reduce heat to 325°, cover and cook slowly until done (about 45 minutes).

TEX MEX BEEF TACOS
Elizabeth Gulley

Serves 10–12

Elizabeth Gulley says the oldest Mexican restaurant in the United States was San Antonio's Original Mexican Restaurant. It closed in 1960. This just might be the O.M.R.'s original recipe for Tex Mex beef tacos.

2 lbs. ground round steak	Dash black pepper
1 tsp. cooking oil	⅓ tsp. salt
1 tbsp. chopped white onion	1½ cups tomato sauce
1 clove garlic, minced	24 taco shells
½ tsp. ground cumin	Shredded iceberg lettuce
½ tsp. oregano	Finely chopped tomato (optional)
½ tsp. hot green chile peppers, minced	Shredded Longhorn cheese (optional)

Brown meat in oil. When thoroughly cooked, add the onion, seasonings, and tomato sauce and mix to make the filling. Simmer, covered, for 10 minutes.

While you are making the filling, heat taco shells in a 200° oven. Fill hot shells with meat mixture, then top with shredded lettuce and finely chopped tomato. Sprinkle top with grated Longhorn cheese, if desired.

OAXACA EGGS WITH NOPALES
Bobbie Covey

Serves 2

2 small tomatoes, broiled or
    blistered over open flame
1 or 2 fresh *chiles serranos* or
    jalapeños, broiled
¼ small onion, chopped
1 clove garlic, chopped
Salt to taste

3 tbsp. peanut oil
3 large eggs
⅓ cup *nopales*, freshly cooked or
    canned
½ cup water
1 large sprig *epazote*

Blend tomatoes, chiles, onion, garlic, and salt. Heat 1 tablespoon
of the oil and fry mixture for 5 minutes.

    Heat remaining oil, beat eggs and cook lightly in oil, stirring
until they are set. Add sauce and *nopales* to eggs and continue
stirring constantly for 1 minute. Add water and *epazote* and cook
for about 3 minutes more. Serve on hot plates. Good with hot flour
tortillas.

HUEVOS RANCHEROS
(Ranch Eggs)

There are a lot of jazzed-up versions of the old ranch eggs recipe.
Some say to poach the eggs. Or to use tomatoes or onions or
lettuce or cheese. It's enough to make Zapata turn over in his
grave.

1 recipe of *Mexican Ranchero
    Sauce*, heated
Lard, oil, or butter

1 corn tortilla per person
2 eggs per person

Heat **Mexican Ranchero Sauce**. Preheat oven to 185°. Place about 1
teaspoon of lard in a 7-inch skillet. (Of course you can use cooking
oil or butter, but lard is the best.) When it is hot enough to make a
drop of water sizzle, use tongs to drop a tortilla in the hot fat. Heat
both sides well, only a few seconds to the side. Hold tortilla up out
of the fat with tongs and allow the excess fat to drip back into the
skillet. Lay each tortilla on a dinner plate and place in warmed
oven. When you have prepared enough tortillas to go around,
cook the eggs to order. For an authentic ranch egg, fry in the same
skillet, sunny side up so that the white is coagulated but the

yellow will still run. Place egg on top of the prepared tortilla, cover with a generous amount of hot **Mexican Ranchero Sauce**, and serve immediately. I always garnish the side of the plate with a jalapeño pickled in oil.

SOPA DE FLOR DE CALABAZA
(Squash Flower Soup)
Melba Chatham

Serves 4

The thing about growing squash in a garden is—you get desperate. Unless the vines are struck with mildew early on, you will have so much squash that you may want to have a squash-carving party. One way to deal with the fertility of this vegetable is to use the blossoms the way Mexican cooks do. If you are guarding your crop, you can use only the male flowers. How do you know a male squash flower from a female? The female has a little squash growing behind the blossom. The male has only a stem. Anyway, you can gather the blossoms early in the morning—either males with no fruit, or the female blossom once the squash is 2 or 3 inches long. Wash the blossoms in cold running water and store in a plastic bag in the refrigerator until you have accumulated about a quart or so of the blossoms. Frankly, I find it works best if you don't tell the children that the soup is made from squash at all. By the time you have accumulated enough blossoms to make soup, the kids are usually so sick of squash they are screaming for Colonel Sanders.

3 tbsp. butter	1 quart half-and-half
1 onion, chopped	2 tbsp. flour
1 quart squash flowers	Salt and white pepper to taste

Melt butter in skillet, add onion and squash flowers. Sauté until the flowers collapse and the onions are transparent. Place in processor with cream and flour. Blend until smooth. Return to heat. Cook and stir until the soup has thickened. Salt and pepper to taste. This pale gold soup looks for all the world like it has saffron in it, but it is delicate as baby's breath.

POLLO FLAUTA
(Chicken Flute)
Betty Hunt

Serves 2

If you have a cup of leftover chicken, a small can of chicken, or even leftover pork or roast beef, you can make a delicious meal for two.

1 cup *Tomatillo Sauce*
1 cup cooked chicken or other
   meat, shredded
6 corn tortillas
Lard or cooking oil
Toppings (any or all of these):
   Mashed avocado squeezed with
   fresh lime juice

Sour cream
Cheddar cheese, grated
Spring onions and tops,
   chopped
Black olive slices
Shredded lettuce
Picante sauce

Put the toppings on the table in little bowls and let everyone choose his or her favorites.

Add chicken or other meat to **Tomatillo Sauce**. Heat.

For best results be sure you are using very fresh tortillas. Old tortillas aren't pliable enough to roll into fine flutes. Roll flutes as tightly as possible without tearing the tortilla.

Using a *comal* or a hot dry skillet, heat each tortilla on both sides for a moment until it is pliable enough to roll easily. Next, spread 1 heaping tablespoon full of the meat mixture along one side of the center and roll the tortilla as tight as possible. Lay the tortilla flute with the flap down and continue the process until you have used all filling and tortillas.

While you are filling the flutes, heat oil in a skillet—about ½ inch. The oil should be so hot that when you sprinkle water into it, it spits back at you. Carefully lay the *flautas* in the hot grease and cook just until the tortilla crisps and turns golden. Use a pancake turner to turn them—only once. Place the flap side down first so that it will seal.

Serve 3 *flautas* to the plate along with the various toppings. These can be eaten out of hand if you have done this properly. I must admit that it takes some practice to get these *flautas* just right. Don't be discouraged if it seems clumsy at first.

One more note about the tortillas. The best *flautas* are made with homemade tortillas because you can press them thinner than the store-bought ones and they are absolutely fresh. See recipe for **Homemade Corn Tortillas** if you'd like to go the whole route.

TEX MEX CHICKEN OR TURKEY MOLE
Leroy Woollett

Serves 8

1 whole cooked chicken or turkey
(about 4 cups)
1 8¼-oz. jar Bueno or Doña María
brand *mole* sauce
1 quart chicken broth
1 7½-oz. can tomato sauce
1 tbsp. smooth peanut butter
1 square dark unsweetened
chocolate

1 tbsp. sugar
Salt to taste
Slivered almonds (optional for
garnish)
Cooked rice or corn tortillas (to
serve with the *mole*)

Stew a chicken in salted water to cover until tender (1½ hours). Remove chicken from broth. Reserve broth. Debone and remove skin from chicken. Tear into pieces with a fork (don't dice with a knife).

In a large saucepan, over low heat, warm *mole* sauce from jar until almost boiling. Add broth, stir to make a perfectly smooth sauce, then simmer 20 minutes. Add tomato sauce, peanut butter, chocolate, and sugar. Cook and stir 20 minutes. Salt to taste.

You may serve *mole* in a couple of ways. Mexican cooks mix chicken with sauce. For aesthetic reasons, I prefer it served this way: heat corn tortillas on a dry skillet for about 15 seconds each, then place one or two on a warmed plate, spoon ½ cup chicken over tortilla, and cover with sauce. You may serve the *mole* over rice and sprinkle almonds on top. In the store you'll also see Mole Verde sauce next to the *mole* sauce; it's quite different, as it is made from pumpkin seeds.

You can make Mole Verde sauce in much the same way you make the original *mole* by leaving *out* the chocolate and tomato sauce. Pour over meats and rice. Mole Verde is preferred by natives of Michoacan and Southern Mexico. It has a rough consistency which may require some getting used to.

CAMARONES Y ARROZ EL PASO
(Shrimp and Rice)
Judy Morriss Jones

Serves 6

¼ cup green onions and tops, chopped fine
¼ cup vegetable oil
1 cup rice, uncooked
2 cups chicken stock
1 tsp. salt
¼ tsp. black pepper
¼ tsp. cayenne pepper
1 tbsp. soy sauce
1 clove garlic, pressed
1 bay leaf
Juice of 1 lemon
½ tsp. thyme

1½ lbs. shrimp, peeled, deveined, washed and dried
1 tbsp. butter
1 tbsp. soy sauce
Dash cayenne pepper
¼ cup Cheddar cheese, grated
½ cup sour cream
½ cup green onions and tops, chopped
1 tomato, sliced
1 avocado, sliced
½ cup black olives, sliced

Chop green onions and set aside. Heat vegetable oil in a heavy 3-quart pot. Add rice, and over high heat cook and stir constantly until rice browns and seems almost to pop—like popcorn. Take care that it doesn't burn. Toss in green onions and stir for about 30 seconds. Add chicken stock, and immediately turn heat down low. Add seasonings: salt, peppers, soy sauce, garlic, bay leaf, lemon juice, and thyme. Cover and cook over low heat until rice is done and all liquid is absorbed (about 20 minutes).

While this is cooking, peel, clean, and pat dry the shrimp. Grate the cheese, cut the onion, slice tomatoes, avocados, and olives. In a heavy skillet (preferably cast-iron) melt butter, toss in shrimp, and sauté over medium-high heat. When they begin to turn pink, add soy sauce and dust the shrimp lightly with cayenne. Try to time the sautéing, which takes about 5 minutes, to coincide with the last 5 minutes of cooking the rice so that everything will be hot at the same time. Once you have the rice cooked and the shrimp cooked, place rice in a serving dish, pour shrimp and pan juices over the rice, then add toppings. First sprinkle the cheese over the shrimp. Then add sour cream, onions, tomato, avocado, and black olives. Serve at once so that the bottom is hot and the top is cold.

HOMEMADE CORN TORTILLAS

If you've ever visited rural Mexico, you know that you're likely to awaken to the sound of applause. Step out of the house into the dry air that, just after daybreak, seems to sigh. Walk toward the clapping, and you'll find Mexican women making tortillas. Forty or fifty pats and they have created a perfect cornmeal disc. Sit down and ask them if you can try it. They'll try to hide their merriment. Faces will pull down into stone masks, eyes will fail to meet yours—until at last, you throw the whole crumbly ball in the air and give up. Then the experts will break into uncontrollable laughter. Want to make tortillas? Buy a press.

2 cups *masa harina*
1 cup water

Combine *masa* and water, mixing until a dough ball forms. (This takes 10 seconds in a food processor, longer if using a fork.) Let dough rest 20 minutes. On a sheet of wax paper, form 15 or so balls about the size of pigeon eggs. Cover with another sheet of wax paper. Now using plastic wrap (not wax paper—it sticks), form the tortillas. The simplest way is to use a tortilla press. Make an envelope of the plastic wrap, put the *masa* ball in the center of the press, and mash. Carefully peel the plastic wrap off the tortilla. If the edge of your pressed tortilla is ragged and crumbly, the dough is too dry and needs a tablespoon or so more water worked in. If you can't peel the paper off, it's too wet—sprinkle *masa* on your hands and work into the dough. Bake on an ungreased griddle (400°) about 1 minute to the side. I know the tortilla aficionado wouldn't approve, but being thoroughly entrenched in Consumer America, I mix the *masa* in a processor, mash it in a press, then bake the tortillas in an electric skillet. This gives me the control I'm used to and turns out a good product. If you are willing to practice, you can make satisfactory tortillas by hand-patting them, or by rolling them out with a rolling pin between two sheets of plastic wrap, or even by pressing a saucer down on top of the plastic-wrapped *masa* ball. You can bake them in a cast-iron skillet on the stove. When you finish baking the tortillas they should still be pliable. Stack them on top of each other and wrap them in a tea towel until you are ready to use them.

It takes a little practice to get them the right thinness. All I can tell you is to keep trying—the thinner the better. Sometimes I drop a whole jalapeño in the processor first and pulverize it, put in a pinch of salt, then proceed with the recipe. This makes a green-flecked hot tortilla that is particularly good with cheese enchiladas.

FLOUR TORTILLAS

Makes about 1 dozen

Why is it that the recipes that sound easiest are always the hardest? Who would think that this primitive bread is hard to make? It is. The trick is the right flour-to-water ratio. The first time I made these they were lumpy. The second time sticky. I finally decided to just keep dribbling in the water until it looked like a nice soft bread dough, and this seems to work out right.

2 cups white flour	1 tbsp. lard or shortening
1 tsp. baking powder	½ cup water, more or less
½ tsp. salt	

Sift together dry ingredients, cut in lard until it looks like small peas in the flour. Add only enough water to make a soft dough. Mix well, then knead on a well-floured board for 5 minutes. Cover and *let the dough rest for 30 minutes.* Form into round balls about 2 inches in diameter; either make the tortillas in a press, or roll between 2 sheets of wax paper. Cook on hot, dry griddle on top of stove until brown, turning once. Wrap in a clean dish towel to keep warm.

BUÑUELOS
Camille Jones

Serves 8–12

Nothing in American cooking quite compares to these sweet, golden-brown puffs of fried dough that are somewhere between wafers and cookies.

4 cups flour	1½ cups water (approximately)
1 tsp. salt	Peanut oil for frying
4 tsp. baking powder	1 cup sugar
2 tbsp. lard or unsalted butter	Cinnamon to taste

Sift together the flour, salt, and baking powder, then cut the lard or butter into the dry ingredients until the mixture is the consistency of coarse cornmeal. Add enough water to make a soft dough. Knead well, adding flour as necessary for handling. The mixture should be soft and elastic but not sticky. Form the dough into walnut-size balls, cover, and allow them to rest for 30 minutes. Roll each ball and cut into a 3-inch square. Fry, a few at a time, in 1 inch of oil at 365°, until golden brown and well puffed. (You may also use a deep-fryer.) Drain on paper towels and sprinkle with sugar and cinnamon before serving.

FLAN ALMENDRA
(Almond Flan)
Ana Rosa Albelais Foster

Serves 6–8

This flan will keep in the pan up to a week in the refrigerator. It is silky smooth. The almonds rise to the top so that when you turn it, you have an almond crust. It is easy to make and elegant to boot.

½ cup sugar
1⅔ cups sweetened condensed
　　milk
1 cup milk
3 eggs

3 egg yolks
1 tsp. vanilla extract
1 cup slivered almonds, coarsely
　　ground

Sprinkle the sugar evenly in a 9-inch cake pan and place over medium heat. Using oven mitts, caramelize the sugar by shaking the pan occasionally until the sugar is melted and has turned a light golden brown. (A little stirring may be necessary when caramelizing the sugar over a gas burner.) Allow to cool; the mixture may crack slightly.

Blend the remaining ingredients at high speed for 15 seconds. Pour over the caramelized sugar. Cover the pan with aluminum foil and place it in a larger, shallow pan containing about 1 inch of hot water. Bake at 350° for 55 minutes or until a knife inserted near the center comes out clean.

Remove the pan from water and uncover; let it cool on a wire rack at least 30 minutes. Loosen the edges with a spatula. Place a serving plate upside down on top of the cake pan and quickly invert the flan onto it.

CAPRITODA
(Mexican Bread Pudding)
Bobbie Covey

Serves 6

2 cups *piloncillo* (or brown sugar, firmly packed)
4 cups water
1 2-inch stick cinnamon
1 whole clove
Butter
6 slices toast, cubed (made from good bread)

3 apples, peeled, cored, and sliced
1 cup raisins
1 cup chopped, blanched almonds
½ lb. Monterrey Jack cheese, cubed

Preheat oven to 350°. Combine sugar with water, cinnamon, and clove. Bring to a boil and cook until the mixture has cooked to a light syrup (about 10 minutes). Remove spices and set syrup aside.

Butter a casserole dish, cover the bottom with toast cubes, add a layer of apple slices, then raisins, almonds, and cheese. Repeat until all ingredients are used up. Pour syrup over all and bake in a preheated oven for 30 minutes. Serve with whipped cream if you wish. Delicious.

PASTEL DE CAMOTE
(Sweet Potato Pie)

Serves 8

1 lb. sweet potatoes
½ cup butter
1 cup sugar
1 tsp. pumpkin pie spice
1 tsp. cinnamon

½ tsp. nutmeg
4 eggs, separated and beaten
1 lemon (juice and grated rind)
1 oz. brandy
1 10-inch unbaked pie crust

Cook potatoes in small amount of water until tender. Drain and mash. Cream butter and sugar; add spices, egg yolks, and lemon. Beat the potatoes in gradually, until light. Add brandy, then fold in beaten egg whites. Turn into unbaked pie crust. Bake 45 minutes to 1 hour at 375°.

POSTRE DE MANGO
(Mango-topped Cream Pie)
Virginia Wood

Serves 8–12

A topping of fresh (or canned) mango slices is the perfect way to finish this cheesecake-like dessert, but peaches or other fruit do almost as well.

Nut Crust:

1 cup walnuts, finely chopped
1 cup flour, sifted
⅓ cup brown or white sugar
Dash of salt
1 tsp. cinnamon

½ cup butter
1 tsp. vanilla extract
1 large egg
1 egg yolk

Chop the nuts (in a rotary hand-held grater or in a blender, no more than ¼ cup at a time). Mix the dry ingredients; cut in the butter until the mixture is the consistency of coarse cornmeal. Beat together the vanilla, egg, and egg yolk and combine with the butter mixture.

Line the bottom of a 9-inch springform pan with wax paper (do not grease the sides) and press the dough to a thickness of ⅛ inch onto the bottom and sides of the pan. Prick the bottom and sides with a fork and bake at 375° for 12–15 minutes or until lightly browned. Cool.

Cream Filling:

16 oz. cream cheese
1 cup sour cream

½ cup sugar
1 or 2 mangos

Beat the cream cheese with an electric mixer at high speed until light and fluffy; add the sour cream and sugar and blend briefly. Trowel the mixture into the cooled nut crust. Arrange slices of mango or other fruit around the edge.

Topping:

½ cup pineapple preserves
¾ cup raisins

¾ cup walnuts, finely chopped
¼ cup curaçao

Heat the ingredients in small saucepan over a low flame for approximately 5 minutes, stirring as necessary. Cool to room temperature. Spoon over top of pie.

EMILY'S MEXICAN CANDY
Emily Mickler

2 cups sugar
¾ cup milk
½ tsp. soda

1½ tsp. vanilla
1 tbsp. butter
1½ cups pecans

In a large saucepan, combine sugar, milk, and soda. Cook without stirring until mixture reaches the soft-ball stage (236°). Remove from heat and add vanilla, butter, and nuts. Beat until it begins to lose its gloss and looks creamy. To form patties, *quickly* drop from a tablespoon onto wax paper that has been sprinkled with a little salt. Cool. Can be wrapped individually in plastic wrap or wax paper.

NOGADA
(Mexican Pralines)

Mexican cooks sometimes use a sugar called *piloncillo* for candy making. This is Mexican brown sugar, corn syrup, and water formed into a cone. But it tastes different from American brown sugar and makes a marvelous praline-like candy. You can buy *piloncillo* in supermarkets in San Antonio. You may have to go to a Mexican specialty market in other cities to find it. But it's worth the search. Mexican vanilla puts the American version to shame. I prefer it for all recipes calling for vanilla.

2 7-oz. *piloncillos*
1 cup water
Pinch salt
1 small stick cinnamon

2 heaping tbsp. butter
1 tsp. Mexican vanilla
1 lb. pecans, halved or broken
    pieces

Dissolve *piloncillos* in salted water over low heat. Add cinnamon stick, increase heat, and boil until a drop of mixture forms a soft ball in water (236°). Remove from fire, remove cinnamon. Add butter and vanilla. Beat until candy starts to thicken. Add pecans and beat by hand until candy begins to sugar. Drop *quickly* onto a buttered pan by the teaspoonful.

Meat

Pan-broiled Steak
Chicken-fried Steak with Pan Gravy
Flank Steak Grill
Hearty Brisket
Best Stuffed Bell Peppers
Stuffed Cabbage Rolls
Beef Jerky
Grillades
Thin Veal for Tom
Broiled Liver
Argyle Ham with Baked Bananas
Ham Balls with Sweet Hot Mustard
Tex Czech Pork Chops
Country Ribs in Orange
Lamb Chops on a Grill

Meat

Cowboys liked their steaks one way. Fried. And done. Through and through. There's the story of the cowboy in a fine hotel in Kansas City who ordered a steak which arrived broiled to a perfect medium rare. He sent it back immediately and complained to the waitress, "I've seen cows git well that was hurt worse'n that."

The cattlemen had some interesting customs when it came to killing beef. They preferred not to eat their own cattle and, if at all possible, would trade meat with a neighboring outfit. They had no use for "aged" beef, but preferred their meat freshly killed. In the spring and summer when the outfit was on the trail, they killed the beef in the late afternoon so that the meat could chill in the cool night air of the high plains. Come morning, they wrapped the meat in tarps and placed it under bedrolls in the wagon to protect it from the heat of the day. Every night the meat was recooled—until it was all eaten, usually just a few days later.

Necessity and the range cook invented what we call chicken-fried steak. Range cattle could be tough. Old Cookie would lay a hind quarter up on the workbench of the chuck wagon, slice off some medium-thick slabs of meat, pound the slabs with a cleaver, salt and pepper and flour them. He knew beef suet was the best cooking fat of all, so he would throw a good-sized chunk of suet into his Dutch oven, render out an inch or so of grease, fish out the cracklings, then drop the steaks into the sizzling fat, cover the oven with a lid, and let 'er rip. Once the steaks were cooked, he'd make "sop" for the boys by throwing a little flour in the drippings, browning it, then adding water to make a good brown gravy. Cowboys never got tired of this meal and would quit an outfit where the boss was too tight to provide a reasonable number of steak dinners.

PAN-BROILED STEAK

I'm not a physicist, but I believe what John Casey told me about salt. Left in its granulated state, it will reflect back on a meat surface and seal in the juices (contrary to popular opinion). Here is the way to cook a steak. I will admit that it creates enough smoke in the house to cause the neighbors to call the fire department, but it does make a terrific steak—crispy on the outside, tender and juicy on the inside.

Using a cast-iron skillet, sprinkle a very fine coating of salt over the whole bottom of the skillet. Place over high heat and get it plenty hot. (You can test it by putting a drop of water in. Should evaporate almost immediately.) Now put in your favorite cut of steak—unseasoned and patted dry, cut as thick as you can afford. Very shortly the fat will begin to expel into the salt and there goes the smoke. Don't worry. Cook the meat about 5 minutes to the side, turning only once. Delicious. Golden reddish brown outside, perfect medium rare inside.

CHICKEN-FRIED STEAK WITH PAN GRAVY

Serves 4

Everyone has a favorite version of chicken-fried steak. Here is the way I like it.

1 round steak	2 tbsp. water (or milk)
Salt and pepper	Cooking oil
Flour	1 tbsp. water
1 egg	

Pound the round steak with the side of a saucer until it flattens and tenderizes. Cut away fat, remove bone, and cut into about 4 serving pieces. Beat egg with water or milk until lemony. Sprinkle all sides of meat with salt and pepper. Dredge in flour, knocking off excess. Dip in egg, then again in flour. Now set aside and begin heating about 1 inch of oil in a cast-iron skillet over medium-high heat. Be sure you put the meat aside so that the coating will set and won't come off in the skillet. When oil is hot enough to spit back at you if you sprinkle water on it, add meat and cook until golden brown on each side, turning only once. Now turn fire down, add 1 tablespoon of water, put a tight-fitting lid on, and steam for 5 minutes. Serve with **Pan Gravy.**

PAN GRAVY

Pour out oil from skillet, but leave any crumbs of the batter (unless they're burned). Return 2 tablespoons of oil to the skillet and add 2–3 tablespoons of flour; stir to make a golden roux, giving the salt and pepper shakers a good shake over it, too; finally, stirring all the while, add about 1½ cups of warm water. Cook and stir until it is smooth and thick. Taste for seasoning. Some people substitute milk for the water. It just depends on what paper-napkin restaurant you began eating chicken-fried steak in. Do whatever suits you, but the milk should be at least room temperature to guarantee a smooth gravy.

FLANK STEAK GRILL

Serves 4

1–1½ lbs. flank steak
⅓ cup mild olive oil
⅓ cup good Mandarin-style soy
   sauce
⅓ cup dry sherry

½ cup mushrooms, sliced
½ cup green onions and tops,
   sliced
2 tbsp. butter
Charcoal grill fire

With a sharp fillet knife, butterfly the steak until it opens out like the pages in a book. Combine oil, soy sauce, and sherry. Place steak in a Pyrex utility pan and pour marinade over, making sure to get it inside the flap. Cover with wax paper. Marinate at room temperature at least 2 hours. Sauté finely sliced mushrooms and onions in the butter. Add a little of the marinade and reduce sauce for 1 minute or so. Open steak out and paste the inside flap with mushroom, onion, and butter sauce. Roll it up, like a jelly roll, secure with stainless steel skewers (I use a long shish kebab skewer and "sew" it closed). Grill over a hot charcoal fire—12–20 minutes to the side (depending on thickness and on how done you want it), basting each side with marinade every 3 minutes or so. Turn only once. Place the *serve* side (pretty side) down first and don't turn the meat prematurely. When ready to serve, place on a board and with a sharp fillet knife, cut into the meat at an angle. You will now have lovely rolls that are brown on the outside and medium rare on the inside. Serve with a robust burgundy, a salad, and a good loaf of French bread. It's all you need.

HEARTY BRISKET

Serves 20

Cooking a brisket recalls an elementary law of physics. What happens to water at 212°? It boils away. By cooking a brisket at 200° all the inherent juices are saved and the meat is made more tender than you ever imagined. It is important that the cooking sack be completely sealed—a good method is to use what is called a drugstore wrap. Here's what you do.

You'll probably notice that a brisket is too wide to seal in one width of foil, so you will need to seal 4 sides. Here's how: Tear off 2 large equal lengths of foil. Lay 1 on top of the other. Now fold 1 side over twice, making a narrow ½-inch double fold. Open out the 2 sheets, and you'll have a good seal on the bottom. Lay the meat on top of the seam. Coat all surfaces with the marinade. Now lift the 2 remaining sides of foil up and, holding them even with each other, fold over and over in ½-inch folds until you have a tight package. Press fold flat against the meat. This leaves only the ends. Fold these like you would a birthday present—into a kite shape—and then fold them *under* the meat. This is what is known as a drugstore wrap. When you are finished the foil should be touching all surfaces of the meat snugly. You just have to be careful not to puncture it during the cooking and handling process.

When I cook this brisket, I do the whole thing after supper. The first night I make the marinade and place meat in the refrigerator; the next night I put it in the oven just before going to bed. By morning it is cooked to a turn. A good working woman's scheme. You can eat this for several days without screaming.

1 8- to 10-lb. brisket	1 tbsp. salt
¼ cup dry red wine	5 cloves garlic, pressed
1 tbsp. molasses	2 onions, minced fine
¼ cup soy sauce	2 stalks celery, minced fine
1 tsp. peppercorns	Pepper, coarsely ground

Make a marinade of wine, molasses, soy sauce, peppercorns, salt, garlic, onions, and celery. (You can put onions and celery in processor until almost pureed.) Lay the boned and trimmed brisket on a large piece of heavy-duty foil and spread the marinade over all surfaces. Wrap the brisket tightly. Place in refrigerator and marinate for 24 hours. Open foil and sprinkle the brisket generously with freshly milled pepper. Reseal, place in a large open roasting pan (or jelly roll pan). Place in a 200° oven and cook for 8 hours. Remove from oven. Rewrap the meat in a clean sheet of foil. Reserve pan juices and serve with warm meat. Good hot or cold on sandwiches.

My friend Shirley Barr makes a great brisket sandwich by slicing paper-thin slices of meat, then layering them on an onion bun topped with equally thin slices of Swiss cheese. She runs this under the broiler and serves the sandwiches open-faced with thin-sliced kosher dill pickles, red onions, and brown-tip lettuce.

BEST STUFFED BELL PEPPERS
Mark DeFoyd

Serves 6

Fortunately, I have one child who likes to cook as much as I do. My boy, Mark, at fifteen the king of the countermen, says he learned to fix stuffed peppers at Camp Stewart. But, he says he'd rather cook them at home because at camp, if you didn't watch your own serving, some ravenous competitor would steal it away. Mark says he ate a lot of half-raw meat just to stay alive when he was cooking at camp.

6 large uniform bell peppers	½ tsp. salt
1 lb. lean ground round	1 egg
1 cup bread crumbs	Chile sauce (preferably *Argyle*
1 jalapeño pepper, chopped fine	*Chile Sauce*)
1 small white onion, chopped fine	Foil
1 clove garlic, pressed	Cast-iron skillet
¼ tsp. pepper	Charcoal fire in a covered smoker

Cut tops from peppers. Remove seeds and stems. Combine remaining ingredients except chile sauce. Stuff peppers almost full. Using your thumb, make a slight indentation in the stuffing to hold the chile sauce. Place a big dollop of chile sauce in each pepper. Cut 6 12″ × 12″ squares of aluminum foil. Place a stuffed pepper in the center of each foil square. Draw up the corners like a dime store Easter egg basket. Put all 6 wrapped peppers in a cast-iron skillet or stew pot with the red chile sauce peeking from a hole in the middle. Pour a cup of water into the bottom of the skillet. Place skillet on the grill, cover the smoker (this should be something like a Weber or an oil-drum smoker), cook covered over hot coals until done, a couple of hours more or less. You can cook these in the oven at 350° for 45 minutes until meat and pepper are tender, but there won't be the undergirding that outdoor cooking gives to the flavor. You could make a jillion of these ahead, freeze them, and serve 1 apiece on a cook-out.

STUFFED CABBAGE ROLLS
Shirley Barr

Serves 6

Give yourself a good ½ hour to prepare the cabbage rolls for cooking. You and I are not as fast as those experienced Fredericksburg Germans. Total preparation time is at least 2½ hours.

Choose a nice big cabbage head or you will scream trying to get off 12 leaves. Save what you don't need for the next day when you can steam the cabbage and serve with hot butter.

12 large cabbage leaves	½ tsp. thyme
1 lb. ground round steak	2 8-oz. cans tomato sauce
2 tsp. salt	1 tbsp. brown sugar
½ tsp. pepper	¼ cup water
1 cup cooked rice (from ½ cup raw)	Juice of ½ lemon
1 small onion, chopped fine	Clean cotton string or toothpicks
1 egg	2 tbsp. cooking oil

Core the cabbage. Place cabbage head in a large stewpot with the core up. Pour boiling water from teakettle over it—say a couple of cups. Put the kettle back on the fire. The outer leaves will soften momentarily allowing you to peel them off whole. Repeat this procedure until you have stripped out 12 leaves as nearly whole as is possible. The leaves may still be somewhat stiff. If so, pour more boiling water over them until they are completely pliable and limp. Trim away the vein end of the largest leaves. Set leaves aside. Now make the filling. Combine beef, salt, pepper, rice, onion, egg, thyme. Mix well. (I can only do this by hand.) Set this aside.

Make the sauce in another bowl by mixing tomato sauce, brown sugar, water, and lemon juice. Set aside. Now place 2 heaping tablespoons of the meat filling in each leaf up near the vein end of the leaf. Fold the end over the stuffing, fold over the sides envelope-fashion, then roll as tightly as possible. Fasten with a toothpick or a piece of clean cotton string. Heat oil in a 10-inch skillet. Brown the rolls, 6 at a time, on all sides. Once the rolls are evenly browned, place all 12 rolls in the skillet, pour the sauce over, cover with a tight-fitting lid, and simmer on low heat for 1 hour, basting once or twice. Remove the rolls to a hot serving platter. Remove string or toothpicks. Take a look at the sauce. Depending on the amount of water in the cabbage and the meat, the sauce may or may not be thick enough. It should look like catsup. If it seems too thin, turn up the fire and, stirring constantly, boil it down until it is thick and dark. Pour over rolls and serve.

BEEF JERKY

1 piece flank steak, 3–5 lbs.
Salt

Coarsely ground pepper
3 cloves garlic, minced

Place meat in freezer and allow it to become about half frozen, so that you can see ice crystals in the meat, but it is still slightly pliable. Using your hands, tear off thin strips of meat—with the grain (this is the way Mexican cooks cut meat). Pound meat slightly with flat side of a wooden spoon. Place meat on a rack in a baking pan. Lightly salt and heavily pepper both sides of meat. Rub with minced garlic. Cook at 200°, turning once, for 6 hours. Store in airtight jar in a dark place.

VEAL

Veal comes to us by way of dairy farming. Cattlemen would have thought butchering calves somewhat akin to cutting up hundred dollar bills and tossing them over your shoulder. The cow was a beef animal to the cowboy—valued by the pound. But in dairy farming the product was milk. And to get milk the cows had to be bred regularly. Once the calf was born, it was usually removed from the cow and bottle-fed for a few weeks, then butchered and served as veal.

In the late 1800s a German nobleman came to the high plains. Like other aristocratic Germans, he dabbled in the breeding of blooded dairy cattle and fine horses, but mostly he was a real estate developer. Walter Baron von Richtofen was an uncle to Manfried Baron von Richtofen, the celebrated flying ace of World War I (as in the *Peanuts* cartoon), and although he seems to have gotten most of his information secondhand, the baron wrote a little book in 1885 called *Cattle-Raising on the Plains of North America*. The book, along with others of its kind, helped to create the great cattle boom of the 1880s. Lots of European money flowed onto the plains as a result of the baron's efforts.

In this fascinating little book, von Richtofen says that the Longhorn, which he calls the "Texas" cow, is the original stock cow of the West. He optimistically predicted that the Texas cow would soon feed all of Europe. One comment this gentleman farmer/author/promoter made was that the calves of the Longhorns were remarkably strong. But why not, he went on to say. These calves were allowed to stay with the cow and, he noted, there were sometimes three generations of cows in one family group that stayed together. He compared these cattle to buffaloes. They were wild and wary and hearty. No cowboy could have milked a Longhorn. No cowboy would have wanted to kill a calf except for an occasional S-O-B stew.

However, in Texas food history, veal is not totally absent. The Cajuns gave us veal. The Alsatians around Castroville gave us veal. It's a cinch the cowboys would have felt about veal the same way they felt about milk—as illustrated by a famous cowboy poem:

> Carnation Milk, Best in the Land
> Comes to you in a little red can.
> No teats to pull, no hay to pitch,
> You just poke a hole in the son-of-a-bitch.

GRILLADES
Nona Morriss

Serves 8

Cajun cooks used to save small trimmings of meat, and when they had accumulated a sufficient amount, would create this dish for brunch. It does not, as I originally believed, rhyme with Rolaids, but is pronounced *gree-ahds*. I must warn you that Cajun cooking requires a lot of patience; the roux must be chocolate brown and the onions, peppers, and tomatoes must be chopped so fine that when you cook them in the roux they totally lose their identity. *Grillades* and grits are the epitome of a Cajun brunch and are often served with baked curried fruit.

3 lbs. veal or beef round, sliced ¼-inch thick and cut into bite-sized pieces
¾ tbsp. salt
½ tsp. black pepper
½ tsp. cayenne pepper
¼ cup flour
2 tbsp. bacon drippings
¾ cup vegetable oil
¾ cup flour
2 cups onions, chopped fine
1 bell pepper, chopped fine
3 cloves garlic, pressed
3 whole tomatoes, chopped fine (if using fresh tomatoes, slip skins)
Dash thyme
1 bay leaf
1 tbsp. Worcestershire sauce
2 cups chicken broth
Salt, red and black pepper
¾ cup parsley

Salt and pepper the meat, then dredge in flour. Heat bacon drippings in a Dutch oven, then brown meat on all sides over high heat. While the meat is browning, chop (but do not combine) onions, pepper, garlic, and tomatoes and set aside. Once the meat is browned, remove from pan. Now add vegetable oil and flour and make a chocolate-brown roux, stirring the mixture over low heat until you think it will burn for sure if you wait another moment. (This could take 15 minutes.) Toss in onions, pepper, and garlic and continue stirring until the onions are completely brown, form a jellied consistency, and seem to disappear. Take your time. If the mixture looks as if it will stick and burn, add a tablespoon of broth—but only if the onions don't have sufficient moisture to brown without burning. Now add tomatoes and stir again until the tomatoes are completely absorbed. The tomatoes give a rosy tint to the brown roux. Add thyme, bay leaf, Worcestershire sauce, and chicken broth. Stir until well blended. Taste the mixture and add salt, cayenne and black pepper to taste. A true Cajun will be very generous with these seasonings—especially the cayenne pepper. Place the meat back in the roux, cover, and cook slowly for 1½ hours. Stir occasionally. The sauce may thin out a little as juices are extracted from the meat. You will want the sauce so thick a spoon laid on the top won't sink. So if it looks too soupy about 15 minutes before you are ready to serve, remove the lid from the pot, turn the fire up some, and stirring frequently, reduce excess liquid. When you are ready to serve, remove bay leaf and stir in parsley. Serve the *grillades* over grits for an authentic Cajun brunch. Also good over rice. This is one of those dishes that are better the second day. Freezes well.

The choice of meats is really up to you. I don't like veal in this dish, even though I know it's authentic, because veal hasn't enough body to suit me. I always use round steak even though my Cajun friends would probably disapprove.

THIN VEAL FOR TOM
Betty Shindler

Serves 4

1½ lbs. veal cutlet
1 large clove garlic
Flour
¼ cup butter
½ lb. mushrooms, sliced thin
½ tsp. salt

½ tsp. coarsely ground pepper
⅓ cup dry vermouth (Noilly Prat best)
1 tsp. lemon juice
2 tbsp. fresh snipped parsley

Pound cutlets with wooden mallet until very thin, then rub all surfaces with the peeled clove of garlic. Dredge in flour and set aside. Melt butter in a heavy skillet. Raise temperature until milk solids begin to precipitate out of butter, then add cutlets, browning on all sides. Lower temperature, add mushrooms, salt, pepper, and vermouth. Cover tightly and simmer 15–20 minutes, or until tender. Just before serving, sprinkle lemon juice and parsley over all.

BROILED LIVER
Sarah Thomas

Serves 4

About 1 lb. calf or pork liver, sliced thin
8 strips bacon, sliced thin
½ tsp. garlic salt

½ tsp. sweet basil, crushed
¼ tsp. oregano
2 baking or cake racks

Wash and dry liver. Arrange on a rack so that pieces touch. Sprinkle with half the garlic salt and half the basil. Cover completely with strips of bacon. Place another rack on top. Flip the racks over and remove the one that was on the bottom. Sprinkle with the oregano, the rest of the garlic salt, and basil. Cover this side with bacon as before. Replace the rack. Put liver between racks over a pan and broil until the bacon is done. Turn entire unit over and cook until bacon on the second side is done.

The bacon keeps the liver moist and gives it a great flavor; the racks keep it all up out of the grease.

Someone told me recently that racks for oven broiling or outdoor barbecue must never be salvaged from an old refrigerator. Some refrigerator racks contain cadmium, which is poisonous.

ARGYLE HAM WITH BAKED BANANAS
Alice O'Grady

Cooking paste for 1 ham

2 tbsp. poupon mustard
2 tbsp. brown sugar
1 tsp. paprika

Mix together to form a paste and coat ham surfaces. Bake thoroughly according to the kind of ham you have (fresh, smoked, or already cooked) until brown on the outside, done on the inside. Serve with **Baked Bananas**.

BAKED BANANAS

Peel bananas and rub generously with cooking oil. Place in a pan and sprinkle generously with sugar, paprika, and parmesan cheese. Bake at 350° for 8 minutes.

SWEET HOT MUSTARD

1 box (1¼-oz.) dry mustard
½ cup white wine vinegar

½ cup white sugar
1 egg, well beaten

In a small saucepan combine dry mustard and vinegar thoroughly. Add sugar and well-beaten egg. Place over medium heat and raise to a boil, stirring constantly. Boil for 1 minute. Refrigerate. This mustard steeps and improves with age. Best if you make it the day before.

HAM BALLS WITH SWEET HOT MUSTARD
Melinda Schmidt

Makes at least 40 balls

2 lbs. ham
1 lb. boneless pork loin
1 cup soft bread crumbs

3 well-beaten eggs
1 cup milk

Preheat oven to 350°. Grind the ham and pork loin using the coarse blade of grinder. Combine with remaining ingredients and form into balls. If you plan to use this as a main dish, make the balls about the size of a golf ball. If you plan to use them for appetizers, make them the size of a walnut. Place the balls, 1 layer deep, in Pyrex baking dishes. (Makes enough to about fill 2 8½" × 11" pans.) Now make the sauce:

4 cups dark brown sugar (2 boxes)
4 cups water
2 cups white wine vinegar

Combine sauce ingredients and heat to a boil. Pour the hot sauce over the prepared balls until they are half submerged. (You may have some sauce left over—it will depend on the size of the baking dishes.)

Place balls and sauce in a 350° oven and cook uncovered for 1 hour. At this point you can freeze the balls, either in the sauce or out, but serve hot with **Sweet Hot Mustard** on the side.

TEX CZECH PORK CHOPS

Serves 6

6 pork chops, ¾-inch thick
Salt and pepper to taste
Flour
2 cloves garlic, pressed

½ cup chopped onion
2 tbsp. peanut oil
1 tsp. caraway seed
½ cup water

Preheat oven to 350°. Salt, pepper, and flour chops. In a cast-iron skillet over medium heat, sauté garlic and onion in oil until golden. Remove onion and garlic. Reserve. Add chops and brown on both sides. Return onion mixture to skillet. Sprinkle with caraway seed. Add water. Cover with a tight-fitting lid and bake in preheated oven until tender (about 45 minutes). Turn the chops after 25 minutes. Good with **Tex Czech Spinach**.

COUNTRY RIBS IN ORANGE

Serves 8

Butchers are always coming up with some new cut with which I am not familiar. About 5 years ago I discovered pork country ribs which are, to my mind, better than spare ribs and cheaper than pork chops. Now I have recently discovered that my butcher will sell me a block of country ribs, which has the same good taste the individual ribs have but with the added advantage of producing a succulent roasted product without the risk of being too dry. Although this is less expensive than a boneless loin, it roasts better because the fat striations and bone keep it from turning into sawdust. This is a versatile cut, standing in place of either more expensive offering—boneless loin or loin chops. If your butcher isn't offering a block of country ribs yet, ask for it. Order it cut through the backbone—to facilitate slicing at the table.

5-lb. block pork country ribs	3 oranges (good Texas juice
6 cloves garlic, pressed	oranges with thin skins are
1 tbsp. salt	the best)
1 tsp. peppercorns	

Select a baking dish that is a close fit for the pork and that has a tight-fitting lid. I use a small enameled chicken roaster. Place meat in pan. Pierce all surfaces with a fork. Combine garlic, salt, peppercorns, and the juice of *1* orange. Rub this mixture over the pork and set aside, covered, at room temperature for 1 hour. Preheat oven to 350°. Look at the meat and make sure the ribs are *up.* Now pour over the juice of the second orange. Cut the orange skin halves into flat pieces and place on top of the meat. Cover and bake for 1 hour. Remove from oven. Discard orange skins. With a bulb baster, remove all juices to a small saucepan and reserve. Turn the meat over. Measure out 3 tablespoons of juices and moisten meat. Replace in oven *uncovered* and cook for 45 minutes. Now, for the final 15 minutes of cooking, turn the meat so that the ribs are again *up,* turn the oven temperature up to 400°, and brown the serve side. You should watch this. The total cooking time could vary according to the accuracy of your thermostat, but should total roughly 2 hours. Don't burn it. During this last 15 minutes, skim any excess fat from the top of the reserved pan juices. Add the juice of the third orange to reserved pan juices. Place over high heat and boil, reducing by half, stirring frequently. Serve the sauce separately or poured over the roast meat.

LAMB CHOPS ON A GRILL
Patricia Slate

Although a lot of sheep are raised in Texas, the natives don't eat much lamb. It goes back to the old rangemen's wars over grass. Cattlemen thought sheep killed grass by biting it off too close to the ground. I don't know what sheepmen thought. I never knew one.

The Easter my mother was six years old, a neighbor drove to the Flag Ranch with a present for the children in his buckboard: A curly lamb decked out in a pink bow. Grandfather didn't bother being courteous to the man bearing the gift. He escorted both man and "stinking sheep" to the edge of his property.

My mother still thinks sheep are unclean and won't eat lamb. If a Texan eats lamb at all, he is likely to grill it, to cover up—as one old codger told me—"the wild taste."

Patricia Slate's pastes are not intended to mask anything. In fact, they enhance the delicate flavor of a perfectly rare-cooked chop.

Lamb chops
Olive oil
Garlic clove, pressed

If you think of it ahead of time, you can marinate the chops for a while in olive oil and garlic—say while the charcoal is getting hot. At any rate, generously baste the chops with olive oil and garlic and grill on hot charcoal grill about 5–6 minutes to a side.

There are a couple of good pastes you can serve on the side with the chops:
1. Combine white-wine mustard and a little fresh rosemary.
2. Or combine:
   1 tbsp. rosemary
   1 garlic clove, pressed
   ¼ lb. butter, softened

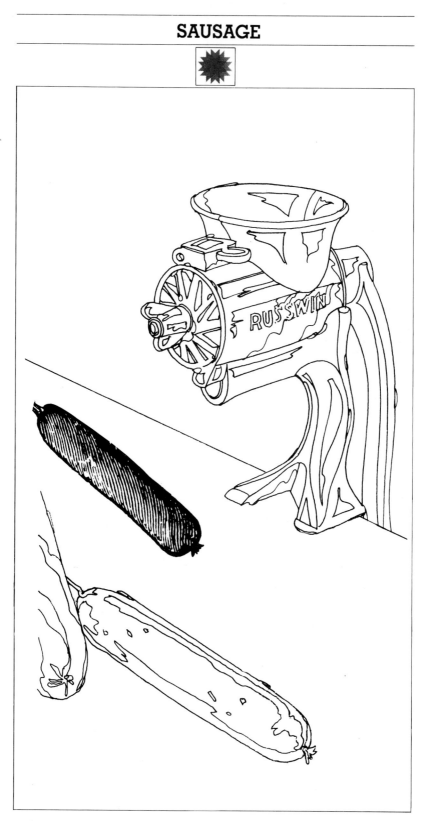

Smoked Venison Sausage
Bernhard's Pan Sausage Seasoning Mix
Bratwurst
Jack Meister's All Beef Salami
Boudin Blanc (White Pudding)
Texas Turkey Ring Sausage
Garlic Sausage
Summer Sausage
Knackwurst-Weiners
Chorizo

Sausage

Some say that sausage making, like law making, is a process you should never watch. An alternative: make sausage yourself.

Sausage making reaches back into antiquity. Originally it was designed to use up scraps of meat left over from butchering which were too good to throw away, but too small to be used any other way. It is one form of cookery which is distinctly regional. Favored meats and spices find their way into sausages from different areas of the world, providing tremendous variety within one classification of food. There is no meat-eating culture which excludes sausage.

I have found sausage making a pleasant day's work with a friend. At the end of the day, we have had a good visit, and the satisfaction of producing a large volume of food for the family.

When I first began investigating the possibility of making sausage at home, I found cookbooks to be woefully vague about details. Every recipe I found assumed I would understand directions to *case*, *stuff*, and *smoke*. I didn't.

The casing is generally animal intestine—pork, beef, sheep, or goat—purchased from a butcher by the yard and salted down. A dollar's worth looks like enough to stuff a whole hog and maybe the neighbor's barking dog.

Casings come in different sizes. Pork casings are the ones generally used for the ring sausages commonly purchased at the grocery store and are the easiest to use at home. Thicker, larger-diameter beef casings are usually used for dried sausage and require more preparation (you must clean fat off the sides). Sheep or goat intestines are used for small breakfast links or frankfurters. Before you begin stuffing, casings should be soaked in water a couple of hours. Change the water twice. When you're ready to attach the casing to your stuffer, cut off a piece about 1 yard long, slip 2 fingers inside, and stretch it over the tap. Turn on the water and rinse. It's a surprise to see this tiny shrivelled white balloon expand. Casings are thin durable membrane. They require no delicacy in handling.

Stuffing may be accomplished in two ways. Most home grinders have a stuffer attachment. This is simply a 6-inch cylinder which fixes to the end of the grinder. To stuff right out of the grinder, merely feed the casing over the cylinder in the same manner as you would put on a sock, crumpling the casing until it exposes the end of the stuffer attachment again. Now turn on the grinder and feed the meat until it just reaches the end of the stuffer attachment. Pull the end of the casing just over the end and tie with common kite string. Turn on the grinder and stuff until the sausage reaches the desired length. Turn off grinder, give the casing a couple of twists, and tie with string. Repeat until you have stuffed the entire casing. This sounds hard but is really simple.

You will discover that air bubbles may form along the length of the casing. Prick with a needle and the casing will reform to touch the sausage again. Natural casing is wonderfully elastic.

If you don't have a stuffer attachment you can stuff in another way. Using a funnel and a wooden spoon, feed the casing over the funnel end. Fill the large end of the funnel with the meat mixture and force through the small end with a spoon until it just reaches the end of the funnel. Tie off one end of the casing. Then simply feed the meat mixture through the funnel with the spoon until the sausage is the desired length. Twist and tie. Repeat until meat mixture is completely cased.

Smoking is a process developed by our ancestors as a method for preserving meat. It is sometimes confused with cooking. Smoked meats and sausages do require additional cooking and may not be eaten without more cooking *unless* during the smoking process the internal temperature of the meat was raised to 160°. These meats are labeled *ready-to-eat* in stores.

Of course, our ancestors never tested internal temperatures of meat, but established safety standards must be followed by commercial packers and would be advisable for home sausage stuffers as well.

If you want to be perfectly safe, you will smoke all sausage to be recooked to an internal temperature of 130° and ready-to-eat sausage to a temperature of 160°.

Smoking may be done in a variety of ways. Many Texas farms had a small wooden smokehouse. You can use one of the modern smokers or a backyard barbecue of the oil-drum variety. The idea is to create a lot of smoke and not much heat. The smoke must be kept moving, so you must create some sort of draft through your closed smoking unit. Slow-burning wood is the ideal smoking fuel, but charcoal sprinkled with a fine layer of sawdust will also work. Before placing sausage in smoker allow fire to burn down so that there are no flames. Hang an oven thermometer inside and do your best to maintain a temperature of 80° to 90°. Add slightly damp wood or charcoal as needed. To improve the taste add twigs from fruit or nut trees such as apple, cherry, and hickory. To test the internal temperature, stick a meat thermometer into a sausage and read. When smoking is completed, refrigerate sausages or store in a cool dry place.

The kind of sausage you make will determine its storage. Ready-to-eat dried sausage which has been smoked and precooked requires no more refrigeration than jerky, its first cousin. Fresh ground sausage, like pan sausage, must be refrigerated immediately and should be eaten within 3 or 4 days, but if you freeze it, it will keep 4 to 6 months. Smoked sausage will keep either in the refrigerator or in a cool (40°–50°) dry place for several weeks. Cured sausage will keep in the refrigerator up to 2 weeks and may also be frozen.

What is the difference between curing and smoking? Both are designed to preserve meat, but curing employs chemical means to extend the shelf life of meats. The old standby in the sausage making business is saltpeter, potassium nitrate. When I asked a commercial sausage packer about the risks of nitrates in the diet (some nutritionists theorize they are carcinogenic), he gave me a withering look and replied, "If you eat meat which is improperly cured, you can be dead the next day from food poisoning. You'd have to eat 50 sausages a day for 40 years before you'd be in danger from nitrates."

If you believe nitrates to be dangerous to your health, simply leave saltpeter out of the recipes that call for it and treat the sausage as if it were fresh meat (in other words, freeze it quickly).

SMOKED VENISON SAUSAGE

Is there a soul in Texas who hasn't been offered venison sausage at some time or other? In a state where deer are roughly the size of an aged jack rabbit, sausage making has come to be one of the prime products of the hunt. Some of the sausage is so bad that folks get real generous and want to give it away. I have tried everything from deer salami, which was dry, tough, and so strong it practically walked off the plate, to breakfast sausage so mild it was like eating hamburger. One of the best compromises I've found is a German links recipe, smoked to give it added resonance and containing saltpeter to retain a nice rosy color. If you object to nitrate, just leave saltpeter out. The color will then be grayish. Don't be shocked at the quantity in this recipe. It assumes you just shot a deer.

14 lbs. venison
7 lbs. pork trimmings—80% lean
1 cup noniodized table salt
⅓ cup coarsely ground black
    pepper
2 teaspoons saltpeter (buy at a
    drug store)

Combine seasonings, sprinkle over meat, then grind once using coarse blade. Mix well with your hands. Stuff into casing 1½" × 10". Smoke about 3 days in a cool smoker, until internal meat temperature is 160°. Sausage may be frozen until ready to use, or dried in a cool, dark, arid place until it's shrunk by ⅓. If fresh-frozen, cook by placing a link of sausage in a skillet with 3 tablespoons water. Cover, cook, and turn until water has evaporated and sausage is an even brown color. If dried, slice off small bites and chew and chew and chew.

BERNHARD'S PAN SAUSAGE SEASONING MIX

For 50 lbs. of sausage

The Bernhard brothers are hill-country butchers who can recall the days when their father used to take them to far-flung ranches for week-long butchering jobs. When Germans say *no waste,* they mean it. Sausage making to a rural Texas German family meant not only trimmings from tougher parts of the animal, but also head cheese and *Blutwurst* (blood sausage), an ethnic treat I've never had the nerve to try. Sausage was stored in large crocks filled and sealed with lard. Milton Bernhard assured me that dried sausage aged from 6 months to 2 years in a lard crock was the best thing one could eat.

The Bernhards sell a pan sausage seasoning mix which can be used for venison sausage or pure pork sausage. Their advice is to use half pork and half venison for optimum results. Ask your butcher for pork trimmings that are 60% lean. Milton Bernhard warns that you will only get out of the product what you put in. Don't expect a deer which has been allowed to remain warm in the field to make decent sausage. The pork trimmings must be absolutely fresh as well. I have used this mix to make pure pork sausage by asking the butcher for pork trimmings that were 80% lean.

14 oz. salt
3 oz. black pepper
½ oz. crushed red pepper with
    seeds (add more for hotter
    sausage)

½ oz. ground red pepper
4 oz. brown sugar
2 tbsp. ground ginger
1 oz. sage

This seasoning mix will keep a couple of years. If you want to make only 15 or 20 pounds of pan sausage, get out a kitchen scale and pencil and divide the mix accordingly.

BRATWURST

Bratwurst is a pale color, what my Texas butcher friend calls "light-complected."

2½ lbs. lean veal
2½ lbs. lean pork
2 tsp. dried sage
3 tsp. salt

1 tsp. white pepper
1 cup white bread crumbs soaked
    in ½ cup milk
1½ cups water

Combine meats and grind twice. Add spices and grind a third time, using coarse blade. Using your hands, combine meat and bread crumbs. Add water and beat until light and fluffy. Stuff into 1½" × 6" casings. To cook, put sausage into a skillet with enough boiling salted water to cover. Lower heat and simmer 10 minutes. Remove sausages from water and dry. To serve, roll sausages in a little flour and brown in butter. If a sauce is desired, pour a little dry white wine into the skillet. Serve bratwurst topped with onions fried in butter and with mashed potatoes.

JACK MEISTER'S ALL BEEF SALAMI
Pearle Koehler

Not everyone who wants to try sausage will have a stuffer or a grinder. If you would like to try your hand at making sausage but don't have a stuffer or grinder, I recommend a recipe which I got from my neighbor, Pearle Koehler. Pearle says her friends from Albuquerque brought samples in a flight bag on the plane, creating quite an aroma in the nonsmokers' section. The spices in this sausage are so heady I'd have to classify it as strong. Because of the spices, however, it requires less refrigeration and will keep for a short trip—even in a flight bag.

4 lbs. common ground beef hamburger	2 tbsp. mustard seed
	1 tbsp. basil
¼ cup Morton's Quick Cure Salt (purchase from a meat market)	1 tbsp. oregano
	1 tsp. onion powder
1 tsp. garlic powder	⅔ cup Parmesan cheese
2 tsp. chile powder	1 tsp. whole peppercorns
2 tsp. crushed dry red pepper	1 4-oz. can diced green chiles
1 tsp. ground cumin	3 tbsp. dry sherry

Mix dry spices, cheese, and salt thoroughly. Break up ¼ of the meat into the bottom of a large pan. Sprinkle ¼ of the dry spice mix evenly over meat. Then add ¼ of the chiles. Continue by fourths with balance of meat, spices, and chiles until the 4 pounds are used. Pour sherry over meat. Now mix by hand a full 15 minutes. After mixing, press meat mixture down flat in pan, cover with lid, and refrigerate about 12 hours.

After cooling, divide meat into 4 pieces. Form an 8-inch roll from each piece. Place each roll into a 10″ × 12″ piece of nylon netting (the kind you buy at the dime store). Twist each end of netting and secure with one of those fasteners off the end of a bread loaf. Place rolls on a rack over a shallow pan to catch the drip and bake in a 225° oven for 4 hours.

Allow rolls to cool and place in a paper bag. Salami will keep in the refrigerator at least 2 weeks and will freeze for 2 months. Don't put in plastic bags or salami will sweat. Slice thin. Tastes better at room temperature. But if you want to tame it, serve cold.

BOUDIN BLANC
(White Pudding)

Serves 6 (2 each)

Don't confuse this version with Louisiana's Cajun-style *boudin*, which is made from rice and pork scraps.

¼ lb. bacon fat	⅛ tsp. ginger
3 cups onions, sliced thin	⅛ tsp. cinnamon
1 cup milk	1 tbsp. chopped parsley
⅔ cup French bread crumbs	2 tsp. salt
½ lb. lean boneless veal	¼ tsp. pepper
½ lb. skinned, boned raw breast of chicken	1 egg
	3 egg whites
⅛ tsp. allspice	½ cup whipping cream
⅛ tsp. nutmeg	Boiling water and milk (to cover)

Cook ½ of the bacon fat until all fat expressed. Add onions and cook slowly until clear. While bacon is cooking, in a small saucepan pour milk over bread crumbs and bring to a boil. Mix gently with a potato masher constantly and cook until mixture has thickened to resemble a pudding. Set aside.

Cube remaining meat and bacon fat, mix with onions and rendered fat, and grind once. Mix dry spices thoroughly in a small bowl. Add all spices and grind twice more. Transfer ingredients to large bowl and beat with electric mixer for 2 minutes, add egg and beat 2 minutes more. Add egg whites and beat 3 minutes. Add bread crumbs, stirring. Add cream to mixture a little at a time, beating between additions. Mixture will be consistency of sticky roll dough. Stuff mixture into casings forming sausages 5 inches long and 1 inch thick. Refrigerate overnight.

Place *boudins* in heavy saucepan and cover with equal parts milk and water. Bring liquid just to simmer and poach slowly for 25 minutes. Drain *boudins*, cool at room temperature, and refrigerate. Makes approximately 12 6-inch links.

Preparation time: 2 hours for 2 people. Use within 3 to 4 days or freeze. Before final cooking prick each *boudin* in 3 or 4 places with a needle to prevent bursting. Cook for eating by brushing with melted butter and grilling or dredge in flour and fry in butter at a low temperature. Serve with mint jelly or sweet gherkins. Also good with a mild cole slaw, French bread, and a white Beaujolais wine.

TEXAS TURKEY RING SAUSAGE

Another popular sausage indigenous to Texas is turkey sausage. The most famous purveyor of this uniquely Texas sausage is Inman's in Llano. Their sausage is cased fresh, then barbecued. The Bernhards smoke the ring sausage first, producing a more resonant product. If you don't want to smoke the sausage, remember that you can barbecue it fresh, although it will be somewhat drier.

10 lbs. boneless turkey meat including skin (you can save money by purchasing turkey parts excluding the breast)	1 oz. black pepper
	1 oz. brown sugar
	1 tsp. ginger
	Pinch cloves
3 oz. Morton's Quick Cure Salt (purchase from a meat market)	Pinch allspice

Grind the turkey meat once, using coarse blade. Mix spices and sprinkle over meat. Mix thoroughly with your hands and regrind. Case in links 1½″ × 10″. With a cotton string tie off both ends and pull into a ring. Each ring should weigh approximately 1 pound. Hang sausages in cool place (38°–45°) to cure and dry for 24 hours. If you wish to make ready-to-eat sausage, place in a smoker at a temperature of 150° for 4 hours, then raise the temperature to 170° and continue smoking until the internal temperature of the sausage reaches 160°, probably about 4 hours. If you wish to make smoked sausage to be recooked, smoke for 8 hours at 155° until the internal temperature of the sausage is 138°. Store in refrigerator.

GARLIC SAUSAGE

6 lbs. pork roast, cubed	½ tsp. marjoram
½ tsp. saltpeter	½ tsp. thyme
1½ tsp. black pepper	½ cup dry white wine
2 tsp. chopped garlic	1¼ lbs. fresh pork rind (ask the butcher to cut this from bacon)
1 bay leaf	
½ tsp. sage	

Court Bouillon

2 cups dry white wine	3 stalks celery, quartered
5 quarts warm water	2 carrots, scraped and quartered
3 sprigs fresh parsley	24 peppercorns
1 bay leaf	

Combine cubed pork roast with spices. Add wine. Cover and let stand overnight in the refrigerator.

Boil pork rind in water to cover for 2 hours in a covered pot. Drain.

Put meat mixture through grinder using coarse blade. Chip the pork rind fine and blend with meat by hand.

Stuff into sausages 6 to 8 inches long. Simmer in **Court Bouillon** liquid for 2½ hours. Serve cold and sliced thin with warm potato salad, cold fresh vegetables, and homemade mayonnaise.

SUMMER SAUSAGE

In Texas, there's a product familiar to delicatessen shoppers usually billed as Summer Sausage. I've never quite figured out why it's called this except perhaps because it's well seasoned and isn't susceptible to spoilage. Good for picnics and sandwiches. In other parts of the country, this same sausage is known as cervelat. It's usually made of pork, a sort of jazzed-up bologna, and is good served cold with thick slices of sharp Cheddar cheese, or grilled briefly and served with beans and potato salad. If you're grilling outside, turn carefully with tongs so that you don't tear the sausages. Their texture is more delicate than anything you buy at the grocer's. They will burn readily and must be watched carefully.

5 lbs. lean pork	1 tsp. thyme
½ lb. bacon	1½ tsp. basil
1 tbsp. chopped green onion tops	½ tsp. ground cloves
3 tbsp. chopped parsley	1 tsp. nutmeg

Cooking Liquid:

8 cups beef broth	1 tsp. pepper
1 onion, sliced	1 tbsp. salt
1 tsp. thyme	1 tsp. nutmeg
1 tbsp. chopped parsley	

Combine meats and grind twice, using coarse blade. Blend in remaining ingredients, using your hands for a thorough mix. Stuff casings 1½ inches thick and 10 inches long. Hang in a cool dry place 4 days. Combine ingredients for cooking liquid and bring to a boil. Prick sausages with a needle and add to liquid, reduce heat, cover and simmer slowly 4 hours. Serve hot or cold.

KNACKWURST-WEINERS

If you stuff this sausage into a 1½-inch casing, you can call it knackwurst. If you stuff it into a ¾-inch casing (probably goat), it will be weiners.

2 lbs. lean beef	1 tbsp. coriander
2 lbs. lean pork	1 tsp. mace
1 lb. fatty bacon ends	2½ tbsp. salt
4 cloves garlic, crushed	2 tsp. sugar
½ cup minced onion	1 cup water

Combine meats and grind coarsely. Add remaining ingredients, knead thoroughly with your hands, and grind again. Stuff into casings 5 to 6 inches long. Place in a heavy kettle with water to cover. Bring to a boil and simmer for 10 minutes. Drain and rinse in cold water. Refrigerate until ready to use (3–4 days) or freeze.

These must be cooked again before eating. You may grill, boil, or fry. Prick each sausage with a needle before cooking to allow grease to run out.

CHORIZO

2 lbs. coarsely ground lean pork	¼ tsp. *each*: coriander, ground
¼ lb. pork fat, finely ground	ginger
2 tbsp. paprika	1 tsp. *each*: oregano, cumin
2 tbsp. chile powder	6 whole garlic cloves, crushed
1 tsp. coarsely ground black	½ cup vinegar (5% acid)
pepper	½ cup sherry
½ tsp. *each*: cinnamon, ground	
cloves	

Mix fat and meat thoroughly. Add other ingredients and mix together, using your hands. Be sure to distribute the vinegar thoroughly through the mixture.

Put the mixture in an earthenware crock or glass jar in a cool place (50°–60°) and allow the sausage to "cure" for at least 24 hours, preferably for 2 or 3 days.

Stuff into hog casings and link, then refrigerate. If you wish to keep for an extended time, freeze the sausage. This sausage *must* be cooked before eating.

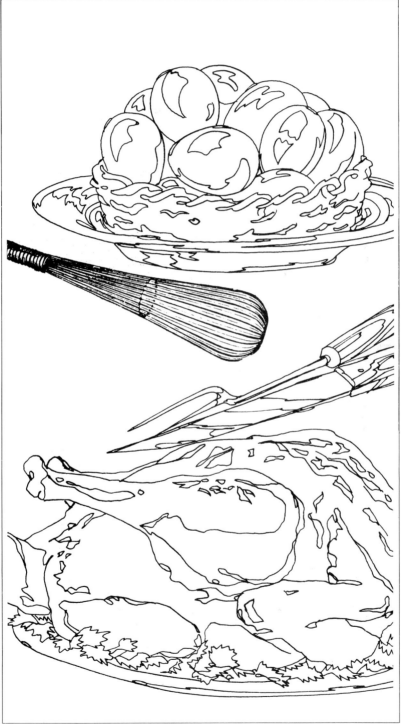

Country Captain
Chicken Guadalupe
Chicken Natural
Southern-style Fried Chicken
Chicken Sweetish Hill
Chicken Texanna
Milk Toast
Irish Eggs
Scalloped Eggs and Cheese
Eggs and Onions
Bad Hombre Eggs

Poultry and Eggs

When I was growing up in Hereford, my mother and grandmother kept a pen of chickens in the backyard. The thing I remember about the chicken yard was that when we gave the chickens a watermelon rind, they were afraid of it and jumped up on the chicken house in terror. I also remember trying to wring chickens' necks the way my grandmother did. She killed them. I made them dizzy. I remember breaking a piece of valuable Bavarian china that belonged to my grandmother and hiding it under the nesting boxes. After my grandmother died, I used to go out in the chicken house and get out that piece of broken china and cry, sure that somehow my deception had killed my grandmother. I was five years old.

When Joe and I moved from Houston to Hunt, the first thing I wanted on our quasi-homestead was a pen of chickens. We already had a chicken house way out in back, and it only took me about two weeks to locate a man in Comfort who sold laying hens. I took a dog crate in the back of the station wagon and headed down to pick up the layers I'd ordered.

After choosing lovely hens I got carried away in the face of all those chickens and asked the old German farmer if that other pen full of small chicks was for sale. Yes, he said. Were they fryers, I asked. Yes, he said, and fifty cents a piece, so on impulse I ordered fifty.

He rigged up some sort of cardboard box for the little chicks, we stuffed the hens in the dog crate, and I whizzed home.

We had a wonderful time with the chickens. They laid beautifully. The eggs were better than any store-bought eggs. As the little chickens grew, we made another discovery. I hadn't bought pullets at all: I'd bought fifty baby roosters. They grew up to stage some splendid White Leghorn cockfights in the backyard. They weren't much good to eat.

Everything went well until the first spring. Then our chicken yard began to be attacked nightly by a persistent 'coon. After the first few times of hearing the terrible ruckus outside, going flashlight in hand only to discover a poor hen with her head neatly clipped off, I soon got over any romantic notions about how cute raccoons were.

The 'coon became our avowed enemy. We plotted and schemed and devised plans to kill the predator. Light was a big problem. Finally Joe thought he'd solved the problem. He affixed a flashlight to the barrel of a 12-gauge shotgun so that he could see out in front of him but wouldn't be blinded by his own light. He kept the gun waiting by the back door.

At last, we heard the now-familiar squawking. Joe leaped out of bed, grabbed the gun, and silently made his way to the chicken yard in the moonlight. Once there, he flicked on the light and saw a pair of red eyes gleaming in the weeds. Trying as best he could to contain his buck fever, he shot directly at the glowing eyes. It was a good clean kill. He murdered two Pearl beer bottles that had fallen off the garbage trailer.

I learned a couple of things from this chicken enterprise. First, you can't beat yard eggs. Second, after plucking feathers from the forty-eighth rooster (we kept 2 for local color), I was grateful for chickens at the grocery store who'd had their feathers sucked off by those rubber suckers they use in chicken plants.

COUNTRY CAPTAIN

Serves 6

1 fryer, cut in pieces
Salt and pepper
½ cup flour
¼ cup cooking oil
1 cup rice
1 green pepper, cut in julienne
   strips
1 clove garlic, pressed
1 onion, chopped coarse
1 1-lb. can tomatoes with juice, or
   4 fresh tomatoes, or 1 1-lb. can
   Ro-Tel tomatoes if you prefer a
   hotter dish

2 cups chicken broth
1 heaping tsp. curry powder
½ tsp. thyme
½ cup raisins, plus more for
   garnish
½ cup sliced almonds, plus more
   for garnish

Preheat oven to 325°. Salt and pepper the chicken. Place flour in a brown paper bag and shake chicken pieces to coat. Put aside so that the coating will set while you heat cooking oil in a 5-quart Dutch oven. Brown the chicken, a few pieces at a time, over medium high heat. Remove chicken pieces to a plate as they brown. Add rice to Dutch oven, stir and brown grains. Now add green pepper, garlic, and onion. Cook and stir until onion is clear. Add tomatoes and juice. Break up tomatoes with spoon, or if using fresh tomatoes, quarter them before putting in the pot. Add broth, curry, and thyme. Stir and raise to a boil. Cover, reduce heat, and simmer for 15 minutes. Stir in raisins and almonds. Replace chicken in Dutch oven, spooning sauce over the chicken pieces. Cover and bake in a 325° oven for 50 minutes. Remove to rimmed serving platter, sprinkle additional raisins and almonds over the top before serving.

CHICKEN GUADALUPE

Serves 4

1 fryer, quartered
Lemon pepper
Salt

Olive oil
Honey

Sprinkle all surfaces of the fryer with lemon pepper and salt. Now coat completely with olive oil. Lay in an open roasting pan, skin side up. Dribble honey over the visible skin surfaces. Bake uncovered at 350° until golden brown—about 45 minutes. Good with rice and shredded carrots.

CHICKEN NATURAL

Serves 2

Try cooking this outside on your next camping trip. It will also cook well on your plain old kitchen stove.

1 fryer, cut in 2 pieces	Salt and pepper to taste
¼ lb. butter	3 oz. mozzarella cheese sliced
1 onion, chopped	1 tsp. capers
1 green pepper, chopped	Anchovy strips (presoaked in milk)
1 clove garlic, pressed	Chopped parsley
2 tomatoes, quartered	

In a cast-iron skillet brown the unseasoned fryer in butter, skin side down first. Remove bird, and cook onion with green pepper and garlic until onion is clear. Add tomatoes. Now put chicken back on top of vegetables. Salt and pepper lightly—just a touch really. Cover skillet tightly and cook over low heat until tender (about 30 minutes). The heat can be a camp fire, a Coleman stove, charcoal, or the kitchen stove. When chicken is cooked, place mozzarella cheese slices on top of chicken. Sprinkle on capers, anchovy strips, and parsley. Put the lid back on and let it stand a few minutes to melt the cheese. Good with broccoli in a French dressing with a twist of lemon peel on the top. Sure beats hot dogs for a picnic.

SOUTHERN-STYLE FRIED CHICKEN
Alice O'Grady

Here is the way the *Argyle Cookbook* of 1942 advised its readers to cook chicken.

Cut chicken into desired pieces and have thoroughly chilled before cooking. Salt and pepper each piece, then carefully roll in flour. Have the frying fat very hot and drop a few pieces into it at a time—do not cook too many pieces at a time. After each piece has been turned, lower the heat and cook until golden brown. Drain on brown paper. To make a delicious creamed gravy, you drain off the surplus fat when the chicken is fried, leaving all the crumbs in the frying pan; these must not be burnt. Add a little flour and stir while browning, then add one-fourth cup hot water and stir until smooth. As this is very thick, thin it to the desired thickness of gravy with milk or cream. Season to taste with salt and black pepper.

A perfect Plantation dinner or Southern dinner consists of fried chicken, butter beans, spinach ring with hard-boiled eggs, green salad of mixed vegetables, lemon pie or a cobbler of fresh peaches or berries. Oh yes, don't forget to have plenty of mint for your tea and no bread could take the place of hot biscuits. Have an extra pound of butter and a dish of preserves.

CHICKEN SWEETISH HILL
Patricia Slate

Serves 2

1 whole chicken breast, boned and
    pounded to stretch and flatten
    it
3 tbsp. cream cheese
1½ tsp. green peppercorns

Dash tarragon and salt
1 egg
1 tbsp. water
Seasoned bread crumbs
¼ cup clarified butter or olive oil

If you don't have a butcher who'll do it for you, skin and bone the chicken breast. I find that the easiest way to get the meat free from the bone is by working my fingers under the breast bone and ribs and tearing it away. If I use a knife, I always seem to lose more meat than I should. Pound the breast lightly with the edge of a saucer or mallet until it is uniformly thin and pliable. Combine cream cheese, peppercorns, tarragon, and salt. Spread evenly over the breast, and roll into neat cylinder, tucking in sides. Should make a nice neat package. It will stay shut with the cheese acting as glue. Now dip in egg mixed with water, then into seasoned bread crumbs. At this point you should refrigerate it at least 30 minutes. It cooks better if it's good and cold to start with. You can bake or sauté this dish. If you are making several for a group it is probably easier to bake. Place in an oiled baking dish, pour on melted butter or olive oil, and bake uncovered for 25 minutes at 350°. Do not turn. For only 2, you can sauté one breast by placing it in a hot skillet, moistened with clarified butter or olive oil, sauté serve side (pretty side) down first. Sauté 10–12 minutes per side, turning only once.

CHICKEN TEXANNA
Anna Kay Brewer

Serves 2

1 whole chicken breast, split in 2 pieces	Soft butter
Freshly squeezed garlic clove	Juice of 1 lemon
Salt, pepper, and poultry seasoning	Tongs for turning
	Hot charcoal fire in a grill
	2 hot serving plates

Rub chicken with freshly squeezed garlic, then sprinkle generously with salt and pepper. On underside only, dust with poultry seasoning. Now coat all surfaces with soft butter. Just before grilling squeeze lemon over chicken. Grill on a hot open charcoal fire. Place the prettiest side (serve side) down first. Grill 10 to 15 minutes to a side. Turn only once. Use tongs. Don't walk away. If fire flames up, sprinkle with water. Grilling requires close attention. Let someone else toss the salad.

Turning meat over and over on a grill only loses juices. So peek at the meat and don't turn it prematurely. The first side that you cook will look the best so look at any meat you are about to grill and always put the serve side down first. Turn once. Then when you are ready to serve, simply scoop it up with a pancake turner onto a hot plate and you've done what a good chef does. You have considered the look of the meat as well as the taste.

MILK TOAST

As I have already mentioned, my daddy thought chili could cure the common cold. But there were other remedies in the family lexicon. My grandmother used to spoon-feed me milk toast whenever I was too weak to eat. I can't imagine now that I was ever too weak to eat, so perhaps it was all some sort of code for love between a grandmother and her grandchild, but I remember well the way it went.

In the first place, she always served the milk toast in a pie tin. It never occurred to me to question this. Why not a soup bowl or a dinner plate? I don't know. But I serve it in a pie tin to my children, too. And she fed me with a tablespoon. Not a soup spoon or a teaspoon. I can't imagine why this was necessary either, but I still serve it with a tablespoon.

There is no doubt that milk toast is of English origin and is probably served with variations, but at our house it was made by first slicing a piece of homemade "light" bread, toasting it well on both sides in the oven, then buttering it and placing it in the pie tin. Over the piece of toast was poured hot milk, probably a cup or so, and into this was dropped a soft poached egg—preferably with the yolk unbroken so that the sick child could watch it being stirred in. This whole concoction was then salted and peppered with the finely milled black pepper that we always used on the plains, and spoon-fed. It sounds so good, I think I'll go downstairs and make myself some for lunch.

IRISH EGGS

Serves 6

Somebody told me to do this years ago when I was in a vegetable co-op and driving to the Houston Farmer's Market at the crack of dawn with a cranky kid in the back seat. This is an out-of-hand breakfast that you can make a day ahead and serve en route to school the next morning, on the way to a picnic, or a camp-out, or any other event that requires that you get going early and when you don't want to cook breakfast. As the kids around here say, it looks gross, but they even admit that once they taste it, they like it. Don't ask me where the name came from.

1 lb. Owens Country Sausage
6 nice large eggs, hard-cooked
    and peeled

Divide the sausage into 6 equal parts and mold it around each hard-cooked egg until egg is completely covered with sausage. Now place the sausage-covered eggs on a rack in a shallow pan and cook at 325° until sausage is completely browned, about 20 minutes.

You can refrigerate this dish, and it will keep a couple of days. Stick it up in the back of the car on a Texas morning, and you'll have hot sausage and eggs in 30 minutes or so.

SCALLOPED EGGS AND CHEESE
Martha Kavanaugh

Serves 6–8

4 cups milk
5 eggs
Salt and pepper to taste
9 slices of day-old white bread (a good kind like French or English muffins)

3 cups grated cheese (can be American, Swiss, Muenster, Cheddar, or Jack)
⅓ cup melted butter

Combine milk, eggs, and salt and pepper to taste. Beat well. Butter a 2-quart casserole dish thoroughly. Cube the bread into bite-sized pieces. Layer the bread alternately with grated cheese. Then pour milk and egg mixture over. Pour melted butter on top. Cover and refrigerate overnight. Next day bake uncovered at 350° for 30 minutes.

EGGS AND ONIONS

Serves 8–10

2 lbs. yellow onions
½ cup (¼ lb.) butter
1 dozen eggs
½ cup flour

4 cups milk, at room temperature
Salt and pepper
Hungarian paprika
Fresh parsley for garnish

Peel and thinly slice onions. Melt butter in a heavy 5-quart Dutch oven (stainless or porcelain enameled better than cast-iron). Add onions and over medium-low heat cook and stir until onions lose their shape and become quite clear (about 25 minutes). Don't brown them. Meanwhile hard-cook the eggs, then cover with cold water, and peel when cool enough to handle. Cut eggs into slices ½-inch thick and set aside.

When onions are cooked to a sort of mush, gradually sprinkle in flour, stirring to mix well. Stirring constantly, blend in milk and cook, stirring until sauce boils and thickens. Taste and season with salt and pepper to suit you. Carefully add egg slices, leaving out a dozen or so for the top. Don't overdo it here; you don't want to break up the eggs. Spoon gently onto a large, heated, rimmed platter. Garnish with remaining egg slices, sprinkle with Hungarian paprika, and use sprigs of fresh parsley around the edge.

Served with sourdough biscuits, this makes a good brunch dish.

BAD HOMBRE EGGS

Serves 2

1 tomato, sliced thin	2 tbsp. salad oil
1 avocado, peeled, pitted, and sliced	2 corn tortillas
	2 tbsp. butter
Juice of ½ lime	4 eggs
2 thin slices of purple onion	Salt and pepper
½ cup shredded Longhorn cheese	Green chile *salsa*

Slice tomato and avocado. Squeeze lime juice over avocado. Slice onion. Shred cheese. Set these ingredients out in a row near the stove along with the *salsa*, salt, and pepper. Warm 2 oven-proof dishes in the oven. Heat salad oil in a 7-inch skillet. Using kitchen tongs, cook tortillas, turning once, one at a time, until lightly brown and crisp. Remove to warmed plates. Pour out any remaining oil. Melt butter in skillet and break eggs into skillet. Cook to order. You can either fry them or scramble them, as you prefer. Place cooked eggs on tortillas, salt and pepper to taste, then add toppings of tomato, avocado, *salsa*, onion, and cheese. Run under the broiler until cheese melts. Serve immediately.

How To Choose Fish
Cowboy Fish Dinner
Breaux Bridge Secret Gumbo
Crawfish Étouffée
How To Make a Roux
Seafood Sauce Piquante
Crabmeat Au Gratin
Deviled Crab
Crabmeat Quiche
Baked Oysters
Oysters Ernie
Fried Oysters
Eggplant Stuffed with Oysters
Galveston Broiled Oysters
Shrimp Jambalaya for 40
Marinated Shrimp
Shrimp Negra
Sautéed Shrimp or Oysters
Squid in Wine Sauce
Bass Acuna
Poached Bass Paella
Fresh Fish Hodgepodge
Fried Fish in Mustard
Baked Stuffed Flounder
Baked Red Snapper with Sour Cream Stuffing
Redfish Fillet
Redfish with Shrimp and Oysters

Fish and Shellfish

Back before refrigerated air and fast transportation, people who traveled to Galveston from the heartland of Texas only wanted one thing to eat. Seafood. Early Galveston versions of shrimp, oysters, crabs, and fish were supremely simple. They were fried in cornmeal, broiled in butter, or stuffed and deviled. The more complex, subtle dishes came from the part of the Gulf Coast that bordered Louisiana where Cajun recipes held sway.

If you'd like to see what early Texas fish houses were like, you should make a trip to Hillman's Cafe at the mouth of Dickinson Bayou. When last I was there, I was struck by a sense of time-lessness. There is no air conditioning. Fans churn the thick air, so heavy and fetid that you can practically cut it. The tables are covered in Naugahyde. The waitresses are encased in red poly-ester pants suits, sweat runs down their faces, and from time to time, each one blows her own breath up into her face in a vain effort to cool off. When a rare whiff of cool air puffs through the jalousied windows, the diners seem to lean into it. The fried fish plates defy description; they're just plain fresh, hot, and good. The menu never changes and neither do the patrons. There is a four-hundred-pound man stuffed into a silky shirt, with a base-ball cap pushed to the back of his head and black rubber boots on his feet. There are foreign-speaking fishermen. There are fam-ilies who have been coming here for fifty years. The air is so warm and close that it makes for conviviality and people talk from table to table.

We know a lot more sophisticated ways to prepare the bounty of the Texas Gulf Coast, but it's damned hard to beat the mixed sea-food platter at Hillman's. Shrimp, oysters, and fish are dredged in cornmeal and quick-fried in deep fat. You don't need a recipe to do it. You just need good Texas seafood.

The big bugaboo in preparing fish is overcooking. Cooking fish at too high a temperature or for too long a time toughens the meat, dries it out, and destroys the subtle flavor. One of the great advantages in cooking fish is that you can have a meal churned out in a hurry if you use this short cooking time to your advantage.

How can you tell when fish is cooked? Raw fish has a watery, translucent look. While cooking, the watery juices become milky-colored; when the flesh has an opaque, whitish tint, the fish is completely cooked.

How much should you buy? For steaks or fillets ⅓ pound per person; for dressed fish ½ pound per person; and for whole fish ⅔ pound per person.

HOW TO CHOOSE FISH

How do you know which fish to choose from the ones on ice? Look him in the eye. His eye should be clear and bulging. Cloudy or sunken eyes are telltale signs of inferior quality. Older fish grow bacteria and even get yellow around the mouth. Don't hesitate to ask the fish seller to let you have a whiff if there is still doubt in your mind. Old fish gets a raunchy smell which is unmistakable, like ammonia—a sure sign of putrefaction.

Choose the fish variety according to your preparation plans. For broiling, for instance, choose a redfish or snapper. For baking, select flounder, snapper, drum or sheepshead. One interesting note: black drum and its fresh-water cousin, sheepshead, contain the highest quality protein, but have been popular only among blacks for one of those mysterious cultural reasons that create food fetishes. At the fish market the price of drum is considerably less than that of redfish; cut and cooked, it looks and tastes like redfish, and is sometimes sneaked under your nose in fine restaurants. Next time you're in a seafood market, try a drum. Choose a size from 8 to 20 inches. Or buy flounder: it's an important year-round fish which has firm, white, delicate flesh that adapts to a wide variety of preparation methods.

Texas produces ⅓ of all the oysters in this country, and they're usually available fresh by the pint in grocery stores that may sell no other fresh fish products. Oysters are of particular value in that they provide many of the so-called trace minerals which have been refined out of other foods. The belief that oysters are only good to eat during months whose names contain an *r* is not true. They actually reach their peak during May and June. Before we had adequate refrigeration, oysters wouldn't keep in summer—these months don't have names spelled with an *r*, hence the old saying. Oysters can be stored up to 7 days if iced down in the refrigerator, but should never be frozen.

Crabmeat is cooked before it is marketed and can be used without further ado. *Lump* refers to the white meat from the body and is most popular and most expensive. *Flake* means small pieces of white meat taken from inside the body and around the edges. Claw meat is much darker meat and is often sold as claw fingers.

If you get the chance to go crabbing, take it. Rotten chicken necks make great bait. It only takes a poor man's fishing rig: a string, a stick, and a dip net. To people who live on the Gulf, fresh-caught crab is virtually free.

COWBOY FISH DINNER
Hondo Crouch

Serves 1

1 can sardines
1 box soda crackers

Open sardine can with key. Place a cracker on pommel of saddle. Carefully lay a sardine on the cracker. Eat. Continue with procedure until you run out of sardines, crackers, or room in your belly.

BREAUX BRIDGE SECRET GUMBO
David Whittaker

Makes 1½ gallons

The thing I love about Cajun recipes is that they all hinge on a secret. Reference books say that *filé* is used to bind a gumbo when okra is not available, but this is a prize-winning gumbo recipe that uses both. The cook swears that his secret rests in the *filé*.

2 lbs. freshly sliced okra
½ cup oil
1 large slice ham, diced (about ¼ lb.)
4 medium onions, chopped
2 tbsp. flour
1 large bell pepper, chopped
3 stalks celery, chopped
Handful of fresh parsley, cut fine with scissors
3 bay leaves
4 cloves garlic, pressed

1 tbsp. thyme
2 8-oz. cans tomato sauce
3 quarts boiling water
1 15½-oz. can peeled tomatoes with juice
1 lb. lump crabmeat
6 whole boiled crabs (crack claws)
2 lbs. shrimp, peeled and cleaned
2 pints oysters and their liquor
Salt and cayenne pepper to taste
Gumbo *filé*

Smother okra in oil over medium-low heat in a heavy pot with a lid for 25 minutes. Add diced ham and onions and cook 10 minutes. Sprinkle flour over this, stir and brown the whole mixture. Add just enough water to keep it from sticking. Add pepper, celery, parsley, bay leaves, garlic, and thyme, stirring constantly. Add tomato sauce and simmer 5 minutes. Slowly add boiling water and undrained tomatoes, stirring constantly. Simmer 2½ hours. During the last 20 minutes add crab, shrimp, and salt and pepper to taste. About 10 minutes before serving add oysters and liquor. Stir well and taste. Now add *filé* until gumbo barely loses its sweetness (start with 1 tablespoon).

CRAWFISH ÉTOUFFÉE

Serves 4

2 lbs. peeled crawfish tails	2 tbsp. crawfish fat
Salt, black pepper, and cayenne	2 cups cold water
pepper to taste	2 tsp. cornstarch
¼ cup oil	4 spring onion tops, chopped
1½ cups chopped onions	Handful of parsley, cut with
½ cup chopped bell pepper	scissors
½ cup chopped celery	

Put enough water in a pot so that crawfish are covered with 4 inches of water. Bring to boil. Drop crawfish into boiling water and turn heat off immediately. Let crawfish stand in hot water for 5 minutes in uncovered pot. Drain. Crawfish are now ready to be peeled and cleaned for use.

After scalding crawfish, separate tails from head. Inside the crawfish head is a yellow substance, which is the fat. Remove this fat from all of the crawfish heads. Store, covered, in refrigerator until ready for use in *étouffée* or stew.

Season crawfish tails with salt and pepper and set aside. Melt oil in heavy pot. Add onions, bell pepper, and celery; cook and stir until onions are clear. Add crawfish fat, 1½ cups water, and crawfish tails. Bring to boil and simmer for 30 minutes, stirring occasionally. Dissolve cornstarch into remaining ½ cup cold water and add to mixture. Stir in onion tops and parsley, cook another 10 minutes, covered. Let stand 10 minutes. Serve over cooked rice.

HOW TO MAKE A ROUX

Cajun cooking often uses a base called a roux (as in *kangaroo*).

1 cup cooking oil (like Wesson)
1 cup flour
3 cups warm water

Pour the oil into a cast-iron pot or skillet over medium heat. When the oil is hot, gradually stir in flour. Lower the heat immediately. (If you are cursed with an electric stove, as I am, you can remove the pot from the coils while stirring in the flour.) You must stir constantly, taking care to keep the flour scraped off the sides and from around the edges. With the fire turned very low, stirring constantly, continue to cook until the mixture is luscious brown. You'll notice a marvelous aroma wafting up which may seduce you into thinking it's done now, but keep stirring until it's the color of walnut.

Add warm water to the roux and stir until thoroughly blended before mixing it into the other ingredients.

The proportions of oil to flour in a roux always remain the same, 1 to 1; the water-to-flour ratio is 3 to 1. Never, never add flour to water. The Cajuns call this a "raw" sauce, and in South Louisiana it's doubtful that even a self-respecting dog would eat it. The cast-iron pot is also mandatory.

You will note a variation on the process for making a roux in some recipes. In some procedures, you are told to toss in onions and garlic and maybe celery at the point when the flour has browned.

Always chop the vegetables before you begin heating the roux. There's no time to do it and brown the flour all at once.

SEAFOOD SAUCE PIQUANTE

Serves 8

Make a roux using 1½ cups of flour and oil and 4½ cups water (see **How To Make a Roux**). In a small saucepan over low heat cook 1 15½-oz. can of tomato sauce until it looks like buttermilk. Stir frequently to get the canned, raw taste out. After adding water to the roux, combine roux, tomato sauce, and:

2 cloves garlic, minced	2 medium white onions, chopped
1 bell pepper, chopped fine	fine
1 stalk celery, chopped fine	

Cook over low heat until vegetables are tender, about 10 minutes. Add:

5 lbs. cleaned, deveined raw	2 lbs. scallops
shrimp	1½ lbs. redfish fillets, cut in strips
1 pint lump crabmeat (pick out shells)	

Simmer over low heat and stir frequently so it won't stick. Add:

Salt and pepper to taste	3 tbsp. gumbo *filé*
Cayenne pepper and Tabasco	
sauce to taste	

Cook until shrimp turn pink and fish fillets become opaque, about 15 minutes. Turn off fire, cover pot, and let stand 30 minutes before serving. Serve in a rimmed soup plate over rice.

Try substituting a boiled, boned hen for the seafood.

CRABMEAT AU GRATIN

Serves 6

1 medium onion, chopped fine	1 tsp. salt
1 stalk celery, chopped fine	¼ tsp. cayenne pepper
½ cup butter	¼ tsp. finely milled black pepper
½ cup flour	1 lb. lump crabmeat
1 cup half-and-half	½ lb. sharp cheese, grated
2 egg yolks, well beaten	

Preheat oven to 375°. Sauté onion and celery in butter until onion turns clear. Add flour and cook and stir to make a golden roux. Add cream. Mix well. Stirring constantly, add well-beaten egg yolks, salt, cayenne pepper, and black pepper. Cook and stir to make a thick, smooth cream sauce. Remove from heat and combine with crabmeat. Butter a casserole dish or six individual ramekins. Place crab mixture in dish, sprinkle with grated cheese, and bake in preheated oven until light brown and bubbly—about 10 minutes. Serve hot.

DEVILED CRAB

Serves 6

1 cup sweet cream	1 tbsp. Worcestershire sauce
4 tbsp. melted butter	½ tsp. salt
1 egg yolk, well beaten	½ tsp. finely milled pepper
6 tbsp. bread crumbs	¼ tsp. cayenne pepper
1 lb. fresh crabmeat	1 tsp. Hungarian paprika
1 whole egg, well beaten	8 drops Tabasco sauce
Juice of ½ lemon	

Preheat oven to 375°. Butter bottoms of 6 ramekins or crab shells and place on a cookie sheet. Heat cream in top of a double boiler. Add 1 tablespoon of the melted butter to cream. When it is too hot to stick your finger in, add well-beaten egg yolk, stirring vigorously. Cook and stir until mixture will coat silver spoon and is slightly thick. Toss remaining 3 tablespoons butter with bread crumbs. Combine crabmeat with the egg. Add crab mixture to cream. Add 3 tablespoons of the buttered bread crumbs. Add lemon juice and remaining seasonings. Cook and stir until thickened. Remove from heat. Heap into ramekins or crab shells. Sprinkle about 1 teaspoon of remaining buttered bread crumbs onto each serving. Dust lightly with paprika. Bake in preheated oven for 15–20 minutes, until brown. Serve immediately.

CRABMEAT QUICHE
Shirley Barr

Serves 6

3 eggs, slightly beaten
1 cup sour cream
½ tsp. Worcestershire sauce
¾ tsp. salt
1 white onion, sliced paper-thin
3 tbsp. butter

1 cup coarsely shredded Swiss
    cheese
½ lb. fresh, white lump crabmeat
    (can use 1 can crabmeat if
    desperate)
1 9-inch baked pastry shell

Preheat oven to 300°. Combine eggs, sour cream, Worcestershire sauce, and salt. Sauté onion in butter. Stir in cheese, crabmeat, and egg mixture. Pour into baked pastry shell. Bake 55–60 minutes or until custard is set and a silver knife inserted in the center comes out clean. Serve hot. Can be eaten by hand.

BAKED OYSTERS

Serves 4

2 tbsp. butter
1 small onion, chopped fine
1 pint oysters, drained
2 eggs, well beaten
1 tbsp. Worcestershire sauce
2 dashes Tabasco sauce

1 tsp. catsup
Juice of ½ lemon
Salt and pepper to taste
Cracker crumbs
Butter
Paprika

Preheat oven to 350°. In a small saucepan, sauté onion in butter until onion turns clear. Add drained oysters and well-beaten eggs. Add remaining ingredients except cracker crumbs, butter, and paprika. Stir gently so as not to break up the tender oysters. Cook over low heat until edges of oysters begin to curl. Now transfer to a well-buttered casserole dish or 4 well-buttered individual ramekins. Sprinkle with cracker crumbs, dot with butter, and sprinkle with paprika. Bake in preheated oven until browned on top (15 minutes for individual ramekins; 25–30 minutes for casserole dish).

OYSTERS ERNIE

Ernest Coker

Serves 4

24 oysters
Salt and pepper
Flour
Melted butter on the side
2 tbsp. melted butter
¼ cup fresh lemon juice

1 cup A-1 steak sauce
2 tbsp. Worcestershire sauce
2 jiggers dry sherry or Madeira
   wine
2 tbsp. flour
3 tbsp. water

Drain the oysters well. Salt and pepper them, then dredge in flour, knocking off all excess flour. Grill on a lightly buttered griddle on the top of the stove until crisp and browned on both sides. If you don't have a griddle use a heavy skillet, but don't ever try to broil them in the oven. Ain't the same. While the oysters are grilling, sprinkle them with melted butter. Sprinkling both sides facilitates the browning.

At the same time you are grilling the oysters, combine in a small saucepan the 2 tablespoons of melted butter, lemon juice, steak sauce, Worcestershire sauce, and sherry or wine. Heat thoroughly but don't boil. Combine flour and water until you have a lumpless thin paste. Stirring constantly, pour this paste into the hot sauce and stir until you have a thick sauce. If sauce is too thin, add a little more A-1 sauce. If too thick, a little more sherry. Place grilled oysters on hot serving plate and pour sauce over. Heaven.

FRIED OYSTERS

Serves 4

1 pint oysters, drained
Salt and cayenne pepper to taste
1 cup yellow cornmeal

Season oysters individually to taste with salt and cayenne. Heat fat or oil to 380°. Roll oysters in cornmeal, drop into hot fat, and deep-fry 2–3 minutes until golden. Do not overcook.

EGGPLANT STUFFED WITH OYSTERS

Serves 4

1 large eggplant	½ medium white onion, chopped
Salt	1 pint fresh, raw oysters
2 slices whole wheat bread	1 2-oz. jar pimientos
¼ lb. butter	Handful fresh parsley
¼ lb. fresh mushrooms, sliced	2 eggs
1 stalk celery, chopped	

The objective here is to create a bowl from the eggplant. Slice side off eggplant lengthwise (that means laying it on its side—do not cut the stem end). Scoop out pulp from large cavity and set pulp aside for later use. Sprinkle inside of eggplant with salt, replace its "hat," and refrigerate in a Pyrex baking dish until time to stuff.

Preheat oven to 300°. Place two slices of whole wheat bread in oven to dry out while oven is heating.

Melt butter in heavy skillet over medium heat. Cover and braise the following chopped items until soft: cubed eggplant pulp, sliced fresh mushrooms, chopped celery, and onion. Be sure to wash well in cold water to avoid grit in the food.

Add drained oysters, pimientos, dried-out bread which you have pulled into small pieces, and parsley. Have you discovered how much easier it is to cut parsley with kitchen shears than with a knife? Stir.

Beat eggs until lemon-colored and add to the above. Turn fire to low and continue cooking for 5 minutes by the clock, stirring constantly. Remove from fire and salt to taste.

Remove eggplant from refrigerator. Discard top or "hat." Stuff. Allow stuffing to mound up over the top. At this point you can put the whole business in the refrigerator, covered of course, and wait until 1 hour before serving time to take it out.

Pour ¼ inch water into the bottom of the baking dish. Make a foil tent which will seal the eggplant in the dish but not mash the top of it. Place in preheated 300° oven and bake 45 minutes. Don't overcook this one. The eggplant will collapse. I learned this through bitter experience: I once served something that looked more like a prune than a shiny balloon.

Good with Christmas turkey.

GALVESTON BROILED OYSTERS
Ada Smith

Fresh oysters, well drained
Good white bread—like
    sourdough or French or even
    an English muffin

Worcestershire sauce
Lemon juice
Melted butter

Trim edges from bread, butter lightly, and toast on both sides. Now mound 4 or 5 oysters on each piece of toast, season to taste with a shot of Worcestershire sauce and lemon juice, dribble melted butter on top, and run under the broiler just until the oysters curl around the edges—no more than 5 minutes.

SHRIMP JAMBALAYA FOR 40

Here's an easy party dish for a large group of about 40 people. Make ahead, then just heat in the oven. Only having 20? Cut it in half. Eight or ten? Divide by 4.

5 lbs. peeled and deveined shrimp
2 cups oil
5 cups chopped onions
2½ cups chopped celery
2½ cups bell pepper, chopped
20 cloves garlic, minced
1 6-oz. can tomato paste
8 cups water

Salt, black pepper, and cayenne
    pepper to taste
2 tbsp. sugar
2½ tsp. cornstarch
2 cups water
15 cups cooked rice
2½ cups green onions and tops
1 cup parsley, cut with scissors

Cook rice separately.

    Chop shrimp and set aside. Melt oil and add onions, celery, bell pepper, and garlic in a heavy pot. Cook uncovered over medium heat until onions are wilted. Add tomato paste and cook, stirring constantly for about 15 minutes. Add 8 cups water. Season to taste with salt, black pepper, and cayenne. Add sugar and cook uncovered over medium heat for about 40 minutes, stirring occasionally or until oil floats to the top. Add shrimp; continue cooking and stirring another 20 minutes. Dissolve cornstarch in 2 cups water and add; cook another 10 minutes. Mix ingredients with cooked rice; add green onion tops and parsley. Mix again. Place in casserole dishes. Cover. Refrigerate until serving time, then heat in 350° oven about 15 minutes, or until thoroughly hot.

MARINATED SHRIMP

Makes 26–30 medium shrimp

1 lb. cleaned, cooked medium to
   large shrimp
1 cup white wine vinegar
2 tbsp. water
3 whole cloves

¼ tsp. pepper
1 bay leaf
1 Bermuda onion, sliced thin
2 tsp. salt
1 tsp. sugar

Place shrimp in a mixing bowl. In a saucepan, combine remaining ingredients and bring to a boil. Pour mixture over shrimp. Cover and refrigerate at least 12 hours.

To serve: drain shrimp and spear with a toothpick. What's even better is to skewer them on hibachi sticks, alternating them with big stuffed green olives; brush with olive oil and broil them over a charcoal grill or in the oven just until the edges begin to brown. Serve hot.

SHRIMP NEGRA
Anna Kay Brewer

Serves 4

Here's a delightful, peppery peel-and-eat communal supper.

2 lbs. medium shrimp, in shells
1 lb. butter (not margarine)
1 whole can (1-oz.) finely milled
   black pepper

Shot of Worcestershire sauce
Loaf of good French bread

Wash and dry raw shrimp. Melt butter over low heat. Add pepper and Worcestershire sauce. Place shrimp 1 layer deep in a 13½" × 8¾" utility pan with sides. Pour butter mixture over. Broil 3 minutes on first side and 2 minutes on the second side. Shrimp are done when they turn from translucent blue gray to opaque pink. The best way to eat this is to spread newspaper on the floor. Put the shrimp out in the middle, sit crosslegged in a circle, tear off chunks of bread to dip in the sauce, and dig in. You won't believe how good this is. About all you need to go with it is a simple salad—something like cucumbers in a sour cream and dill sauce—and a good California Gewurztraminer. The German gewurtz is too sweet. Chill the wine icy cold. You will love it. This is a 3-paper-napkin meal. Don't be surprised if you have the urge to lick your fingers, rub the butter all over you, or take off your clothes.

SAUTÉED SHRIMP OR OYSTERS

Serves 2

Now this is easy.

1 pint of oysters, drained, or ½ lb.
    shrimp, cleaned and deveined
¼ lb. butter
1 garlic clove, pressed

2 green onions and tops, chopped
½ cup fresh parsley, cut with
    scissors
½ cup fresh mushrooms, sliced

Heat butter in a sauté pan, then add garlic and green onions. Cook until onion begins to get clear and butter is hot enough to make the solids precipitate. Keeping fire hot as possible without burning the butter, add oysters or shrimp. Toss and turn until shrimp begin to turn pink or until oysters begin to curl. Now add parsley and mushrooms, cook another minute, and serve immediately. A great meal in about 5 minutes.

SQUID IN WINE SAUCE

Serves 4

Squid has been available in Texas Gulf Coast fish markets forever. I'll grant you more people buy squid for bait than for eating, but they are missing a bet. Squid is cheap. It is exotic-tasting—not "fishy" at all—and it is one sure way to run the kids away from the table. Mine won't touch it, so if I want a quiet dinner with Joe, I just announce *squid* and they all head for the nearest pizza joint.

    First you have to clean it. Fill a large pan with cold water and place the squid in water. One at a time, lay squid on a cutting board, and with a sharp knife cut off the tentacles right below the eyes. You will feel a hard thing that feels like a round fingernail in the center of the tentacles. This is the mouth. Pop it out and place in a plastic bag for disposal. Don't put the leavings down your garbage disposal unless you want to shop for a new house in about 3 days. After popping out the little mouth, drop the tentacles in a pan of clean cold water. Run the knife up the back of the hood and open the squid out flat. Dispose of gut, ink sac, and backbone (lovely looking, kite-shaped, clear and plastic-like). Holding the flat piece of meat in your hands, rub the skin off and discard. Now you have a white, clean piece of meat shaped like a kite with a couple of wings on it. Rinse it completely free of sand and skin. Sniff. See, no smell at all. Lay it on the cutting board and cut crosswise into ½-inch strips. Place this in the cold water along with the tentacles. Repeat until you've cleaned a pound or so. When the strips cook, you'll notice that they curl up like flutes and are really splendid looking. I once ruined a pair of Anne Klein pants cleaning squid because I forgot for one fatal moment that the ink is permanent. Don't get it on your clothes.

¼ lb. butter
2 garlic cloves, pressed
6 green onions and tops, cut fine
Chopped parsley, a good handful
¼ lb. fresh mushrooms, sliced
    vertically

2 tbsp. cornstarch
2 tbsp. soy sauce
¼ cup sherry
Juice of ½ lemon
1 lb. cleaned and sliced squid
Dry red wine

Sauté in butter the garlic, green onions, parsley, and mushrooms until onions turn clear. Mix together cornstarch, soy sauce, sherry, and lemon and add to sautéed vegetables. Stir. Keep fire low. Now add squid and cook covered until the squid is done. You can tell it's done when the strips curl into flutes and the color turns from white to a washed out pinkish purple. Cut the sauce with red wine until it is the consistency of a fine translucent gravy. Remove 1 squid from the skillet and try to cut it. It should cut very easily. If the squid is young and thin, it will cook in less than 10 minutes. If, however, the squid is thick and rubbery, you will have to cook it 20 minutes or so. Serve over rice. A green salad and a good Burgundy, that's all it takes.

BASS ACUNA

Serves 6

½ medium onion, chopped
2 cloves garlic, pressed
1 large bell pepper, sliced
1 8-inch *chile serrano*, minced
2 tbsp. bacon drippings

1 8-oz. can tomato sauce
½ cup water
½ tsp. cumin
Celery salt to taste
1 bass (2–3 lbs.)

Sauté onion, garlic, bell pepper, and chile in hot bacon drippings until onions are soft. Add tomato sauce, water, and seasonings and simmer, covered, about 20 minutes. Fillet bass and cut meat in chunks. Add fish to sauce, cover, and steam 5 minutes. Serve fish with the sauce alone or over rice.

POACHED BASS PAELLA

Bass is a fish that's fun to catch but fairly tasteless. Here's a good treatment. You may substitute any firm, white-meated, mild fish from the market with good results. Allow ½ pound of fish per person. How many you can serve depends on size of bass.

½ cup cooking oil
2 small yellow onions, sliced
2 cloves garlic, pressed
1 cup long-grain rice
½ tsp. saffron
3 cups hot water
1 whole bass (3–5 lbs.)
1 fresh *chile poblano* (*ancho*),
    seeded and coarsely chopped
    (you may substitute jalapeños
    for a hotter, more Tex Mex
    taste)

1 tsp. ground *chiles pasillas*
½ cup chopped parsley
2 cups fresh or frozen green peas

This preparation needs a stove-to-table pan. You are going to cook the whole fish on a bed of rice, and it's best if you can get it to the table undisturbed. If you try to remove the fish to a serving dish you may break it up and that would be a shame. Choose something fairly shallow but long enough to accommodate the whole fish, head to tail. A fish poacher is, of course, suitable. This recipe makes an attractive, dramatic presentation if cooked in an appropriate vessel.

    Heat oil in pan and sauté onion and garlic. Now add rice, and stirring constantly continue to cook until the rice grains turn a nice golden color. Place saffron in hot water and let it stand while you are browning the rice. Once the rice is a lovely caramel color, lay the fish on top of the rice and add remaining ingredients—remove the pan from the heat while you're adding these ingredients if you think there is a danger of burning the rice, because you can't stir it once you've laid the fish on top. Pour saffron water over all, cover with a tight-fitting lid, and simmer until the fish flakes and the rice has absorbed all water. It takes 6–8 minutes per pound to poach a fish—roughly 30 minutes for a 4-pound fish.

FRESH FISH HODGEPODGE

Serves 6–8

This is how I used to combine the garden vegetables and Joe's catch from the Guadalupe. You can use any kind of mild white-fleshed fish, salt or freshwater. It will stretch a small catch and is an interesting blend of flavors and textures.

1 lb. skinned fish fillets	Basil, oregano, salt and pepper to taste
1 white onion, cut into rings	
2 garlic cloves, pressed	1 eggplant, peeled and sliced into thick rounds
2 jalapeños, seeded and chopped	
1 sweet red pepper, cut into julienne strips	1 cup Monterrey Jack cheese, grated
Olive oil	Loaf good French bread
4 tomatoes, quartered	

Wash and dry fish fillets. Sauté onion, garlic, jalapeños, and red pepper in olive oil until onion is clear. Add tomatoes. Don't stir this dish once you add the tomatoes because you want the various ingredients to be in identifiable pieces and not some sort of mush. Keep the fire low and just *lift* the bottom vegetables slightly if they seem to be sticking. Season generously with basil, oregano, salt and pepper. Simmer, covered, for 10 minutes. Taste. Add eggplant slices and cook covered until eggplant is tender (about 20 minutes). Add fish and cook until fish flakes (about 20 minutes more). Cover with grated cheese and run under the broiler until bubbly and brown. Serve in soup bowls with French bread and a Burgundy. If you have some sort of stove-to-table vessel to cook this in, it will save you a pot to wash.

FRIED FISH IN MUSTARD

If you get hold of some big fish fillets, say from big redfish or gasper goo' or drum, here is a good way to cook them out in the backyard like they do in East Texas. Using a Coleman stove or other guaranteed high heat source, heat up a big pot of oil. Smear fish all over with French's yellow mustard. Now dredge in flour. Cook in hot oil until brown. Delicious. Of course you can also do this on the kitchen range, and you can use frozen fish fillets if you need to. It's just a good way to cook fish. The funny thing about it is that the fish won't taste like mustard. It just tastes seasoned and delicious.

BAKED STUFFED FLOUNDER

Serves 4

1 whole flounder (3–5 lbs.)
Salt and white pepper
½ cup melted butter

Stuffing:
1 cup dried bread cubes
2 saltine crackers, crumbled
1 stalk celery, cut fine
½ small onion, cut fine
2 dashes Tabasco sauce
1 tsp. sage
½ cup lump crabmeat, chopped
   coarse

½ cup scallops (2 or 3), chopped
   coarse
6 medium shrimp, chopped
   medium
2 tbsp. parsley, cut fine with
   scissors
2 well-beaten eggs
Pinch salt

Garnish:
Hungarian paprika
1 lemon, sliced
Fresh parsley, cut fine

Preheat oven to 500°. Make a lengthwise cut in the flounder from just below the gill almost to the tail. Make two crosswise cuts— one below the gill and one just above the tail. Slip the knife into the long cut and slice, releasing meat from the backbone. Open up flaps. Coat all surfaces of fish, inside and out, with melted butter, salt, and pepper. Place in a buttered baking dish. Make stuffing with remaining ingredients. Use a light hand in mixing so that stuffing doesn't become leaden. Stuff fish, fold flaps back in place. Place fish uncovered in preheated oven and bake for 10 minutes. Reduce heat to 350°, cover fish, and cook for 10 minutes more. Check for doneness by raising flap of fish. Flounder meat should now be an opaque white, shrimp should be pink, and scallops should be opaque white. If, after 20 minutes of cooking, the fish isn't done, replace in oven and check at 5-minute intervals. When thoroughly cooked remove from oven, sprinkle with paprika, and garnish with lemon slices and parsley.

BAKED RED SNAPPER WITH SOUR CREAM STUFFING
Linda Clarkson

Serves 6

Try to choose an oven-to-table cooking vessel so you won't have to juggle the fish to a serving platter.

1 3- to 4-lb. dressed whole red
    snapper (can use other
    dressed fish)
1½ tsp. salt
Sour Cream Stuffing

Sprinkle washed and dried fish (did you remember to scale it?) inside and out with salt. Place the fish in a buttered baking dish and set aside while you make the stuffing.

SOUR CREAM STUFFING

¾ cup chopped celery
½ cup chopped onion
½ cup melted butter
1 quart bread cubes or crumbs
½ cup sour cream
¼ cup peeled, seeded, and diced
    lemon with juice

2 tbsp. grated lemon rind (the
    yellow part only—discard
    white membrane)
1 tsp. paprika
1 tsp. salt
½ cup warm water

Preheat oven to 350°. Cook celery and onion in half the melted butter (¼ cup) until onion is clear. Combine with bread cubes, sour cream, lemon, and seasonings. Toss lightly. (Many dressings are ruined by a heavy hand. Don't mash it down.) Stuff the fish loosely. Close opening with toothpicks or skewers. Coat outside of fish with remaining ¼ cup of melted butter. Pour ½ cup warm water in bottom of baking dish, add fish, and bake uncovered in preheated oven. Cook 40–60 minutes or until the fish flakes when you stick a fork in it. Baste occasionally.

REDFISH FILLET
Nona Morriss

Serves 4

1–1½ lbs. redfish fillets (can use other mild fish such as cod or sole with good results)
Juice of 1 lemon
½ cup milk
½ cup flour

Salt and pepper
½ cup seasoned bread crumbs
¼ cup butter or olive oil
½ cup chopped parsley
½ cup white wine

Pour lemon juice over fish fillets and marinate in the refrigerator. All day is best, but an hour or so will do. When ready to cook, heat oil or butter. Meanwhile, generously season flour with salt and pepper. Now dip fillets in milk, then in flour, then back in milk, and finally in seasoned bread crumbs. Place in skillet serve side down and fry until golden brown (about 10 minutes), turning only once. Remove to hot serving plate. Place chopped parsley and white wine in drippings and raise to a vigorous boil. Pour thin sauce over fish and serve.

REDFISH WITH SHRIMP AND OYSTERS
Patricia Slate

Serves 1

¼–½ lb. redfish fillet per person
Seasoned flour
Clarified butter or olive oil

For each fillet:
2 shrimp and 2 oysters
1 tbsp. dry white wine
1 chopped shallot
1 tbsp. fresh parsley (cut with scissors—it's easy)

1 tbsp. heavy cream
Salt
Dash cayenne pepper

Dredge redfish fillet in flour seasoned with salt and white pepper. Now heat clarified butter or olive oil in a sauté pan until the oil thins and runs to the edge of the pan (that's how you can tell it's hot enough). Keeping the pan good and hot, place the fillet in the pan, serve side down, and cook 2½ to 3 minutes to the side, turning only once. Remove fillet to a warm plate. Toss in shrimp and oysters with wine. Toss 2 minutes in the very hot skillet. Add shallot and parsley. Toss 1 minute. Now add cream, salt, and cayenne pepper. Simmer until the sauce begins to thicken. If fat runs out of the sauce, just add more wine or cream until you get a good-looking emulsion—like Mama's gravy. If the sauce is too thin, boil it down to reduce it. When it looks and smells so good you think you might scream out loud, pour it over the fish and serve. It's so good, you won't believe it. Serve with rice, Gewurtztraminer, and a salad. I can do about 4 of these at a time in a 10-inch skillet. Any more than that pushes the procedure. Probably best not to try more than 4 at a time unless you're awfully agile.

Brunswick Stew
Clear Game Soup
Dove How-To
Chile Pequín Doves
Dove Rosemary
Sesame-fried Dove
Preparing Duck for the Table
Duck Gumbo
Smoked Duck Deluxe
Roast Goose with Pear Stuffing and Sauce
Pheasant Madeira
Hunter's Bagged Quail
Quail in Wine Sauce
Froglegs Brazoria
Chicken-fried Rattlesnake
Fried Wild Turkey Breast
Roast Wild Turkey
Texas Paté
Venison Backstrap
Braised Haunch of Venison

Game

I am not a hunter. I have only killed game once in my life. It was a deer. A doe, with a few white spots. The weapon I used was the front end of a Chevrolet. It was a good clean head shot that catapulted the animal into the ditch and only dented the license plate. A lucky shot.

When it happened, my daughter Katherine and I were on our way to Kerrville to pick up some chicken feed. The whole thing—sun in my eyes, flashing deer, screeching brakes, and shocked silence—was so overwhelming that I had to pull the car over and catch my breath. I got out to examine the damage to the front end of the car, then took a long look at that deer, stone dead in the ditch. I called to my daughter in the back seat. Open up the trunk. Let's take it home. No, she screamed with all the moral certainty that goes with being thirteen. It's against the law.

Get out of that car and help me, I barked, trying to sound authoritarian. They'll put you in the penitentiary, she wailed. Get out of the car, I said, through clenched teeth.

The deer didn't weigh much, maybe forty or fifty pounds, and we got it into the trunk with no trouble. I must say that driving back to our house in the country, I did feel a little like the fellow who just robbed the First National Bank. I was scared and excited all at once, but kept telling myself that it was just plain wasteful to leave a perfectly good venison out in the sun to bloat.

Katherine hid in the back seat. I suppose she figured if the highway patrol stopped us for our heinous crime, they'd never see this quivering teenaged lump in the back.

Somehow I got overwhelmed with the adventure of the whole thing, and told Katherine that when we got it home we were going to dress it out ourselves. After all, it would be hours before Joe would be home and the meat would be ruined if we just threw it into the backyard. At that point she began to cry, long bitter sobs at the injustice of having been born to such a rotten, insane parent.

I had watched Joe dress out deer on more than one occasion. Katherine had, too. But as we took knife in hand and began to skin and gut the deer, we suddenly got an idea of what a complicated job it was. At least Joe had been to medical school and understood anatomy.

It took us hours. To tell the truth, we got the thing quartered and couldn't figure out what to do next. When Joe came home that night and we showed him our nicely white-wrapped meat now cooling in the refrigerator, he grinned from ear to ear. He thought perhaps he'd have a couple of new hunters to take to the field. I told him the only thing I'd learned from the whole experience is why lawyers don't want butchers on juries.

BRUNSWICK STEW

Serves 6–8

After receiving instructions from an East Texas hunter, I once tried to roast a squirrel. Served on a platter, it looked like a roasted brown rat, so I gave up on ever serving the squirrel on his own bones. Brunswick Stew is mostly method. You could use stewed rabbit, or squirrel, or even a chicken. It's great on a winter night.

3 squirrels, cut in serving pieces (about 3 lbs. of meat—can combine with other small game such as rabbit, or can also substitute a stewing hen with good results)
1 stalk celery
1 scraped carrot
1 onion, quartered
1 tbsp. salt
3 quarts water

2 slices bacon, uncooked and diced
¼ tsp. cayenne pepper
Salt to taste
¼ tsp. finely milled black pepper
1 cup chopped onion
4 cups stewed tomatoes
2 cups potatoes, diced fine
2 cups lima beans
2 cups corn

Place meat in a Dutch oven. Add celery, carrot, onion, salt, and water. Bring slowly to a boil, reduce heat, and simmer 1½–2 hours, or until meat begins to fall away from the bone. Skim the surface occasionally. Lift meat and vegetables out of the broth. Discard vegetables. Remove meat from bones and return to broth. Add bacon, cayenne pepper, salt to taste, pepper, onion, tomatoes, potatoes, and limas. Simmer for 1 hour or so. Add corn (marvelous if it's just been cut from the cob) and cook 10 more minutes. Taste again and adjust seasonings. You may want more salt and pepper here. Serve in soup bowls. Corn bread is the only suitable bread.

CLEAR GAME SOUP

Makes 4 quarts

Making soup from the bones of game is one of those chores that can make you feel so righteous. And the smell in the kitchen is so hearty and fecund that if you close your eyes you will think you're in some castle somewhere, preparing for one of those feasts where people threw bones over their shoulders to the dogs. In truth, all you are doing is making ordinary broth. But, oh, that gamey flavor.

3 lbs. bones of venison, elk, or
    antelope, broken up with a
    cleaver
1 lb. meat scraps (more or less—
    just toss in what you have)
4 stalks celery
Handful of fresh parsley

1 tsp. salt
2 onions, quartered
2 carrots, scraped and cut in half
2 cloves garlic, minced
1 tsp. peppercorns
4 quarts of water

Combine, bring to a boil, and simmer covered until liquid is reduced to 1 quart (about 3 hours). Skim off any fat, then strain broth
through cheesecloth and chill. Break off any additional fat. Reheat
when ready to serve, season to taste with salt and pepper, and
serve in cups as a first course. You can sprinkle croutons over the
top, or you can break up a couple of tomatoes in the soup. Try it
different ways and see what suits you. Good with Parmesan
cheese sprinkled on top.

DOVE HOW-TO

How you cook dove should be determined by the age of the birds.
A young bird will taste good fried. An older bird must be cooked
with some moisture. You can tell a young bird by its whitish skin
and pinfeathers. An old bird has dark skin and no pinfeathers. It
will take 3 or 4 doves to serve 1 person. Sometimes I pick the
whole bird, but other times I merely tear out the breast and cook
that. Breasting them is easier, but you lose skin and the basic
shape of the bird.

    One Helen Corbitt technique which applies to all game has to
do with aging. Once the birds are shot, gutted, washed, and iced
down, leave them be for 3 or 4 days. Just put them in a paper
sack in the bottom of the refrigerator. Don't put them in plastic—
it's not good for them to sweat. Pluck the feathers on the day you
want to cook the birds. A lot of fastidious people turn up their lip
at a refrigerator full of birds in the feather, but I've never seen
them turn away from the table. Plucked birds dry out fast and
must be either cooked or frozen quickly—preferably in a block of
ice, say an old milk carton filled with water. They will keep up to
a year without getting freezer burn if you use the ice method. I
have served game birds to a lot of dubious people who discover
the real delicacy that game birds can be.

CHILE PEQUÍN DOVES

3 doves per person
2 dried chile pequín per dove
1 slice bacon per dove

Salt and pepper
Enough gin to cover the bottom of
    the pan

Preheat oven to 350°. Place a couple of chiles in the cavity of each dove, and salt and pepper. Now wrap the dove breast in bacon. Lay the birds in a flat pan, one layer deep, with sides touching. Use as small a pan as possible so that the birds will be packed tightly in the pan. I use a little Pyrex cake pan. Now pour gin into the pan until it's about ½ inch deep. Cover the pan and bake in preheated oven for about 1½ hours. Remove the foil and stick a fork into a breast. If the meat gives way and seems loosened from the bone, the birds are about done. Leave in the oven uncovered until the bacon browns (about 20 minutes). Remove to a hot platter. Don't try to make gravy from the drippings unless you like the real raunchy flavor of game, combined with bacon grease.

DOVE ROSEMARY

3 doves per serving
Salt and pepper
Roughly ½ tsp. dried rosemary per
    bird
Flour
1 small onion sliced in rings for
    every 3 birds

Ample butter to cover bottom of a
    skillet, about ¼ pound for a
    dozen birds
Good sherry—such as Sandeman
    dry

Salt and pepper the birds, then sprinkle a generous amount of rosemary in the cavity—about ½ teaspoon per bird. Now dredge in flour. Set aside. Sauté sliced onion in butter until clear. Turn the fire up and brown the birds on all sides. Here you have a choice. You can finish this on the top of the stove or in the oven. If you choose to cook the birds on the top of the stove, simply turn the fire to low, add about ½ cup of sherry to the skillet, cover with a tight lid, and simmer until the flesh falls away from the bone—about 40 minutes. Or you can transfer the birds to a casserole, pour the juices and sherry over the birds, cover tightly, and bake at 350° for about 1 hour. The oven method is a little more foolproof, but the birds don't glaze quite as nicely as they do on the top. If you choose to cook on the top of the stove, be careful not to boil away all the liquid. Keep the fire low. If necessary, add a splash or so of sherry during the cooking time. The pan juice from these birds is divine and should always be poured over the birds. It's too thick and gloppy to work well in a gravy boat.

SESAME-FRIED DOVE

Serves 4

12 doves	1 tbsp. salt
1 egg	1 tbsp. freshly cracked pepper
½ cup milk	4 tbsp. sesame seeds
1 cup flour	Oil for deep-frying

Choose only young doves with white skin for frying. Mix egg and milk. Place flour, salt, pepper, and sesame seeds in a kid's lunch sack. Shake birds in flour, then in egg and milk, then in flour again. Let the birds stand while the oil gets hot so that the batter will set. Deep-fry in oil at 375° until golden brown.

PREPARING DUCK FOR THE TABLE

Start with a good table duck. Some ducks are fish eaters and they are not considered suitable for the table. Mallard, Sprig, Teal, Canvasback, and Wood duck are suitable table ducks. Widgeon and Gadwall are edible if they have been eating grain.

Most hunters know ducks need careful handling in the field. A beautiful mallard left ungutted and allowed to become warm will be inedible. The birds should be gutted as soon after shooting as possible, preferably in the field. Generally duck weather is cold enough so that the birds are in no danger of spoiling before they arrive home, but they should never be left in a warm car or a warm house for very long.

Aging is a vital step in the proper preparation of the duck. The gutted duck should be left in his feathers in a cool place (not frozen) from 5 to 10 days. An enzyme action takes place which makes the meat more palatable. The duck can be aged outdoors if you live in a cold climate (daytime temperatures below 45°) and provided it's safe from backyard predators such as cats and dogs. Otherwise, you can put the duck in a brown paper bag and refrigerate. Remember the magic phrase "heavy aged beef"; aging does as much for duck as it does for beef.

After the birds have aged from 5 to 10 days with their feathers intact, they are ready to be dressed. Whack off the head and neck with a sharp butcher knife. Next, cut off the wings at the joint closest to the body and the legs at the joint where the feathers start. You may find poultry shears help. Cut off the tail high enough to remove the oil gland that is located at the base of the tail. There are no feather-picking shortcuts. Simply line the sink with newspaper and start pulling feathers from the dry carcass in the same direction that they grow. When you have removed as many feathers as possible, there will still be a few pinfeathers (if it is a young bird) and some soft underfeathers which you can rub off under running water. If you are a perfectionist, singeing will help to remove them, or you may decide, as I have, that a few little feathers never hurt anyone and can be covered up with gravy.

If properly aged, cleaned, and frozen, ducks are as tasty cooked next August as they are in November. Pack them 2 to a package, in a ½-gallon milk carton. Fill carton with water and freeze.

Recipes for roast duck abound. Most of them call for an apple and onion in the cavity. What the cookbooks don't tell you is that roasting requires a young bird. You can tell a young bird by his pinfeathers (dark projections through the skin, about the size of a grain of rice).

If you don't know how many winters your duck has flown south, the byword is *braise* (cook in liquid). When using this method, I add spirits—whiskey, vermouth, or a dry wine. Spirits tenderize the bird and add a delicious flavor. You may adapt **Quail in Wine Sauce** to duck with good results. The ducks will need a minimum of 3 hours cooking time when braised.

DUCK GUMBO
Nona Morriss

Serves 8

4 wild ducks, plucked, washed, and dried	2 quarts warm water
Salt and pepper	2 quarts chicken broth
4 onions, chopped fine	¼ cup Worcestershire sauce
4 celery stalks, chopped fine	Salt to taste (begin with 2 tsp.)
1 bell pepper, chopped fine	Generous use of black pepper and cayenne pepper
5 cloves garlic, pressed	¼ tsp. thyme
1 cup cooking oil (or bacon drippings)	½ cup fresh parsley, cut fine with scissors
1 cup flour	½ cup green onion tops

After ducks are plucked, washed, and dried, salt and pepper them generously and set aside. Chop onions, celery, and bell pepper, press garlic, and set aside. In a 5-quart cast-iron Dutch oven over low heat, make a dark brown roux using oil and flour. When it is just this side of burning, add vegetables and stir vigorously. Keeping heat low, cook and stir until vegetables seem to blend completely with the roux. Now add warm water, chicken broth, and Worcestershire sauce. Season with salt, black and cayenne pepper, and thyme. Taste. Place ducks in liquid, cover, and simmer for at least 3 hours, until duck is falling off the bone. Remove ducks, debone, and replace meat in gumbo. Add parsley and onion tops. Serve immediately over rice.

SMOKED DUCK DELUXE

Wrap cleaned ducks completely in thin-sliced bacon secured by toothpicks. When you have finished wrapping the ducks, very little skin should show through. Place in a smoker and cook 8–12 hours, turning occasionally, taking care that water remains in the pan at all times. It's a long wait, but you will have meat so flavorful it can be cut into pieces and served as a cocktail party tidbit as well as a main course. Served cold, it makes a superb sandwich on brown bread.

ROAST GOOSE WITH PEAR STUFFING AND SAUCE

1 goose, 7–12 lbs. (a 7-lb. goose
  serves 6)
2 apples, halved

2 stalks celery, quartered
2 onions, quartered
Salt and coarsely ground pepper

Preheat oven to 350°. Wash goose and wipe dry. Rub inside cavity with salt. Place ½ apple, 1 stalk of celery, and 1 quartered onion in the wishbone or neck cavity. Skewer the neck skin to the back and fold the wings behind the back. Stuff the rear cavity with remaining apple, celery, and onion. Skewer the cavity shut. Salt and pepper the goose generously and place on a rack inside a roasting pan with a lid. The rack is needed so that the goose will not fry in the accumulated grease. Cover pan tightly and roast 3 to 5 hours or until the leg joint moves freely. If the level of grease creeps up to touch the bird, remove it with a bulb baster. Uncover pan the last 30 minutes to complete browning. Remove stuffing. You should allow the bird to stand 20 minutes before carving. Save the legs for leftovers and cut the breast into paper-thin slices, each bordered by a strip of crisp skin.

  The stuffing which is served with the bird is cooked in a separate pan during the 30 minutes the goose is browning. The quality of the stuffing will be determined largely by the bread you use. A firm homemade or sourdough bread is recommended.

PEAR STUFFING

2 cups dried pears, stewed
2 quarts white bread, cubed
½ cup diced onion
¾ cup butter
2 cups chicken broth

1 tbsp. salt
¼ tsp. coarsely ground pepper
1 tsp. poultry seasoning
1 6½-oz. can salted cashew nuts

Stew pears in a small amount of water until soft, then dice fine. Meanwhile cut bread into small cubes. Sauté onion in butter, mix with the bread, and toast mixture in the oven until dry. Moisten with the broth, add seasonings, pears, and cashews, place in bread pan, and bake for 30 minutes at 350°. This is so good the second day, you can make it a day ahead and reheat it with fine results. Whatever you do, mix with a light touch. A heavy hand results in a sodden, brick-like stuffing.

SAUCE

Giblets and neck of goose
2 cups water
Salt and pepper to taste

2 tbsp. cornstarch
¼ cup water

While the goose is roasting, place the giblets and neck in a small pan and cover with 2 cups of water. Salt and pepper to taste. Simmer 3 hours, adding water as necessary. Just before you're ready to serve the dinner, strain sauce into a second pan, cut giblets fine, and add them to the sauce. Discard the neck. Bring sauce to a rolling boil and add the cornstarch moistened in water. Taste again and season to suit. Cook and stir until you have a clear, thick gravy.

PHEASANT MADEIRA

Serves 6–8

2 pheasants, cut into serving
  pieces like a chicken
Salt and pepper to taste
½ cup butter
2 medium onions, sliced thin

½ cup fresh mushrooms, sliced
  thin
1 cup Madeira wine
1 egg yolk, beaten

Preheat oven to 350°. Salt and pepper the pheasant pieces. In a Dutch oven, brown a few pieces at a time in the butter. Remove the browned pieces and set aside. Now sauté onions and mushrooms in drippings until the onions turn clear. Place pheasant pieces on top of the vegetables, pour wine over, cover, and place in preheated oven. Cook until tender—about 2 hours. Remove birds to warmed serving platter. Place Dutch oven on top of the stove and raise the temperature to boiling, reducing the sauce by almost half. Beat the egg yolk in a cup. Using a tablespoon, begin *slowly* spooning hot sauce into egg yolk, stirring all the time, until you have a cup full of hot egg yolk and sauce. (If the egg yolk strings, you have added the hot sauce too fast. You'll have to start over.) When you have a well-blended cup of hot egg yolk and sauce, pour this back into the boiling sauce, stirring vigorously, and cook and stir until it thickens like gravy. Place in a gravy boat and serve with the birds.

Remember that a pheasant is little more than a fancy chicken. You can adapt about any chicken recipe to pheasant, increasing the cooking time a little to account for the pheasant's tendency to be a little leaner and perhaps drier than his domestic plain-plumed cousin.

HUNTER'S BAGGED QUAIL

Darrell Staedtler

1 bird per person	Onion
Salted water with juice of 1 lemon	Apple
Cooking oil	Bacon
Salt, pepper, thyme, poultry seasoning	Small brown bags
	Cotton string

Preheat oven to 350°. Soak birds in lightly salted lemon water for 20 minutes. Remove birds from water and pat dry. Coat body inside and out with oil. Rub generously inside and out with salt, pepper, thyme, and poultry seasoning. Stuff cavity of each bird with a 2-inch piece of onion and a 3-inch piece of apple. Lay 2 strips of bacon (actually 1 strip cut in half) over the breast of each bird. Oil each bag inside and out and let the excess oil drip off. Oil an open roasting pan and place ½ inch water in the bottom to prevent sticking. Place each seasoned bird in its own bag, tie bag closed with string, then place the bags in roasting pan. Place pan in preheated oven for 1½ hours. Slice open bag and remove bacon, onion, and apple before serving. Good with wild rice and a crab apple.

QUAIL IN WINE SAUCE

Serves 6

This is a good basic game bird recipe which can be adapted to any variety of bird and will tenderize an old bird. In my kitchen it's called "old faithful."

½ cup cooking oil
2 medium onions, minced
2 whole cloves
1 tsp. peppercorns
2 cloves garlic, pressed
1 bay leaf
6 quail

2 cups dry white wine
½ tsp. salt
¼ tsp. pepper
Pinch cayenne pepper
1 tsp. chives
1 pint heavy cream

In a stew pot cook the onions in oil until clear, with cloves, peppercorns, garlic, and bay leaf. Add quail and brown on all sides. Add wine, salt, pepper, cayenne pepper, and chives. Simmer with a lid on the pot until tender (from 45 minutes to 1½ hours). Remove quail to hot serving dish. Strain sauce. Place sauce in saucepan and boil, reducing by half. Now add heavy cream and stir. Adjust seasonings. Heat to boiling and pour over quail.

This makes a thin sauce. If you prefer more of a gravy, thicken sauce with 1 tablespoon of cornstarch dissolved in ½ cup cold water. Pour in a thin stream into hot cream. Cook and stir until sauce becomes thick and translucent. The recipe begs for wild rice served on the side.

I have tinkered with this recipe a lot. Sometimes I use vermouth. Sometimes I use tequila. I have used doves instead of quail. If you use doves and tequila you can call it Tequila Paloma. You could also try it with Cornish hens or ducks.

FROG LEGS BRAZORIA

Serves 6

Frog legs are a delicacy we harvested from our Brazoria pond. On the spring nights we ran the trot line, we also rowed around the edges of the pond, silently slipping the paddle into the water and forcing the boat deep into the reeds, closer and closer to the sawing of the bullfrogs.

Since bullfrogs' eyes glow red in the dark, the best way to see them at night is to hold a flashlight up against your forehead. This keeps the light out of your eyes and makes a headlight, like a miner's. We probably looked pretty crazy gliding around that pond, holding flashlights against our heads and hunting for glowing red eyes at the base of the reeds.

And that moment of truth always came when the frog, mesmerized by the light, would stop his sawing. Then there was nothing to do but hold your breath. Would he jump? Would you get him? It is a moment of unbearable tension. Some of the biggest and wisest ones who had a particular territory staked out became familiar adversaries to us. Let's try the spot over by the willows, we'd say. Maybe tonight we can get old Granddad. But old Granddad would just stare back at us, those eyes glowing like coals, and hold his ground until the very last instant; then dive. We finally decided he owned the pond. We left him alone.

Here is a good way to cook frog legs.

12 good-sized frog legs, skinned and cleaned	½ cup flour
	Juice of 1 lemon
½ lb. unsalted butter	1 tbsp. minced parsley
2 tbsp. mild olive oil	1 tsp. minced chives
½ cup milk	Cayenne pepper
Salt and pepper	2 cloves garlic, pressed

After you have skinned and cleaned the frog legs, you may wish to cut the tendon that leads to the toes so that the legs won't jump around in the skillet. You may also leave it and ignore the wiggling toes. Depends upon your sensibilities. Heat 2 tablespoons of the butter and the olive oil in a 10-inch skillet. Season the milk with salt and pepper, then dip the frog legs in milk, then in flour. Shake off excess flour. Cook over medium heat, turning once, until browned on all sides, 10–15 minutes. Now add lemon juice, parsley, chives, and a dash of cayenne pepper. Put a lid on the skillet, turn heat down as low as possible, and prepare the sauce.

Place remaining butter in a smaller skillet, squeeze in the garlic, and brown the butter, stirring until it begins to smell like caramel. You will have to watch this every minute so that it doesn't burn. It's one of those things that you have to hold back on until the very last instant. Cook the butter until you think any moment it might burn, then whisk it away from the fire, and place the pan on a cold trivet to cool it quickly.

Place the cooked frog legs on a hot serving platter, pour the browned butter over, and garnish with lemon slices. Serve it with a rice ring and a simple green salad. I promise you, people will fall away from the table in a dead faint because it's all so divine.

CHICKEN-FRIED RATTLESNAKE

Every year on opening day we hunt doves with a group that includes two maniacs. They not only hunt doves, they also hunt rattlesnakes. And they don't even use a gun. They use a stick and a rope. They always take along some poor sucker who acts as bag man. The initiate has to hold open a croaker sack while these fools drop the live snake into the bag. Then he has to hold it at arm's length until they get back to the camp where they kill the snakes. Don't ask me how they kill them. I haven't the faintest idea. I sure didn't watch. These guys take the skin and make belts and hatbands and get paid a lot of money by other maniacs who want to wear such rigging.

Knowing that any Texas cookbook worth its salt had to have a recipe for rattlesnake, I asked these guys if they'd give me the meat. Sure, they said. The first one they brought over was about 3 feet long, all white meat and—this is the really disgusting part—the skinned, beheaded snake the maniac held in his hand was still coiling itself around his arm. When he dropped it on ice, it wiggled violently. I am going to cook that? I asked myself.

All night long I worried about that writhing snake in the ice chest. But sure enough, by morning it had gone into blessed rigor mortis. Now here comes the bad part. These guys thought I really meant business, so the next day they brought over the snakes they had killed that day—all skinned and gutted and in a white plastic bag. How many? I asked. Eight, they answered proudly. I nearly fainted.

I took the heavy bag and put it in the ice chest without even looking. I did promise them I'd cook the meat that night so we could all try it. One glance in the sack and I lost my nerve, a bundle of various-sized coiled white snakes. I couldn't face it. I shoved the sack into the refrigerator.

Finally, after 2 days, I took the sack out of the refrigerator and dumped the whole thing in the sink. Gads. I took a deep breath and a butcher knife and went to work.

Now you've all heard that rattlesnake meat tastes like chicken. The only chicken I've eaten that was as tough as a big snake came from a ranch outside La Grange. I will say this. The 3- to 4-footers which were about the circumference of a silver dollar were edible. The really big 6-footer, which was as thick as your wrist and had the most apparent meat, was as tough as the proverbial boot.

So, if you must, cook a young, tender rattler, not some old devil who has lived by his wits so long he's tough.

Here's what the boys told me about cooking them. Lay 'em out and look for black spots on the meat, cause sometimes when we're gittin' them out of the rocks they get excited and bite theirselves. So them black spots is venom. Got it? Cut out black spots. There was a little old lady up at camp this year who has spent so many years outdoors training bird dogs that her skin looks like saddle leather. She said she loves to sauté rattlesnake in butter with a splash of white wine. Frankly I couldn't look at that section of rib cage unvarnished, so I never tried this method. I knew if I was going to eat one, it had better be breaded. Asking all the good old boys and reading all the books I could find, here is what I came up with. How many will it serve? That depends.

1 3- or 4-foot rattler	Salt and pepper
1 egg	1 cup flour
½ cup milk	Fat for deep-frying

Cut the cleaned, skinned snake into 1- or 2-inch lengths. Combine egg and milk. Salt and pepper the sections. Place flour in a kid's lunch sack. Shake snake in flour. Now place snake in egg and milk mixture, then again in flour. Let it stand to set the batter while you are heating the oil to 375°. Deep-fry until golden brown.

Joe says there is an art to eating rattlesnake. The best meat is up against the backbone. He calls it backstrap of snake. There are a lot of tiny rib bones which give you an all too graphic reminder of the original shape of the snake, so Joe says to hold the snake in both hands with the backbone facing you, take a deep bite, get the backstrap, then suck the meat off the ribs. When I called nine-year-old Jay in to dinner, he rather enjoyed strutting past his city-slicker friends and taunting them. Wanna come to my house for a good snake dinner? They ran home faster than an invitation to eat liver would have warranted.

We had a big discussion as to what the snake tasted like. We knew it wasn't chicken. It wasn't quite frog legs. I don't quite know. Later somebody told me that if I had parboiled the big snake for 15 minutes in water seasoned with onion and garlic, it would have become tender. Frankly, I doubt that I'll ever get the opportunity to try that method. It isn't every day that one gets a gift of 8 snakes in a sack.

FRIED WILD TURKEY BREAST

Serves 6–8

2 whole turkey breasts	¼ tsp. nutmeg
½ cup flour	1 cup cracker meal
2 eggs	1 cup cooking oil
2 tbsp. water	

Cut the meat off the bone and remove the skin. Slice about ½ inch thick. Flour thoroughly. Beat eggs with water and nutmeg, then dip breasts in egg mixture and in cracker meal. Fry until golden brown.

ROAST WILD TURKEY

One of the primary differences between a wild turkey and a domestic one is that the wild bird has foraged for his dinner and run for his life. Wild turkey is inherently drier, darker, and stringier than his pen-raised cousin. This does not necessarily mean that the bird has to be tough. If you will observe a few basic principles of cooking, you can prevent that.

First of all your cooking temperature should be no more than 250°. Second, don't salt the surface of the bird before cooking. Rather, seal the surface in some manner, such as with a butter and flour paste. This will hold in the juices and insure a good final product.

Many people like to smoke game birds, and turkey can be prepared this way within certain important limits. Smoking a wild turkey by conventional means can be disastrous. Only if you can control the temperature so that it remains *below* 180° at all times should you attempt to smoke a wild turkey. Most commercial meat processors won't touch a wild turkey for this very reason. One processor in Kerrville told of the shock on a hunter's face when he looked at his shriveled, naked, bronzed smoked bird. The hunter accused the processor of switching birds. The true culprit was shrinkage—commercial smokers are too hot. Only if you have a smoker with a water pan and can build a very modest fire should you attempt to smoke a lean wild bird. It may take all night, but at least you won't have turned it into turkey jerky.

To roast the turkey in the kitchen stove, preheat oven to 400°. Place the cleaned dry bird on its back on a rack in an open roasting pan. Coat the cavity with softened butter, then truss the cavity and legs closed with string and skewers. Over the body and legs, spread a combination of 3 tablespoons butter and 2 tablespoons flour mixed until creamy. Place in preheated oven until the bird begins to brown (about 20 minutes), then immediately reduce temperature to 250°. Baste the bird every 20 minutes or so with a combination of ¼ cup butter melted in ⅔ cup water. When you have used all of this mixture, use a bulb baster to baste the bird regularly with the pan juices until the bird is cooked through.

If the bird seems to brown before the leg joint will move freely—an indication that the bird is cooked through—make a foil tent which will cover the bird loosely. Because of variation in the age of birds, it is difficult to estimate cooking time other than by moving the leg joint or pressing the breast to see that it "gives." A young bird might get done a full hour before a more mature bird. In cooking game you must learn to account for variables which never come with the supermarket meats. You must learn to look at the product itself, not just the clock or a chart.

This shouldn't cause too much of a crisis, however, if you remember that the bird should stand at least 20 minutes before slicing and up to 1 hour. Just give yourself plenty of time to prepare the bird—about 4 hours—and you shouldn't have any problem.

TEXAS PATÉ

If you are ever associated with a hunter, you will run up against several hard truths. The first being that the hunter will want you to make use of the game. All of it. The first time my husband presented me with an enormous quivering deer's liver I nearly fainted. What was I supposed to do with *that*? Fortunately, I had just written a piece on kosher cooking and had at hand a recipe for chopped liver. Improvising from that, I came up with this recipe, which will get rid of a large portion of the liver and tastes good.

This year when we were cooking cabrito, I tried the recipe using the liver of a goat kid. It was equally delicious. This paté won't freeze, so you'll have to eat it up pretty quickly, have a party, or give some of it away. That won't be hard.

½ deer liver (or 1 goat kid liver), roughly 3 lbs.
3 eggs
¼ lb. bacon
2 onions, chopped

1 fresh jalapeño, chopped
½ tsp. salt
1 tsp. coarsely ground pepper
2 slices bread
1½-quart fancy mold

Cut the liver into thin slices. Carve out any blood vessels and discard. Broil liver, 2 minutes on each side. Once the liver is broiled, wash and dry. Hard-boil the eggs. Now fry the bacon. Remove bacon and sauté the onions in the bacon grease. While onions are sautéing, run the liver through the food grinder, using a coarse blade. Now place the chopped liver in the bacon grease with jalapeño and onion mixture. Add salt and pepper to taste. Cook and stir over medium heat for 5 minutes. Peel the eggs. Remove liver, jalapeño, and onions from the grease and run through the grinder again, along with the hard-cooked eggs, bacon, and bread. (You may have to run this mixture through twice to get a nice fine mix.) Mix with your hands. Moisten the mixture with some of the bacon grease. Grease a mold lightly with bacon grease, letting excess drip out, press the liver mixture into the mold, and chill. Turn out onto a flat plate and serve with crackers—I like stone-ground crackers. Don't botch up the flavor of the paté by using seasoned crackers.

VENISON BACKSTRAP

1 backstrap serves 3–4

The backstrap is the choicest part of a venison carcass. It is equivalent to filet mignon of beef. You can treat it in much the same way.

Cut thick slices of the backstrap (about 1 inch). Wrap bacon around the outside and secure with toothpicks. Smear butter on the surfaces of the backstrap. Sprinkle with a dash of rosemary and cayenne pepper. Run the fillets under the broiler and cook about 7 minutes to the side. Best if served medium rare.

Many hunters like backstrap chicken-fried, but it has always seemed to me a waste of choice meat. It seems more appropriate to cut steaks from the shoulder or ham for chicken-frying.

BRAISED HAUNCH OF VENISON

Most of the deer from Texas are White Tail. Since the eradication of the screwworm, Texas deer have proliferated like jackrabbits and reduced in size until you may think you have an overgrown jackrabbit in your kitchen. An average deer may weigh no more than 80 pounds. I like to cook the whole venison ham or haunch, which usually weighs in the neighborhood of 10 pounds. There is never any fat on the deer which are brought to my kitchen, so I think roasting them is pretty hopeless. Braising seems to me the cooking method of choice. Of course, if someone showed up at my kitchen door with a nice fat Colorado deer, I might just roast that, but for those poor little fellows bounding in the South Texas bee brush, I think it's safer to braise. You don't want to ruin a three-hundred-dollar piece of meat (average cost of one hunt).

1 venison ham	Good handful of fresh parsley
½ lb. butter	½ cup mushrooms, sliced
Salt and pepper	2 bay leaves
4 yellow onions, sliced	1 tsp. thyme
2 stalks celery	1 cup dry red wine
4 carrots, scraped and cut in rounds	

Coat all surfaces of meat with soft butter, salt, and pepper. Place in a roaster on a bed of vegetables sprinkled with thyme, add bay leaves and wine. Cover and cook at 350° allowing 12 minutes per pound. If you are real persnickety you can stick a meat thermometer into the ham, taking care not to touch the bone, and cook to the desired measure of doneness. Rare roast venison is divine, but some of the good old boys will insist on having it well done. Once it's cooked, remove to a serving platter and make a gravy from pan drippings.

VENISON GRAVY

½ cup dry sherry
1 cup beef broth
1 cup sour cream

Place the roaster on the top of the stove, add sherry and beef broth to the pan drippings, and over high heat cook and stir until it is reduced by half. Strain. Stir in sour cream until smooth. Taste and adjust seasoning with salt and pepper.

Country Biscuits
Jalapeño Corn Bread
Country Corn Bread
Hush Puppies
Mexicorn Fritters
Five Spice Gingerbread
Raleigh House Blueberry Muffins
Sourdough Starter
Sourdough Biscuits
Sourdough Bread
Deaf Smith County Whole Wheat Bread
Swedish Rye Bread (Vörtlimpa)
Kolaches
Raleigh House Orange Rolls
Bread Crumbs

Breads

Making bread is one of the things Texans do especially well. From the good Central Texas bakeries that specialize in German and Czechoslovakian breads and pastries, to the tortillas of the Texas Mexicans, to the quick breads favored by ranch families, biscuits and corn bread, breads are well executed by Texas cooks.

Depending on the part of the state you live in, or grew up in, you may have access to good commercially prepared regional breads. But Texas is too big. You won't have it all. What I have tried to do here is give you a good sampling of the different types of breads and pastries that you can prepare at home.

In James Beard's superb book, *Beard on Bread*, he notes that all-purpose flour isn't the best choice for making yeast breads. According to Beard, the best flour is made from hard wheat, and one of the best areas for raising this wheat is Deaf Smith County—which just happens to be the county in which I was raised.

Frank Ford, a Deaf Smith County farmer who got interested in the natural foods movement years ago, owns a company known as Arrowhead Mills, which markets a good whole-grain, hard-wheat flour. It is sold in some grocery stores and in most health food stores. It makes a superior bread.

When it comes to corn bread, you will get a more nutritious bread with stone-ground cornmeal. This means just what it says: that the whole kernel of corn was ground between stones to make a meal. This differs from the commercial method in which a complicated procedure removes the main nutrients from the grain before producing a meal. In my experience, there is no difference in procedure when using stone-ground meal instead of regular meal as far as the way the recipe reads. You don't have to alter measurements in any way. Purchasing stone-ground meal is just a good habit to get into. You should buy fairly small quantities, as its shelf life is not as long as that of its cousin. Just buy what you need for 3 or 4 weeks.

One complaint I sometimes hear about untreated flours and meals is that they get weevils. It's true, they do. In the old days when my grandmother lived on a ranch and bought flour in 100-pound sacks, weevils were a constant. There was a standard method of getting rid of them. The good old-fashioned sifter works wonders. Weevils aren't cockroaches. They won't hurt you.

Another technique I learned was to freeze flours and meals. I can't swear this is true, but I was told that the eggs of weevils are in all flours and that if you freeze the product you simply kill the eggs. I have done it for years. I have even frozen flour after it had active weevils in it, then simply sifted them out. This may sound ghastly to you, but we all have to remember that pesticides are a fairly new invention and that our ancestors managed to survive in spite of these small pests. I don't think anyone would argue that weevils are the lesser of two evils.

Making bread is one of the more adventuresome things you can do in the kitchen. Yeast is a live thing. It may grow at different rates. You may make the same recipe 10 times and get 10 different loaves. There are other variables. The moisture content in flour varies—even in flour from the same sack from one day to the next. The weather varies. Your own mood varies. Bread making is a mysterious proposition. It's an art as much as a science. Part of its joy lies in the surprise.

There is nothing as rewarding as kneading dough. Granted, I have a dough hook on my mixer and frequently use that to do part of the kneading. But there is nothing like getting my hands in that dough, kneading it and patting it and feeling it and smelling it. The character of the dough changes so that I can watch it mature, so to speak, until it is as smooth and satiny as a baby's skin. And that wonderful aroma that pervades the house. Rising bread makes a house smell like a home.

There is no doubt about it. For most of us bread making is a luxury. Few of us are home long enough to go through the process that—although it takes only moments of active attention from time to time—requires several hours. I advise you to consider bread making a luxurious experience. I find it positively therapeutic to knead dough, to watch bread rise, and to see glistening loaves cooling on a rack. I love the process of making bread. It must be somewhat akin to the pleasure that potters get from throwing and firing pots. A golden loaf of bread is a work of art. It's kind of a toss-up as to who enjoys it most, the baker or the diner.

If you have never baked and want to learn the art from the beginning, go buy James Beard's book, *Beard on Bread*. I will only remind you of a few necessities before you begin.

1. Yeast is alive. You can kill it with too much heat. When you are dissolving dry active yeast, turn on the hot water and stick your wrist into the water. If the water gets hot enough to burn your wrist, it will kill the yeast. Just use water that feels comfortably warm. Cold water won't activate yeast at all. It's the same idea as heating baby's bottle. Just warm enough to feel good.

2. You cannot depend upon a hard-and-fast measurement for flour. You must eyeball it and add just enough flour so that the dough loses its stickiness. If you get carried away and add so much flour that the dough won't stick to itself, just hold the entire ball of dough under running water, shake off the excess, and continue mixing and kneading. You can add water and flour alternately several times without doing violence to the dough. It's all a matter of practice and of being alert to the amount of flour the dough will take.

3. Kneading is simple. Put the dough on a well-floured board, turn it over and over on itself, press down the flap with the heel of your hand. You'll see it change in appearance. At first it will look lumpy, but gradually will become smooth and elastic and beautiful. You may want to use a clock at first. I'd say a minimum of 5 minutes is always necessary when hand-kneading yeast doughs.

4. When you set the dough aside to rise, always place it in a bowl that is clean and oiled. Coat all sides of the dough with oil or butter, cover the bowl with a tea towel, and set in a warm, draft-free place. Heat rises, so you will usually have good luck if you set the dough up high in a room—unless you have the central air conditioning on, then you may find that placing dough in the oven with the door propped open and the light on works best.

5. After the dough has doubled and you have punched it down and formed the loaves, you'll find the second rising will take place quicker. If you go off and leave it, you can wind up with very dry loaves that are riddled with enormous holes. Some people like bread that way, but big holes in the bread mean that you have let it rise too long or too fast.

6. The length of cooking time can vary depending on several factors. How accurate is the thermostat in your oven? When I began the testing for this book, I purchased an oven thermometer for my range. I discovered the top oven was 25° hotter than the setting indicated and the bottom oven was 25° colder. I had the range calibrated. You don't have to do that. Just adjust the thermostat. But I do recommend the use of an independent thermometer. The second factor has to do with the bread itself. How much has it risen? What is the moisture content? What size are the loaves? You need to watch bread. When it turns an even golden brown, you can remove it, hold a tea towel in your hand, turn the loaf out of the pan, and knock on the bottom of it. It should sound hollow. A dull thud means the loaf is probably not quite cooked in the middle and needs a little more time.

Everything I have said about yeast doughs (and that includes sourdough yeasts) can be turned around when you are talking about biscuits. The main reason for doorstop biscuits is too much handling. You should add as little flour as possible to get the dough to a nonsticky stage. You should turn it out on a board and barely knead it three or four times. I don't even roll biscuit dough with a rolling pin. I just pat it out, leaving the center of the dough kind of sticky. The less flour you have in biscuit dough and the less handling the dough gets, the lighter and flakier the biscuits.

As for corn bread, it's the best, simplest bread there is. Just mix it up quickly. You don't have to beat it a long time. Any Texas farm wife can have corn bread in the oven in 3 minutes flat—and chances are she won't even use a recipe.

My final word on bread is this: please serve it with real butter. It makes me want to cry when I go into a Central Texas restaurant that smells so good and yeasty I think I'm going to swoon and they bring over divine homemade bread and serve it with pale, tasteless margarine. If you have gone to the trouble to make a decent loaf of bread, do the bread the honor of serving it with first-class butter. You'll be glad you did.

COUNTRY BISCUITS

Hazel Stalcup

Makes about 1 dozen medium biscuits

2 cups flour	¼ tsp. soda
½ tsp. salt	1 tbsp. baking powder
1 tsp. sugar (to make 'em brown pretty)	5 tbsp. shortening
	1 cup buttermilk

Preheat oven to 450°. Sift together dry ingredients, then cut in shortening with a pastry blender. If you want to do it the real old-fashioned way, mix it with your hands. This is a good sit-down job. You can even read while you're doing it. Make a well in the middle of the flour mixture and pour in buttermilk. With a fork, mix *very lightly*, just until the flour is thoroughly moistened.

Turn out on a floured board and knead just *2 or 3 times*. Pat out dough until it's about as thick as an ear of a prickly pear cactus (½ inch), then cut with an inverted drinking glass or a biscuit cutter. At this point you can freeze what you don't want to bake for this meal. Then just pull them out of the freezer 30 minutes before baking time. Bake in preheated oven 12–15 minutes on a pan well greased with butter or fresh bacon grease. I always turn them over once to mop their tops with oil.

JALAPEÑO CORN BREAD

Katherine Thurber

Makes 9 3-inch squares

1 cup cornmeal	⅓ cup melted shortening or bacon drippings
½ tsp. salt	1 cup grated Longhorn cheese
½ tsp. soda	¼ to ½ cup canned jalapeño
1 cup canned cream-style corn	peppers, drained, seeded, and
2 eggs, beaten	chopped fine
⅔ cup buttermilk	

Preheat oven to 350°. Stir cornmeal, salt, and soda together. Combine corn, eggs, buttermilk, and shortening and mix with dry ingredients. Pour half of the mixture into a well-greased 9″ × 9″ × 2″ pan. Sprinkle with cheese and peppers and add remaining mixture. Bake in preheated oven 30–40 minutes until the bread browns slightly and springs back at the touch.

COUNTRY CORN BREAD
Hazel Stalcup

Serves 6

3 tbsp. bacon grease	1 tbsp. sugar
1 cup cornmeal, preferably yellow	1 cup buttermilk, well mixed
½ cup flour	1 egg
½ tsp. *each*: salt, soda, baking powder	

Preheat oven to 500°. Place 3 tbsp. bacon grease in 10-inch cast-iron skillet and heat until almost smoking. Mix cornmeal, flour, salt, soda, baking powder, and sugar. Add buttermilk and stir well. Add egg and mix. Pour hot grease into batter and stir quickly. Test skillet with a drop of water. If it sizzles, pour batter into skillet. If it doesn't sizzle, reheat skillet on top of stove until piping hot, then add batter. Put into hot oven immediately. The top will look shiny. Cook it until the top looks dull (probably no more than 10 minutes). When you touch it with your finger it should feel firm. Now turn on broiler and brown the top. Serve immediately.

For Mexican corn bread, fry 4 thin slices of bacon and crumble into batter. To the hot grease add 2 tablespoons finely chopped onion and 2 tablespoons finely chopped green pepper. Sauté until clear, drain, and add to batter. Now add 1 seeded chopped jalapeño (preferably canned). Pour hot grease into batter and proceed as above.

Grandmothers sometimes put 1 cup of raisins which had been softened in hot water into the basic corn bread batter and served the bread with butter and syrup for a dessert.

HUSH PUPPIES

Makes 36

2 cups corn meal	¼ tsp. sage
1 cup flour	¼ cup parsley, cut fine with scissors
¼ cup sugar	
¼ tsp. soda	1 onion, cut fine
3 tsp. baking powder	2 eggs
2 tsp. salt	1 cup buttermilk
1 tsp. finely milled white pepper	1 tbsp. butter, melted

Combine ingredients and beat well. Drop from teaspoon into hot oil. Deep-fry at 360° until brown.

MEXICORN FRITTERS

Makes 12–15 fritters

2 eggs
½ cup milk
1 cup flour
1 tsp. baking powder

1 tsp. salt
1 tsp. cooking oil
1 12-oz. can Mexicorn (can use
    plain corn if you prefer)

Beat eggs, then add remaining ingredients, stirring well after each addition. Heat fat to 375° and drop by teaspoonfuls into fat. Deep-fry a few at a time until golden brown. Drain and serve hot with cane syrup.

FIVE SPICE GINGERBREAD

Makes 9 3-inch squares

½ tsp. salt
1½ tsp. soda
1 tsp. ginger
¾ tsp. cinnamon
½ tsp. allspice
½ tsp. nutmeg
½ tsp. cloves
½ cup shortening
1 cup sugar

1 large egg
1 cup molasses
½ cup sifted all-purpose flour
1 cup whole wheat flour
1 cup hot water
½ cup raisins
½ cup pecan halves
Whipped cream

Preheat oven to 350°. Combine first 8 ingredients and mix well. Gradually blend in sugar. Beat in egg. Add molasses alternately with flours. Add hot water, a little at a time, beating after each addition. Turn into well-greased, lightly floured 9″ × 9″ × 2″ pan. Sprinkle top with raisins and pecans. Bake in preheated oven 55–60 minutes or until a toothpick inserted in the center comes out clean. Serve warm or cold, topped with whipped cream.

RALEIGH HOUSE BLUEBERRY MUFFINS
Martha Johnson

Makes 1½ dozen

⅔ cup shortening
1 cup sugar
3 eggs
3 cups flour

2 heaping tsp. baking powder
1 tsp. salt
1 cup milk
1 14-oz. can blueberries, drained

Cream shortening and sugar until smooth, then add eggs one at a time. Sift together flour, baking powder, and salt, then add to first mixture alternately with the milk. Fold in blueberries. Fill well-greased and floured muffin tins ⅔ full and bake at 375° 25 minutes or until browned and done.

SOURDOUGH STARTER
Ruth Schup

Sourdough biscuits were the pride of the range. Cowboys had little use for what they called "bacon powder" biscuits, and they referred to light bread as "wasp's nests." The range cook's skill was measured by his ability to make sourdough. In the spring, after he had scrubbed down the chuck wagon with good strong lye soap, he began the process for sourdough which carried him through the whole season. In a 5-gallon nail keg the cook would make a mixture of water and flour to which he added a pinch of salt, maybe a potato, or a little vinegar. He stirred this mixture around, covered it with a piece of cheesecloth, and set it out in the sun to ferment. At night old Cookie would wrap the keg in blankets to keep it warm. On cold nights he might even take it to bed with him. If the yeast got cold it would quit working. The first batch was usually made just to season the keg and was thrown out after a couple of days of bubbling.

After Cookie was satisfied that fermentation was well under-way, he'd make a new batch, let it bubble a couple of days, and he was ready to go. The idea was to keep the process going, so he replaced the sponge he used in the biscuits with equal parts of flour and water, and he was all set for the season. Before long, the keg would have a dried coating of dough on the inside and flour splotched down the outside. Cookie swore this was a sign the biscuits would be the best.

He didn't bother with a biscuit cutter, but merely pinched off bits of dough, rolled them in bacon grease or lard, and cooked them in a Dutch oven over the coals.

Breads

As finicky as yeast is, it occurs to me that the bad disposition of a range cook might have been caused by his constant preoccupation with keeping the sourdough sponge warm and working. How would you like to sleep with a 5-gallon nail keg that smelled faintly sour and got little wads of flour dough all over your bedding?

I'm sure the story is apocryphal, but the tale of the flat-eyed cook who was praised for his sinkers credits the superiority of his biscuits to the bullfrog he kept in the sponge.

There are many ways to get a sourdough sponge going. Some people use milk and yogurt with flour. But a good approximation of the genuine cowboy version simply calls for water and flour, with dry yeast thrown in to guarantee a good start. You can make your own sourdough sponge this way. You may discover you aren't too keen on baking-powder biscuits after you taste sourdoughs.

1 package dry yeast
2 cups warm water (the same
    temperature as a baby's
    bottle. Test it against your
    wrist. It shouldn't feel hot
    enough to burn your skin.)
2 cups all-purpose flour

In a 1½-quart glass or earthenware container, mix together yeast and water until yeast is thoroughly dissolved. Add flour and mix until there are no lumps. Cover with cheesecloth or a piece of an old sheet. Don't use wax paper or plastic wrap. The idea is to keep the sponge clean but to allow airborne wild yeasts to get to the sponge and make the process work. Store in a warm, draft-free place. (I put this up on top of a cabinet—out of harm's way and where the air is warm and still. Can be a problem if you have central air conditioning.) The yeast won't work if the air is chilled. It will work well in the oven, door slightly ajar with the light on for added warmth. During the following 48 hours, stir the sponge a couple of times. You should notice bubbles forming and the volume should increase some (not a whole lot however; don't think it's failed if it isn't rising like bread). After 2 days you can store the sponge in the refrigerator. You may notice a clear liquid that separates out. Simply stir it back in. If, however, the liquid on top of the sponge is pink-tinged, throw it out and begin again.

When you use some of the sponge to make biscuits or bread, replace what you have taken out with equal parts flour and water, mix thoroughly, let it stand out overnight in the same warm place to get the fermentation going again before you refrigerate.

You will notice a pungent smell somewhat akin to leaves on a forest floor. Never add anything to the starter besides flour and water.

SOURDOUGH BISCUITS
Ruth Schup

Makes 1 dozen

1 cup flour
1½ tsp. sugar
1 tsp. baking powder
¼ tsp. salt

¼ cup butter, shortening, lard, or
    bacon grease
1 cup sourdough starter

Preheat oven to 425°. Sift flour, sugar, baking powder, and salt into a large bowl. Cut in fat with a pastry blender until mixture looks like bread crumbs. Make a well in the center and pour in starter. Stir with a wooden spoon until all flour is combined with the starter.

Flour a board and your hands generously. Turn out dough onto the board and knead just enough to make it smooth. Don't overdo this. Every extra motion toughens a biscuit. Pat the dough out to a thickness of ½ inch and cut with biscuit cutter or a small inverted glass. Place on a lightly oiled cookie sheet or in an oiled Pyrex dish. Oil dish with the same fat which you used in the biscuits (this depends on your preference). You can decide how you want the biscuits to look here. If you want them to rise the most, place them in the vessel with the sides touching. This will make a pan full of pull-apart biscuits. If you like crisper, thinner biscuits, mop both sides with fat and place them slightly apart in the pan. Now cover the pan with a piece of wax paper, place the biscuits in a warm, draft-free place, and set them aside for ½ hour to rise. (If you have a double oven, you can preheat the second oven to 150°, then turn it off when you put the bread in to rise.) Bake for 20–25 minutes in preheated oven until biscuits are lightly browned. Serve immediately, and pass the butter, please.

SOURDOUGH BREAD
Ruth Schup

Makes 1 loaf

1 cup sourdough starter
1 cup warm water
2 cups flour

2 tbsp. sugar
2 tsp. salt
About 2 cups flour

Place starter in a large mixing bowl. Stir in warm water and 2 cups of flour. Mix thoroughly. Cover with cheesecloth or old clean sheet and let it stand in a warm, draft-free place for 36 hours (more or less). Add sugar, salt, and 1½ cups of flour. Stir. Add more flour, a little at a time, until dough just loses stickiness. Turn dough out onto a well-floured board, flour your hands well, and knead for 5 minutes. Let dough rest for 10 minutes. Now shape into loaf, either round or oblong.

Butter all surfaces of loaf. Let it rise in buttered bread pan or cookie sheet in a warm, draft-free place for 1½ hours, or until the bread has doubled in bulk. Bake in a preheated 400° oven for 40–50 minutes until the top is golden brown. Cool on a rack. This bread will have a dense, fine texture and a delicate sour taste. Cut into very thin slices.

DEAF SMITH COUNTY WHOLE WHEAT BREAD

Estelle Elliston

Makes 2 loaves

1 cup canned milk	1 package dry yeast
1 cup water	¼ cup warm water
⅔ cup molasses	6 cups whole wheat flour
3 tbsp. shortening	Oil or butter to coat surfaces
2½ tsp. salt	

Heat canned milk and water to 160°. Add molasses, shortening, and salt. Stir to dissolve shortening. Set aside and let cool to lukewarm. Dissolve yeast in warm water and add to milk mixture. Work in flour and mix until dough begins to lose its stickiness. Turn out on a well-floured board and knead for 5 minutes. Grease a large bowl. Place dough in bowl, coat all surfaces with oil, cover, and place in a warm draft-free place to rise. When dough has doubled in bulk (about 1½ hours but don't rush it) punch down and knead on a floured board for 3–4 minutes. Shape into 2 loaves and place in greased bread pans. Coat all surfaces with oil or butter, place in warm, draft-free place, and allow to rise until double in bulk. Bake at 375° for about 50 minutes—or until loaves are an even brown. This makes a dense, coarse-grained bread.

SWEDISH RYE BREAD
(Vörtlimpa)

Makes 3 loaves

Two types of Swedes immigrated to Texas during the latter half of the nineteenth century and were instrumental in the development of Texas. Agrarian Swedes, led by a man named Swanson, settled in the village of New Sweden. From farming, the prosperous Swedes branched out into banking; one Texas Swede was an original board member of New York's Chase Manhattan Bank and another rescued Freeport Sulfur Company from bankruptcy and led it to worldwide prominence. In Texas City around the turn of the century, another distinct social class gathered. These were the fishermen who came from the rocky islands and inlets of the cold North Sea, some of whom dredged out the Houston Ship Channel.

3 cups stout or dark beer	6 cups rye flour
1 tsp. salt	3 cups white flour
¼ cup butter	Peel of 4 whole oranges, finely
1 cup molasses	chopped (remove any white
2 packages dry yeast	pulp before chopping)
1 tsp. sugar	2 tbsp. fennel seed, well pounded
¼ cup lukewarm water	

Heat stout, salt, and butter in a large pot. Add molasses and cool to lukewarm. Mix yeast, sugar, and water and let stand.

Sift 3 cups of the rye flour and 1 cup of the white flour into stout mixture. Beat well. Add yeast mixture, orange peel, fennel, and remaining flour, turn out on floured board, and knead well. Put back in pot which has been washed, dried, and generously buttered; cover with a damp towel and let rise until doubled in bulk.

Turn out on a floured board and divide into 3 parts. Shape into long loaves. Place on a buttered baking sheet and let rise until double. Prick all over with a toothpick and bake in a slow oven (300°) 30–40 minutes. When half done, brush with water to which a little molasses has been added; brush again when done. When cool, wrap in foil to keep crust soft.

KOLACHES

Makes 6 dozen

We can thank the Texas Czechs for kolaches. Lots of trouble but delicious. Organize the work this way: first make kolache dough and while it is rising the first time make the filling and set aside to cool. Make topping while dough is rising a second time and set aside.

1 pkg. dry yeast	3 cups flour
½ cup lukewarm water	1 tsp. sugar
1½ cups lukewarm milk	

Dissolve yeast in warm water, then combine with milk, flour, and sugar. Mix until smooth. Cover and let rise in a warm, draft-free place for about 45 minutes.

1 whole egg	½ cup shortening
2 egg yolks	4 cups flour
1 tsp. salt	¼ lb. melted butter
½ cup sugar	

Combine eggs, salt, sugar, and shortening. Add to risen dough. Mix well, then add 3½ cups of flour and mix well. Knead until smooth, about 5 minutes. Let rise again for 45 minutes. Now sprinkle on final ½ cup of flour and knead for 3 minutes. Spoon dough the size of a pigeon egg onto your hand and roll into rounds between the well-greased palms of your hands. Place on well-greased cookie sheets and flatten slightly. Press indentation in center of each kolache with your thumb. Brush with melted butter. Let rest 15 minutes.

FRUIT FILLING

1 cup dried fruit (apricots, prunes,
    apples, raisins)
Water to cover
1 cup sugar
4 tbsp. butter (½ stick)

Cook fruit in water until soft (12–15 minutes). Drain. Chop thoroughly and combine with remaining ingredients. Cook and stir over low heat until it begins to thicken like jam (15 minutes). Cool. After kolaches are formed and have rested 15 minutes, place ½ teaspoon filling in center of each dough round.

KOLACHE TOPPING

½ cup sugar
4 tbsp. butter at room temperature
½ cup flour
½ tsp. vanilla

Combine topping ingredients. Place ½ teaspoon of topping over the fruit filling. Let kolaches rise in a warm, draft-free place until double in size (about 15–30 minutes). Bake at 350° for 20 minutes until light brown. Remove from oven and brush with melted butter.

You can also use jam or preserves for the kolache filling. Just add melted butter to jam and mix well.

Kolaches don't keep much better than doughnuts so you must either eat fast, give some away, or store in airtight container; realize they become a little tougher every day.

RALEIGH HOUSE ORANGE ROLLS
Martha Johnson

Makes 36 rolls

2 packages dry yeast
1 cup lukewarm water
1 tsp. salt
⅓ cup sugar

⅓ cup salad oil
2 eggs, well beaten
4 cups flour

Dissolve yeast in water, then add salt, sugar, and salad oil. Beat eggs and add. Now add flour, a little at a time, until you have a smooth mixture. Beat until the dough is elastic. Place in a well-greased bowl, cover, and let rise in a warm, draft-free place until doubled in bulk. Form into rolls, place in well-greased muffin tin or cookie sheet, and allow to rise again. Bake at 375° for 25 minutes. Serve with **Orange Butter.**

ORANGE BUTTER

¼ cup frozen orange juice
    concentrate, undiluted
¾ cup butter
1 box powdered sugar

Cream together and spread over warm rolls.

BREAD CRUMBS
Peggy Vineyard

Here's how Peggy Vineyard makes bread crumbs.

Use any kind of bread that's left over: heels of white, rye, diet, pumpernickel, English muffins. Start saving old bread and freezing it for 3 or 4 months. Then take it out of the freezer and place it on a cookie sheet, 1 layer deep. Brush the bread with a little melted butter. Place it in a 250° oven and dry it out—about 30–45 minutes.

Now break up the bread into manageable pieces and crumble it into blender or food processor, a little at a time. Transfer crumbs to a bowl. Season with lots of Parmesan cheese, fresh or dried parsley, garlic, oregano, sweet basil, and a dash of celery salt. Taste and adjust seasonings until it suits you. Store in jars in the refrigerator or in plastic bags in the freezer.

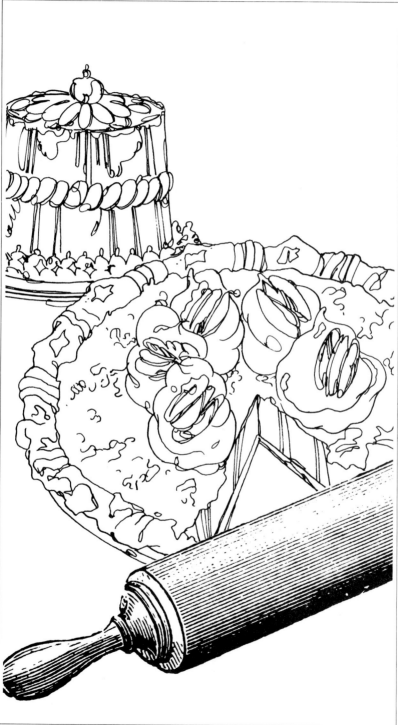

Lela's Special Cobbler
Dropout's Pastry
Buttermilk Chess Pie
Mustang Green Grape Pie
Dewberry Pie
Meringue
Chocolate Meringue Pie
Lemon Meringue Pie
Best Pecan Pie
Fudge Pecan Pie
Drunken Punkin Pie
Fresh Apple Cake
Mother Lively's Hickory Nut Cake
Benbow's Cold Oven Pound Cake
Caramel Icing
Sauerkraut Kuchen (Sauerkraut Cake)
Cocoa Buttercream Frosting
Buttermilk Bundt Cake
Fruitcake for People Who Hate Fruitcake
Texas Kuken (German Coffee Cake)
Sunshine Cake
Texas Prune Bourbon Cake
Plum Pudding

Pies and Cakes

Texas desserts are dominated by flour and sugar. Flavorings such as chocolate and fruit occasionally complement the primary ingredients. I suppose the basis for this choice has to do with the country itself. Flour and sugar were stocked in household kitchens in 50-pound sacks. The wild berries that ripened, the fruit that matured, and the extracts that could be procured from the grocer were then added and combined to make good sturdy desserts. But the cook had one constant on the frontier and that was dry staple goods.

The Germans and Czechs made the most of desserts, using their old-country recipes and their new-home ingredients. The Cajuns didn't seem to want dessert. The Mexicans favored candies—almost unbearably sweet. The farm wives who had an abundance of eggs perfected wonderful meringue pies and angel food cakes.

The choices in this section would all stand well alone. It seems to me that Texas cooks don't think of desserts as an element to be combined in a series of coordinated courses, but rather as some sort of separate event, perhaps best eaten in mid-afternoon with a cup of tea, and even then knowing full well that you won't be able to eat your supper.

BAKING WITH HONEY

You can substitute honey in almost any recipe which calls for sugar by cutting the amount in half. For example, if a recipe calls for 1 cup of sugar, simply substitute ½ cup of honey, shave ¼ cup from any other liquid in the recipe, and you're back to the ratio of the original recipe.

Another sweetener, which was used when sugar was rationed in World War II, is good old Karo syrup. Using Karo, you double the amount of sweetening called for. For example, if the recipe requires 1 cup of sugar, use 2 cups of Karo. Of course, you will have to halve the other liquids.

LELA'S SPECIAL COBBLER
Lela Jowell

Serves 8

In Texas, the word *cobbler* can mean a lot of different things. Essentially, it is a shortcut for a pie, combining a flour and baking-powder batter with fruit. You can use whatever fresh fruit or berry is available in the summer or, in the winter, some sort of canned or frozen fruit. If you are using fresh fruit or berries, simply wash, peel, and cut the fruit into large chunks. Measure out about 1½ cups of fruit (the quantity isn't crucial, just use what you have), cover with ½ cup of sugar, and let stand. Just keep the ratio the same: about 3 times as much fruit as sugar. Let the fruit mixture stand while you are making the batter. If you are using berries, leave them whole. If you are using canned or frozen fruit, simply lift them out of their fruit syrup with a big spoon and place them in the cobbler, allowing some juice to go with the fruit.

Certain flavors seem to go together, and you can jazz up the cobbler by adding these seasonings. With cherries, add a touch of almond extract; or try peaches and nutmeg; apples and cinnamon; dewberries, raspberries, or strawberries and a shot of lemon juice.

You can be inventive with a cobbler by combining two fruits: red sour cherries and apples, peaches and apricots, strawberries and bananas. You could also throw in some nuts: almonds with cherries, pecans with peaches, walnuts with apples. I'll bet you can come up with even better combinations than these. Be inventive.

This method of making a cobbler comes from one of my mother's friends who grew up on a Panhandle cattle ranch. God knows what kind of fruits they had up on that arid treeless prairie to begin with. But I like this one because it's easy, it's flexible, and it's pretty in the pan.

¼ lb. butter	½ tsp. salt
1 cup flour	½ cup milk
½ cup sugar	Roughly 1½ cups fruit, give or take
1 rounded tsp. baking powder	½ cup

Preheat oven to 400°. In the oven, first melt butter in a 10″ × 13″ Pyrex baking dish. Meanwhile, mix flour, sugar, baking powder, and salt. Add milk and mix well. Once the butter has melted and spread over the bottom of the pan, weave the batter into the pan, around and around, leaving spaces where only butter shows. Fill the spaces with fruit, piling it on, sugar or syrup and all. (About 1½ cups of fruit works well, although this is flexible.) Place cobbler in oven and bake until it browns on the edges and the sugar begins to caramelize in the spaces—about 35 minutes. Serve hot with cold heavy cream. Not whipped cream, just cream poured from a pitcher. The cobbler should be served in a bowl, not on a flat plate.

DROPOUT'S PASTRY
Shirley Barr

Makes 2 9- or 10-inch shells or 1 2-crust pie

I could never make a decent pie crust, no matter how broadly Betty Crocker smiled at me, until I found this recipe.

3 cups sifted flour
1¼ cups shortening
1 tsp. salt

Work ingredients together until consistency of meal. Sounds just like your old recipe, right? Here comes the secret.

Beat together slightly: 1 egg, 5½ tablespoons water, and 1 teaspoon vinegar.

Make a well in the flour mixture and add liquid mix. Work well, divide in half, roll out with light strokes from the center to the size desired. Easy to handle and flaky. Good.

If recipe calls for a cooked pie shell, roll out crust, fit into pan, prick pastry with a fork to prevent puffing, and bake at 475° 6–8 minutes or until brown. Otherwise, bake according to particular pie's directions.

BUTTERMILK CHESS PIE
Ora Calloway

Makes 1 10-inch pie or 2 8-inch ones

1 large or 2 small uncooked pie
    shells
½ cup butter
2 cups sugar
3 rounded tbsp. flour

3 eggs
1 tsp. vanilla
¼ tsp. almond extract
1 cup buttermilk
Dash nutmeg

Preheat oven to 425°. Prepare pie crusts and set aside. In processor or mixer bowl cream butter with sugar. Add flour and combine thoroughly. Add eggs, one at a time, beating well after each egg. Combine vanilla and almond extract with buttermilk and stir. Add to original mixture. Add a dash of nutmeg. Mix well. Pour into prepared pie shell(s), dust top with more nutmeg, and bake in preheated oven 10 minutes. Reduce heat to 350° and cook 35–40 minutes, until custard sets. It should be firm if you wiggle the pan. Good warm or cold.

MUSTANG GREEN GRAPE PIE
Minnie Junek

Serves 6

Snook, Texas, has a Czech heritage which combines with the native flora and fauna to produce good "gathered" pies.

1 uncooked pie shell in a deep
    dish
2 cups wild green grapes, English-
    pea size, stemmed, washed,
    and drained (seeds are soft
    and needn't be removed)

2 cups sugar
1 tbsp. flour
1 small can evaporated milk,
    undiluted

Place grapes in pie shell. Combine sugar and flour. Sprinkle over grapes. Pour milk over flour and sugar. Bake 1 hour at 325°.

DEWBERRY PIE
Marie Lewis

Serves 6

1 uncooked pie shell in a deep dish	1 cup sugar
2 cups dewberries, washed gently, stemmed, and drained	1 tbsp. flour
	3 beaten eggs
	¾ cup cream or canned milk

Place dewberries in shell. Mix sugar, flour, eggs, and cream. Pour over berries. Make topping and cover.

1 cup sugar
1 cup flour
¼ lb. butter

Mix sugar, flour, and butter to a lumpy consistency and sprinkle over pie. Bake 1 hour at 325°. If crust browns too fast, cover edges with foil until center is firm. Substitute other fruits for dewberries for an equally good result. Peaches are great.

MERINGUE
Cathy Abercrombie

For 1 pie

Here's how to make a foolproof meringue that won't "weep."
First, add sugar a little at a time. Second, spread meringue over hot filling.

3 egg whites	¼ tsp. cream of tartar
¼ tsp. salt	1 tsp. baking powder
1 tsp. vanilla	⅔ cup sugar

Beat egg whites and all other ingredients except sugar until foamy. Add sugar, 1 tablespoon at a time, while beating vigorously until the whites will hold a firm peak and are satiny looking. Spread meringue over hot filling, starting with small amounts at edges and sealing to crust all around. Spread pie with remaining meringue, making hills and valleys. Bake in preheated 350° oven until peaks are lightly browned, about 15 minutes.

CHOCOLATE MERINGUE PIE

Serves 6–8

I hate it when I find a more expensive product that is actually better. Last week I bought a tin of Dutch-process dark Jersey cocoa from Williams-Sonoma and discovered that it is superior to Hershey's. The chocolate pie I made bore no resemblance to those hideous Jello pudding travesties and was, I regret to report, even better than when I make it with grocery-store cocoa. The color was deep mahogany, the flavor—honest chocolate. If you plan to make an old-fashioned chocolate meringue pie, let me caution you to read the label on the cocoa box. So many cocoas now have sugar mixed in, and these cocoas won't make a decent pie. The other piece of advice I have regarding the making of this or any other pudding is that, if your life is really fractured, you can make the pudding in a double boiler, stirring from time to time. Then if the telephone rings or your kid scrapes his knee, you won't have ruined the pudding. But, on the other hand, if time is more crucial, you can make pudding directly over a low-medium heat; stir it *every* moment and you'll be done with the whole procedure in about ¼ the double-boiler time.

1 9-inch pie shell, baked	3 eggs, separated
½ cup pure cocoa, unsweetened	2 cups milk
¼ cup cornstarch	2 tsp. Mexican vanilla
1¼ cups sugar	2 tbsp. butter
¼ tsp. salt	1 recipe for *Meringue*

Combine dry ingredients in a medium saucepan and stir to mix thoroughly before you add liquids. Now add egg yolks (save the whites for the meringue) and milk and mix until there are absolutely no lumps. A wire whisk works well for this. When you place the pudding mixture directly over medium-low heat, switch to a wooden spoon and stir constantly until the pudding thickens and comes to a plopping boil. Don't get impatient and turn up the fire or you'll burn it. Remove from heat and stir in vanilla and butter. Pour into baked pie shell. Top with meringue. Bake at 325° until meringue browns, 15–20 minutes. If you get in a hurry with the pudding and remove it from the heat before it thickens completely, you will wind up with a tasty chocolate soup, a dessert that my son Jay calls Mount Saint Helen's pie. Not bad, but not pie.

LEMON MERINGUE PIE

Mary Elizabeth Barnard

Serves 6–8

1½ cups milk
1¼ cups sugar
¼ tsp. salt
1 tsp. grated lemon rind
4 tbsp. cornstarch
4 tbsp. flour

¾ cup cold water
3 egg yolks, well beaten
1 tbsp. butter
10 tbsp. fresh lemon juice
1 9-inch pie crust, baked
1 recipe for *Meringue*

Combine milk, sugar, salt, and lemon rind and bring to a boil over medium heat. Blend cornstarch and flour with cold water until free of lumps then pour in a thin stream into boiling milk mixture, stirring constantly. Cook and stir until thick, about 5 minutes. Remove from heat, cool slightly, and separately add egg yolks, butter, and lemon juice, mixing well after each addition. Pour into prepared pie crust and top with meringue. Bake at 325° until lightly browned, about 15 to 20 minutes.

BEST PECAN PIE

Emily Mickler

Serves 6–8

1 unbaked pie shell
1 cup sugar
½ tsp. salt
1 cup dark corn syrup

3 eggs, well beaten
½ cup butter
1½ tsp. vanilla
2 cups coarsely chopped pecans

Prepare the uncooked pie shell. Refrigerate.
Preheat oven to 375°. In a small saucepan combine sugar, salt, and corn syrup. Heat until the sugar dissolves. Meanwhile beat the eggs until foamy. When the syrup is hot add butter and stir until butter melts. Now add vanilla, chopped pecans, and eggs. Pour into prepared pie shell. Bake in preheated oven for about 40 minutes, or until a knife inserted in the filling comes out clean. Cool on a rack. Can be served with or without whipped cream.

FUDGE PECAN PIE
Linda Clarkson

Serves 6–8

1 unbaked 9-inch pie shell
½ cup butter
3½ tbsp. cocoa
1 cup hot water
2 cups sugar

½ cup flour
Pinch salt
1 tsp. vanilla
1 small (5-oz.) can evaporated milk
¾ cup chopped pecans

Melt butter in small saucepan. Add cocoa and stir to dissolve. Now add hot water and stir again. Add remaining ingredients except nuts. Stir with wire whisk to dissolve all lumps. Must be perfectly smooth. Add pecans, pour into pie shell, place in preheated 350° oven and cook until the custard sets—about 50 minutes.

DRUNKEN PUNKIN PIE
Ernest Coker

Serves 6–8

1½ cups cooked pumpkin,
    whipped
¾ cup sugar
1½ cups half-and-half
3 egg yolks
½ tsp. cinnamon
½ tsp. nutmeg

¼ tsp. ginger
Dash salt
3 egg whites, beaten stiff
1 9-inch pie crust, unbaked
Bourbon
Whipped cream

Preheat oven to 350°. Combine ingredients except egg whites, and then fold into beaten whites. Pour into prepared pie crust. Bake in preheated oven for 45 minutes. Cool slightly. When ready to serve, poke a few knife slits in each slice of pie and pour one scant teaspoon of bourbon into each slice. Then top with a dollop of whipped cream.

FRESH APPLE CAKE

Serves 10–12

This very old recipe for apple cake is one of those windows through which you can see the pioneers. Rural Texas women were practically magicians. They took the barest list of staple goods, augmented them with the desert's pitiful harvest, applied knowledge they brought with them from their native culture, assimilated information from their neighbors, and came up with a cuisine that has its own identity, is original, and is aesthetically pleasing. And that, you'll notice, is a definition for art. Who would ever believe that the common apple, along with the most ordinary ingredients, could be raised to such a level?

Of course, if I told my grandmother that she was an artist, she'd just snort. But being an artist is a way of seeing. It has to do with seeking beauty in whatever you see or hear or touch or smell or taste. It has to do with divining order in seemingly chaotic parts. If you have ever tackled a recipe that seems too hard, or too complicated, or too much trouble and had it all turn out right, then you have felt the sensation an artist feels upon completing a work.

Women used to know this intuitively. Back when the sheer maintenance of an even heat source was an accomplishment, women tried to outdo themselves in combining foods to produce new and aesthetically pleasing dishes. Granted, beauty is sometimes in the mouth of the beholder, and there were worlds of combinations that wouldn't stand the test of time, but it's the process that counts. The process keeps people searching for better, more pleasing combinations. That's art. It's also a fresh apple cake.

3 cups flour	2 cups sugar
1 tbsp. baking powder	1 cup cooking oil
1 tsp. soda	2 tsp. vanilla
1 tsp. salt	4 apples, grated (Pippin are best)
1 tbsp. cinnamon	1 cup pecans
3 eggs	

Preheat oven to 350°. Generously coat a Bundt pan with shortening and flour. Sift together flour, baking powder, soda, salt, and cinnamon. Set aside. Beat eggs, then add sugar and beat well. Add cooking oil and vanilla and beat well. Combine with flour mixture. This will produce a very heavy oily batter. Stir until completely mixed. Core (but do not peel) apples, then grate and add to batter. Stir well. You will notice that the moisture in the apples lightens the batter considerably. Finally stir in pecans. Pour into prepared cake pan and cook in preheated oven for 1 hour, or until the top springs back when you touch it. Turn out of pan immediately. Keeps well. Very moist.

MOTHER LIVELY'S HICKORY NUT CAKE
Clementine Lively

Serves 10

In East Texas, hickory nuts begin to fall 'long about October. Clementine Lively remembers autumn at her grandmother's river farm when a brick and hammer became a fixture on the hearth. Whoever sat down for a few minutes was expected to pick out nut meats. It was tedious work. There were smashed thumbs and tears. But when Christmas came the hickory nut cake stood proudly with mince and raisin pies, fruit cake, and date loaf candy, the traditional Christmas desserts in early East Texas.

1 cup butter	½ tsp. salt
2 cups sugar, sifted twice	1 cup milk
2 tsp. vanilla	6 egg whites
3 cups cake flour	1½ cups hickory nut pieces, dusted
1 tbsp. baking powder	with flour

Cream butter, adding sifted sugar gradually; continue creaming until light and fluffy. Add vanilla. Sift flour, baking powder, and salt together 3 times. Add alternately with milk to creamed mixture, ending with flour. Beat until smooth. Gently fold in stiffly beaten egg whites. Shake nuts in flour, add last. Bake in greased and floured 10-inch tube pan in moderate oven (350°) for about 50 minutes. Cool about 15 minutes before turning out on rack or plate. Serve without icing. You may substitute pecans or walnuts with good results.

BENBOW'S COLD OVEN POUND CAKE
Kathy Benbow

Serves 10

½ lb. butter	2 tsp. vanilla
2 cups sugar	3 cups flour
6 eggs	½ pint heavy cream

Grease and flour large tube pan. Cream butter and sugar. Add eggs one at a time. Add vanilla. Add flour and cream alternately. Pour into tube pan. Place in a *cold* oven. Set oven temperature at 325° and cook for 1 hour and 25 minutes.

CARAMEL ICING
Kathy Benbow

This recipe is over 100 years old.

For 2 layers:

2 cups sugar
1 cup butter
½ cup buttermilk

½ tsp. soda
Scant 2 tbsp. white Karo syrup
½ tsp. vanilla

For three layers:

3 cups sugar
1½ cups butter
¾ cup buttermilk

¾ tsp. soda
Scant 3 tbsp. white Karo syrup
1 tsp. vanilla

Combine all ingredients but vanilla and cook over low heat to soft ball stage—236°. Remove from heat. Add vanilla. Cool a little and ice cake.

SAUERKRAUT KUCHEN
(Sauerkraut Cake)
Emily Mickler

Serves 10

⅔ cup butter
1½ cups sugar
1 tsp. vanilla
3 eggs
½ cup cocoa
1 tsp. baking powder

½ tsp. salt
1 tsp. soda
2¼ cups sifted flour
1 cup water
⅔ cup drained, thoroughly rinsed, and chopped sauerkraut

Preheat oven to 325°. Grease and flour 3 8-inch cake pans. Cream butter and sugar until smooth. Add vanilla and eggs, one at a time. Sift dry ingredients together and add alternately with water. Mix well. Fold in drained sauerkraut. Turn into cake pans. Bake in preheated oven for approximately 30 minutes or until cake springs back at the touch. Remove from pans immediately, cool on a rack, then frost with **Cocoa Buttercream Frosting**.

COCOA BUTTERCREAM FROSTING

¾ cup cocoa
Pinch salt
2 cups powdered sugar

½ cup butter
1 tsp. vanilla
¾ cup whipping cream

Combine cocoa, salt, and sugar. Cream butter and vanilla. Add cream. Combine sugar mixture and cream mixture a little at a time, then beat 2 minutes at high speed with an electric mixer. Spread on cooled cake.

BUTTERMILK BUNDT CAKE
Sylvia Morrison

Serves 8

When Joe's mother used to come to our house to eat I always tried to outdo myself, because she had been a rather famous cook in the family and especially acclaimed for her marvelous renditions of San Antonio German dishes. No matter what I served, no matter how hard I worked, she would invariably turn to me at the end of the last course—even if it was flaming something or another—and ask in her always bland voice: Darling, could I just have a little plain cake now? This recipe falls into the category of a little plain cake.

2 cups sugar
1 cup shortening
4 eggs
1 tsp. vanilla
½ tsp. almond extract

1 cup buttermilk
3 cups flour
½ tsp. baking powder
½ tsp. soda
¼ tsp. salt

Preheat oven to 325°. Coat Bundt pan with shortening, then dust well with flour. Cream sugar with shortening until well mixed. Add eggs, one at a time, beating vigorously after each egg. Pour vanilla and almond extracts into buttermilk. Sift flour, baking powder, soda, and salt together. Add liquid and flour mixtures alternately to sugar and egg mixture. Beat 2 minutes after all ingredients are added. Pour batter into prepared Bundt pan and place in preheated oven. Cook at least 1 hour and 10 minutes. Cake is done when you press on top and it springs back. Turn out of pan immediately. Serve plain or dusted with powdered sugar.

FRUITCAKE FOR PEOPLE WHO HATE FRUITCAKE
Mary Elizabeth Barnard

Serves 10–12

½ lb. candied pineapple
½ lb. candied cherries
3 cups pecans

½ lb. pitted dates
2 cans coconut
1 can Eagle Brand milk

Stir to mix all ingredients. Pack mixture down firmly in a greased bread pan and bake 1 hour at 250°. Anyone will eat this. Even the most adamant fruit cake haters. Keeps for weeks in a tin.

TEXAS KUKEN
(German Coffee Cake)

Serves 10

1 package dry yeast
¼ cup lukewarm water
2 cups milk
4 tbsp. butter

⅓ cup sugar
2 tsp. salt
2 eggs, well beaten
4 cups flour (more or less)

Dissolve yeast in warm water. Combine milk, butter, and sugar. Heat just enough to melt butter. Cool to lukewarm. Combine with yeast, salt, and well-beaten eggs. Add flour to make a very soft dough; knead gently. Let rise in a warm, draft-free place until double in bulk (about 1 hour). Knead gently again. Spread thinly over bottom of a jelly roll pan. Top with **Streusel**.

STREUSEL

1 cup granulated sugar
2 tbsp. flour
3 tsp. cinnamon

¼ lb. butter at room temperature
1 cup chopped pecans

Combine sugar, flour, and cinnamon. Add softened butter to make crumbly mixture. Spread mixture thickly over dough. Sprinkle with chopped pecans. Let rise in warm, draft-free place until dough is light. (When you stick your little finger into the dough, it should yield and indent readily. Feels sort of like a baby's skin.) Bake at 350° 15–20 minutes until it is golden brown. Cut in squares while still warm.

SUNSHINE CAKE

Emily Mickler

Serves 12

If there is another way to go wrong on a recipe besides the ways I have gone wrong on this one, I can't believe it. Joe's cousin, Emily, has a reputation in the family for being a splendid baker. It's all true. Her grandchildren said I had to get the Sunshine Cake which Emily and her mother, Mimi, always baked for birthdays. She said, honey, it's easy. You just take 9 eggs, a cup of flour, an orange, 1½ cups of sugar. I said, don't you have it written down? Sure, she says, and pulls out the 1934 *San Antonio Public Service Manual for Homemakers*, and there on a blank page in Aunt Mimi's fine spidery hand is the recipe—sort of.

So I get it home. I know it's an angel food process. I know from eating Emily's that it's light as air. But then I try to follow the directions. I do everything wrong. One falls apart. One is heavy as lead. Another collapses. At one point, Jay calls it an Earthquake Cake. Those old recipes written for expert cooks were little more than a listing of ingredients. But after a lot of trial and error and gnashing of teeth, I have gotten this down into a form which makes it fairly easy and good.

I have thought about Aunt Mimi and Emily making this cake on a wood stove, beating the eggs by hand, grating off half their fingernails to get the orange rind. And we can't face life without the microwave.

9 eggs, at room temperature
1½ tsp. cream of tartar
1½ cups sugar

1 cup flour
Rind and juice of 1 orange

Preheat oven to 375°. Separate egg yolks from whites. Beat whites first. When they are frothy and foamy add the cream of tartar. Measure out half of the sugar (¾ cup) and add this 1 tablespoon at a time while beating egg whites. When the egg whites are ready, they should be white and glossy and hold nice firm peaks. Now beat the egg yolks until they look thick and sort of ropey. Juice the orange. Strain out seeds and add orange juice to egg yolks. Here is where I kept going wrong on the old recipe. You must use the rind of the whole orange, but just use the colored part. Here's how I do it. Cut off the yellow part of the rind and throw it in the food processor and grate. Or you can do it by hand. Combine grated rind with egg yolks and orange juice; set aside. Emily says to sift the flour and other half of the sugar 9 times. Can't you see the patience when time meant less than money? I have one of those so-called triple sifters, so I just sift it 3 times. You decide. Now you have 3 bowls full of stuff that you've got to get together without losing the air you've worked into each mixture. First pour about ⅓ of the egg yolk and orange juice liquid over the top of the egg whites. Using a slotted spoon or rubber spatula, cut in the liquid just until it disappears. Now sprinkle top with flour and sugar mixture (about ⅓ of it) and fold it in, bringing scraper across bottom of the bowl, up the side, and over. Turn the bowl and continue until just blended. Repeat until all egg yolk and flour mixtures are blended into whites. Don't overdo this. Extra movements cut out air. Carefully push batter with rubber scraper into a 10-inch tube pan that has been dusted with flour. Pull a knife gently through the batter to break up air bubbles. Bake in a preheated oven for about 45 minutes, or until the imprint of your finger bounces back when you touch the top. Now here is another crucial point. When you get this cake out of the oven immediately place it upside down and allow to cool completely before you touch it. I once loosened the sides while it was hot and the whole thing went down like an inner tube hit by an air gun. Another thing. Don't try this in a Bundt pan. Somehow it doesn't rise as well and it is impossible to get it out. For this cake you need a 10-inch springform angel cake pan. I've probably made this sound so hard you'll never try it, but honestly, it's not so bad if you just follow the directions. Needs no icing and the kids will love it.

TEXAS PRUNE BOURBON CAKE

Serves 12

1 cup prunes, cooked, cooled,
   pitted, and mashed (begin
   with about 1½ cups before
   removing seeds)
2 cups flour
1 tsp. soda
½ tsp. salt
1 tsp. *each*: ground cloves,
   allspice, nutmeg, and
   cinnamon

2 cups sugar
3 eggs
1 cup oil
1 tsp. vanilla
½ cup buttermilk
1 cup chopped pecans

Preheat oven to 350°. Barely cover prunes with water and boil in a small saucepan until they are plump, about 10 minutes. Remove from heat and set aside to cool. Sift together flour, soda, salt, and dry seasonings. Mix together sugar and eggs. Add oil and vanilla. Stir. Pit prunes and chop fine. Now add flour mixture and buttermilk alternately to sugar, eggs, and oil. Mix well. Stir in prunes and pecans. Pour into a greased and floured tube, Bundt, or ring pan. Bake 1 hour in preheated oven, or until cake is brown on top and springs back at the touch. Remove from pan immediately. Glaze while still warm with **Bourbon Glaze.**

BOURBON GLAZE

1 cup powdered sugar
2 tbsp. bourbon
Enough water to make a thin paste

Mix sugar, bourbon, and water together until it is free of lumps, then pour over warm cake.

PLUM PUDDING
Mary Elizabeth Barnard

Serves 20–25

English concoctions frequently catapulted onto the prairie in an almost pure state. This recipe for Plum Pudding came from my Aunt Mary's grandmother. Aunt Mary still cooks the pudding in cans that her grandmother gathered. She uses a sort of baking powder can the size of which is no longer available. She says you can use a Campbell's soup can or a big peach can and get good results.

The cans should first be seasoned. Once you get them going, you can save them and use them year after year. Aunt Mary's cans must be 75 years old by now. To season new cans, wash and dry them, then rub a small amount of cooking oil inside, and place in a 275° oven for 1 hour or so. Remove, wipe out the oil with a paper towel, and you are ready to make plum pudding.

Another thing Aunt Mary told me about the way her mother and grandmother made plum pudding is interesting. The first step calls for blending suet with flour until the suet disappears. In the old days, women would sit down, get a good book, and work the suet into the flour by hand, all the while reading the latest novel; after an hour or so, or probably when they got to a good quitting place in the book, they would combine the remaining ingredients. Of course, today you can combine the suet with flour in a food processor in 2 minutes flat. But you sure will miss a lot of good reading.

Aunt Mary had a little clipping out of the Amarillo newspaper glued onto her old flour-spotted recipe. The clipping said that in the eighteenth century plum pudding was known as "hackin" because its ingredients were hacked before being mixed together.

⅓ lb. suet, ground very fine	1 lb. raisins (2 cups)
4 cups flour	1 lb. currants (2 cups)
½ tsp. salt	3 oz. citron
3 well-beaten eggs	8 oz. mixed candied fruits
1 cup sugar	11 oz. candied cherries
2 cups buttermilk	8 oz. candied pineapple
1 tsp. soda	1 cup flour
1 tsp. cinnamon	
½ tsp. *each*: ground cloves, ground allspice, ground nutmeg	

First, thoroughly mix suet with flour and salt. You can do this by hand, or you can do it in a food processor. The suet should absolutely disappear. Now add eggs, sugar, buttermilk, soda, cinnamon, cloves, allspice, and nutmeg. Mix thoroughly. Combine all fruits with the 1 cup flour. You can best do this with your hands, too. The fruits are sticky, and the object here is to coat and separate each piece of fruit. Once the fruits are thoroughly coated with flour and separated, combine gently with the first mixture. Now grease and flour cans.

How many cans you use will depend on the size of the cans. At least 3 or 4. Fill each can about ⅔ full of the pudding mixture. Seal tops tightly with aluminum foil.

You will need a large pot to put the cans of pudding in for cooking. A turkey roaster with a rack inside works well; but whatever you use, rig up some sort of rack in the pot, fill pot with about 1½ inches of water, and place the covered cans on the rack without letting any sides touch. Now cover the pot and simmer gently for 3 hours. You should adjust the heat so that whenever you remove the lid, steam escapes; but there is no point in raising it to a hard boil or you will just boil the water away. Check the water from time to time and don't let the pot become dry.

After 3 hours remove the cans from the pot. Remove foil caps and let cans cool for about 10 minutes, then run a thin-bladed knife around the edge and slide the puddings out of the cans. Let them cool thoroughly, then wrap tightly in aluminum foil, and store in the refrigerator. The puddings will keep for months stored in this manner.

When you are ready to serve, cut as many slices as you want to serve and either re-steam or zap them in the microwave for a few seconds. Plum pudding isn't good cold.

You can make different sorts of sauces to go with them. Children like a lemon sauce: melt a little butter, mix in powdered sugar and lemon juice to make a thin paste, and pour over. Grownups may want their sauce flavored with rum or sherry.

Black Lebkuchen
Blond Brownies
Texas Toffees
Molasses Biscotti
Coconut Jumbles
Pfeffernuesse (Peppernuts)
Springerle
Eggless Buttermilk Sugar Cookies
Aunt Bill's Brown Candy
Piloncillo Pecans
Peppermint Candy (Polkagrisar)
Pine Nut Pralines
Swedish Hard Candies (Knack)
Toffee
Banana Fritters
Tres Sistres Ice Cream
Camp Stewart Ice Cream
Nanny's Prune Whip

Whenever I think of sweets I have to think about Christmas. In Texas, German cookies and English candies were made and swapped and given for gifts and eaten for weeks.

We used to sing Christmas carols in our Panhandle town. It didn't look like a Dickens Christmas, though. There was no snow. There were no velvet dresses. There were no ragamuffin children staring back at us. But there were plates of cookies to be passed and candies that made your fingers so sticky you thought you'd die before you got home. There were always plenty of volunteers to go caroling. I don't know if it was the Christmas spirit that made us all so willing to brave the frigid blast that came directly from the North Pole. I think it was more likely the promise of cookies.

BLACK LEBKUCHEN

Emily Mickler

At least 60 squares

1 cup dark molasses
½ lb. German sweet chocolate
6 egg yolks
3 whole eggs
½ cup brown sugar
½ cup soft butter
1 tsp. *each*: cinnamon, cloves,
   allspice, nutmeg, and vanilla

2 cups pecans, chopped and
   lightly floured
Juice and rind of 1 orange
Juice and rind of 1 lemon
2 cups flour
2 tsp. baking powder

Heat molasses and chocolate in top of double boiler until chocolate melts. Cool and add egg yolks, whole eggs, brown sugar, and butter. Beat well. Now add spices and vanilla and stir to mix. Chop the pecans coarsely and coat with a little flour. Add pecans to mixture. Grate only colored part of orange and lemon rind, then add juice and rind to mixture. Stir well. Sift baking powder and flour together, then add to mixture and mix thoroughly.

Grease and flour 2 cookie sheets with sides. Spread batter evenly over sheets in a layer ½-inch thick. Bake at 350° until barely brown, about 20 minutes. Remove from oven. Allow to cool about 10 minutes in the pan, then cut in small squares. You can sprinkle powdered sugar over the tops or you can ice with **Chocolate Icing**.

CHOCOLATE ICING

1 cup milk
¼ cup butter
2½ cups powdered sugar

½ tsp. salt
¼ cup cocoa
1 tsp. Mexican vanilla

Heat milk over low heat in a medium saucepan. Add butter and stir to melt. Sift together powdered sugar, salt, cocoa. Add to milk and butter with vanilla. Beat until smooth and thick. Spread on cooling Lebkuchen. Store in a tin with layers of wax paper in between.

Remember that any time you are storing cookies in a tin, you must allow them to cool completely before putting them away. Otherwise they will sweat in the tin and the texture will be ruined.

BLOND BROWNIES
Shirley Barr

36 squares

½ cup butter
2 cups brown sugar, packed
2 eggs
1½ cups sifted flour
2 tsp. baking powder

1 tsp. salt
1 tsp. vanilla
1 cup walnuts, coarsely chopped
Powdered sugar

Preheat oven to 350°. Melt butter over low heat. Remove from heat and stir in brown sugar until well blended. Stir in eggs. Sift together and stir in flour, baking powder, and salt. Stir in vanilla and walnuts. Spread in a well-greased jelly roll pan, 10″ × 15″. Bake in preheated oven for 25 minutes. Don't overbake. Sprinkle with powdered sugar and cut into squares while warm. Keeps well in a tin.

TEXAS TOFFEES
Martha Kavanaugh

Makes 24 bars

½ lb. butter
1 cup sugar
Pinch salt
1 large egg, yolk and white
    separated and beaten
    separately

2 cups flour
1 tbsp. cinnamon
2 cups coarsely chopped pecans

Cream butter, sugar, and salt (easy in a food processor). Add egg yolk and blend. Stir in flour and cinnamon. Spread mixture very thin onto well-buttered jelly roll pan(s). Spread top with lightly beaten egg white. Cover with chopped pecans. Cook in slow oven (200°–250°) until firm to the touch. This will take 45 minutes to 1 hour. When firm and slightly browned on top, remove from heat and turn out onto wax paper. Cut into bars *while hot* and allow to cool. Store in a tin. Will keep for weeks.

MOLASSES BISCOTTI

Makes about 36 cookies

The thing that drives me crazy about cookie making is that it takes so much time to form the cookies and the kids eat them up so fast that I usually seem to have a sink full of dirty dishes and nothing to eat all at the same instant. The Italians make a type of cookie called *biscotti* which is baked in the shape of a long skinny French roll, then sliced while hot. It takes a lot less time, uses one cookie sheet, and works. So when I got this good molasses cookie recipe that had one of those long-drawn-out procedures that included chilling the dough and rolling it out into little balls, I thought, what the hell? Why not *biscotti* this Texas recipe and see how it goes. Delicious and quick.

¾ cup shortening
1 cup sugar
¼ cup molasses
1 egg
2 cups flour

2 tsp. baking soda
½ tsp. ground cloves
½ tsp. ground ginger
1 tsp. cinnamon
½ tsp. salt

Melt shortening over medium heat. Mix sugar, molasses, and egg, and add hot shortening. Beat well. Sift together flour, soda, cloves, ginger, cinnamon, and salt; add to first mixture. Mix well. Form into 2 12″ × 2″ French rolls. Roll in granulated sugar (really cake it on) and place on an ungreased cookie sheet, leaving at least 3 inches between the 2 rolls. Bake in moderately hot oven (375°) for 10–12 minutes. Cut into slices while hot. This makes a bar cookie that is soft on the inside, hard on the outside. If you overcook these, they will be hard as rocks. The roll should be quite soft when you cut into it.

You can alter the spices to suit you in this recipe. Just taste the dough before you form the rolls. If the cookies seem too bland, dust the dough with more spice and work it in before rolling the dough into the baguette shapes.

COCONUT JUMBLES
Emily Mickler

Makes 48 cookies

1 cup butter
2 cups sugar
2 eggs
1 8-oz. package of coconut

1 tsp. vanilla
½ tsp. baking powder
2 cups flour

Preheat oven to 325°. Cream butter. Add sugar and beat well. Add eggs and beat until smooth. Now add coconut, vanilla, and baking powder and stir. Stir in flour until all flour disappears and mixture is well blended.

Turn out on a floured board and roll out to a ½-inch thickness. Cut into small squares or diamonds. (Use a knife instead of a cookie cutter. The dough is too soft to handle and won't hold a definite shape.) Using a spatula place the cookies on an ungreased cookie sheet, leaving a ½-inch margin around cookies. Bake in preheated oven 12–15 minutes, or just until the cookies brown well around the edges. Remove from hot cookie sheet immediately. Cool on a rack.

PFEFFERNUESSE
(Peppernuts)
Betty Hunt

Makes 14–16 dozen

1½ cups butter
1½ cups sugar
½ cup molasses
¼ cup brandy
8 drops anise oil
5½ cups sifted flour
1 tsp. baking powder

½ tsp. soda
2 tsp. cinnamon
½ tsp. cloves
½ tsp. finely milled black pepper
1 tsp. vanilla
Powdered sugar

Cream butter and beat in sugar. Add molasses, brandy, and anise oil. Sift flour with baking powder, soda, and spices. Add to butter mixture with vanilla. Line a 13″ × 9″ pan with wax paper. Pound dough into pan. You will have a pan full of dough at least ¾-inch thick. Refrigerate overnight. Invert pan on board and remove paper. Cut in 8 strips, 1½ inches wide. Cut each strip ¼-inch thick. You should now have cookies approximately 1½ inches by ¾ inches by ¼-inch thick. Bake on greased cookie sheets 10 minutes at 350°. Shake in powdered sugar when cool. Store airtight. Will freeze.

SPRINGERLE
Georgia Graeber

Makes 6 dozen

You've seen those funny looking rolling pins with the designs cut out in them? Those are for *springerle*. Some of our family have *springerle* molds that came from Germany. These cookies are a Christmas tradition with German-Texans. You might have to go to the drugstore for anise oil. Not all grocery stores have it.

4 eggs	**4 cups flour**
2 cups sugar	**½ tsp. baking powder**
4 drops anise oil	**Anise seed for pan**

Beat eggs until lemon-colored and thick. Add sugar gradually and beat for 15 minutes. Stir in anise oil and flour that's been sifted together with baking powder. Mix thoroughly. The dough is fairly soft. Chill in the refrigerator at least 1 hour.

On a well-floured board roll out dough ½-inch thick. Dust the *springerle* pin or molds well with flour and press firmly into the dough as you roll to make the patterns. Cut the shapes apart with a paring knife.

Now lightly grease cookie sheets and sprinkle lightly with anise seeds. Place cut-out cookies on sheets. You can put them close together. They don't spread out. The remainder of the dough can be pressed together and re-rolled and cut again and again until you've used it all.

Let the cookies stand overnight in a cool place. Bake at 300° for 10 minutes to set shape, then reduce heat immediately to 275° and continue baking for 25 minutes more.

The cookies should be light colored, looking almost as if they'd been iced. Store in a tin for 2–3 weeks to ripen. If you want them softer, put a cut apple in the tin.

Joe says when he was a kid they were always so hard they nearly broke his teeth out.

EGGLESS BUTTERMILK SUGAR COOKIES
Sophie Hohmann

Here is a German cookie recipe designed for when the hens quit laying. It makes a zillion cookies. You should roll them out as thin as is humanly possible—well, maybe not that thin, but thin—and cook them only until they brown on the edges. Kids love these cookies cut in shapes. If you're in a hurry, just cut them into squares with a knife. These are about the best sugar cookies I've ever found. Mrs. Hohmann, who used to keep Jay when he was a toddler, kept all the little kids happy with a never-ending supply.

2 cups sugar
1 cup butter
¼ tsp. salt
1 cup buttermilk
1 tsp. soda
5¼ cups flour

1 tsp. vanilla (You could vary this. Try almond. Or do as my grandmother did. Rinse the spoon in almond flavoring just before measuring in vanilla.)

Preheat oven to 400°. Cut butter into sugar, then add all ingredients and mix well. Roll out ¼-inch thick and cut any way you wish. Sprinkle tops with sugar. Bake on an ungreased cookie sheet at 400° just until edges brown, 8–12 minutes. Remove from sheet to cooling rack immediately.

AUNT BILL'S BROWN CANDY

I got into a terrible argument about the origin of this recipe. I thought it was my grandmother's. One of my friends thought it was her grandmother's. I guess we both thought there was some long-lost relative of ours named Aunt Bill. Turns out this recipe was in an Oklahoma newspaper 50 years ago and everybody wanted to be related to Aunt Bill because her candy was so good.

6 cups white sugar
2 cups cream (or half-and-half)
¼ lb. butter

¼ tsp. soda
1 tsp. vanilla
2 cups pecans

Place 2 cups of the sugar in a cast-iron skillet over low heat. Stir constantly until the sugar begins to melt and caramelize. When it has liquified completely, remove from heat. At the same time (this is one of those recipes where you'll wish you had 4 hands) cook 4 cups of sugar and 2 cups cream in a large stainless steel stewpan. As soon as the sugar has caramelized, pour it in a small stream into the boiling cream and sugar. Cook to soft-ball stage (236°). I always use a candy thermometer, because this syrup heats up faster than other types of boiled candies, and you don't want it to get too hot. The instant it reaches 236°, remove from heat (it helps to set the pan on a cool dish cloth). Add soda, stirring all the time, then the butter and vanilla. Cool until you can put your hand on the bottom of the pot. Beat with a wooden spoon until mixture is thick and dull. Add pecans and pour quickly into a buttered dish or onto wax paper. Cut into squares when cool.

PILONCILLO PECANS
Emily Mickler

You know by now that Emily is the best cook in the family. She knows a lot of things by heart and when she told me how to make this candy, it sounded easy. Emily has always lived in San Antonio and she picks up *piloncillo* the way you or I would pick up a loaf of bread. *Piloncillo* is that Mexican sugar cone that has such a distinct raw sugar taste. Emily still lives in the house her father built and didn't even have a thermostat on her oven until 4 or 5 years ago. When she said, cook just past the soft-ball stage, I knew I'd have to get out the candy thermometer. Well, as luck and bad organization would have it, I couldn't find the damn thing, so I just sighed and started out with Emily's simple directions.

First off it was Sunday, and I had my old conflict of interest that comes from the ritual of reading the Sunday paper. I started reading some boring analysis of the presidential election and burned the first batch of syrup so thoroughly that it set off the smoke alarm in the house before I even noticed. Second time I stayed in the kitchen. Like a lot of Mexican recipes, this one has the simplest ingredients and procedures, but does call for watching.

After looking at that burned pot, making the candy, and seeing a sticky mess on wax paper, I tore up Emily's recipe and threw it in the trash. This time you blew it, Emily. But after an hour or so, when the candy looked as good as any in a San Antonio Mexican restaurant, Jay fished the torn-up recipe out of the garbage and said, Mama, this is a winner. He's right. But watch it, and don't be discouraged by the way the candy looks when you first turn it out of the pot. It will lose its stickiness. It just takes time for sugar to crystallize.

1 7-oz. *piloncillo*	1 tsp. **Mexican vanilla**
½ **cup water**	1 **cup broken pecan pieces**

Over medium-low heat cook *piloncillo* and water to just past the softball stage (238°), breaking up the *piloncillo* as it softens in the water.

Keep a lid on the pan until the *piloncillo* has thoroughly dissolved, just removing it from time to time to break up the sugar cone with a wooden spoon. Once you have a syrup, keep the lid off and raise the temperature of the syrup to 238°. Remove from heat. Add vanilla. Tear a big piece of wax paper and place nearby. Add a cup of pecans to the mixture and beat until the pecans begin to separate, then drop by spoonfuls on the wax paper. It will still look kind of sticky. Let it cool thoroughly, and you'll have a wonderful praline candy just like they serve in Mexican restaurants.

PEPPERMINT CANDY
(Polkagrisar)

2 cups sugar
1 tbsp. white Karo syrup
1 cup water
2 tsp. vinegar

3 drops peppermint oil (never use extract)
Red food coloring

Mix sugar, Karo syrup, water, and vinegar in a saucepan and let stand until dissolved. Bring quickly to a boil and cook over low heat until mixture becomes brittle when dropped into cold water (275°). Remove from heat and allow to cool 4 minutes. Pour ¾ of the mixture onto an oiled baking sheet. Add peppermint and turn edges constantly toward middle with spatula. When cold enough to handle, stretch with oiled hands. Fold, stretch, and fold continuously until it loses its gloss. Then pull into 1 long strip and place on an oiled baking sheet. Color remaining candy red and pour onto baking sheet in 2 strips, 1 on either side of white candy. Twist strips together and cut immediately into different shapes with oiled scissors.

PINE NUT PRALINES

Makes 36 pralines

There are a lot of recipes for pralines. If you are feeling particularly flush, you might want to try this Panhandle recipe which uses pine nuts in place of pecans. Don't faint when you step up to the counter to pay for the pine nuts. They are expensive.

1 cup buttermilk
1 tsp. soda
3 cups sugar
4 tbsp. butter

1 tsp. vanilla
2 cups pine nuts (or pecans if you wish)

In a large stainless steel stewpan, dissolve soda in buttermilk. Stir in sugar. Cook over medium heat to soft-ball stage (236°). Remove from heat. Add butter, vanilla, and nuts. Stir to mix. Cool until you can comfortably hold your hand on the bottom of the pot. Beat by hand with a wooden spoon until the mixture loses its gloss, then drop quickly onto wax paper by the heaping tablespoonfuls.

SWEDISH HARD CANDIES
(Knack)

1 cup sugar
1 cup dark syrup
¼ cup butter

1 cup heavy cream
⅓ cup blanched almonds, coarsely
   chopped

Mix sugar, syrup, butter, and cream in skillet. Cook over low heat, stirring constantly until the mixture forms soft balls when dropped in cold water (236°). Add almonds and pour into small fluted foil-lined paper candy cups. Allow to set. Candies can be kept for months in a covered tin.

TOFFEE
Edith West

Don't try this with margarine. It costs a lot to use butter, but it's worth it.

2 cups butter
2 cups sugar
2 cups salted almonds, slivered
6 tbsp. water

2 tbsp. white Karo syrup
1 tsp. vanilla
8 oz. milk chocolate, melted

Melt butter in a large heavy pan. Gradually add sugar, stirring constantly. Add *1 cup* of the almonds, and the water and syrup. Cook over medium heat, stirring from time to time until temperature reaches 300°. Remove from heat. Stir in vanilla. Pour into a well-buttered 10″ × 15″ pan with sides. Meanwhile, melt chocolate in a water bath. (You know—a homemade double boiler. Some sort of Pyrex container set into a pan with 1 inch of water over heat. Doesn't even have to boil really.) Once you have poured the toffee into the buttered pan, quickly spread melted chocolate over the top and finish off by sprinkling remaining almonds on top. Some chocolates spread easier than others. I prefer Hershey's. Allow it to cool completely, then break into chunks using a small mallet or the handle of a knife. Store in a tin.

BANANA FRITTERS

Serves 8

4 large bananas	Juice of 1 lemon
½ cup powdered sugar	3 tbsp. dry sherry

Batter:

2 eggs	1 tbsp. sugar
2 cups flour	Pinch salt
1 tsp. baking powder	Oil for deep-frying
1 cup milk	

Peel and quarter bananas. Sprinkle with powdered sugar. Combine lemon juice and sherry and sprinkle over. Cover and refrigerate for 30 minutes. Combine remaining ingredients for batter. Dip bananas in batter and deep-fry at 360° until golden brown (about 3 minutes each). Drain on absorbent paper. Serve hot with powdered sugar sprinkled on top.

TRES SISTRES ICE CREAM
Emily Mickler

1 gallon

3 cups sugar	3 bananas, mashed
3 cups water	3 cups rich milk, cream, or canned
Juice of 3 oranges	milk
Juice of 3 lemons	

Bring sugar and water to a boil. Remove from heat and add orange juice, lemon juice, and bananas. Put into a jar in the refrigerator and chill completely—preferably overnight. Pour into the clean canister of your ice cream freezer, add milk, and freeze. If you let this fruit syrup stand overnight, the bananas in the ice cream won't be rock-hard. But you can make it the same day—the results just won't be optimum.

CAMP STEWART ICE CREAM
Kathy Ragsdale

1 gallon

Nowadays, I almost always find homemade ice cream disappointing and I wonder: why is it that ice cream doesn't taste as good as it did when I was a kid? I think I've finally figured out why. I went to visit one of our kinfolks on a July day in San Antonio. There was no air conditioning. It was four o'clock in the afternoon. Sweat dripped down my spine. She offered ice cream. Suddenly, it was marvelous. It occurs to me that ice cream is good in an inverse ratio to the heat. But there is ice cream and there is ice cream. Here is an authentic version that begins with a cooked custard. Kathy Ragsdale says it was her grandmother's recipe that she adapted to quell a mob of sweaty campers.

6–8 eggs	Dash salt
2 cups sugar	1 quart whipping cream
2 tbsp. flour	1 box ice cream salt
½ gallon warmed milk	Crushed ice
1 tsp. vanilla	Ice cream freezer

In a large saucepan, beat eggs until frothy. Add sugar and flour. Mix. Add warmed milk. Stir until sugar dissolves. Cook over medium heat, stirring constantly, until mixture coats a silver spoon (just before boiling). Remove from heat. Place pan in a larger container filled with ice water. Don't let water run over the top into the custard. Cool undisturbed in the ice water. Add vanilla, salt, and cream. Turn in ice cream freezer until frozen.

You can flavor this any way you please: chocolate, coffee, lemon, fruit. Just add the flavoring, tasting all the while, until it tastes about right—but make it strong. Remember that chilling calms down the taste buds. If you want to add fresh fruit, it's best to start the day before. To 2 cups of fresh, sliced fruit, add ½ of the sugar called for in the recipe (1 cup). Sprinkle the fruit with a little Fruit Fresh. Allow to stand covered overnight in the refrigerator. This makes a good fruit syrup and prevents fresh fruit from becoming rocks in the ice cream. Add fruit and syrup to the cooled custard and proceed. Don't forget you put 1 cup of sugar on the fruit. Make custard with 1 cup of sugar only.

NANNY'S PRUNE WHIP

Louise Ayers Stevenson

Serves 6

This is the sort of dish grandmothers used to make for children with sore throats. A lot of trouble but delicious.

First make a soft custard:

2 cups scalded milk	**⅛ tsp. salt**
3 egg yolks	**1 tsp. vanilla**
¼ cup sugar	

Heat milk over low heat until just below boiling. Beat eggs slightly in a bowl. Add sugar and salt. Stir constantly while adding to hot milk, very gradually. Cook and stir over low heat until mixture thickens and coats the spoon but does not boil. Add vanilla and chill. (If it curdles, you have overheated it. Don't worry. You can use a food processor or mixer to brush out the knots. If you don't wish to watch it so closely, you can cook it in a double boiler, but that is slower and means another pot to wash. Just be careful and don't let the milk scorch or even the cat won't touch it.)

After you have placed this in the refrigerator, make prune whip:

⅔ cup stewed pitted prunes (from 1 cup unpitted prunes)	**½ tbsp. lemon juice**
½ cup sugar	**5 egg whites**

Cook prunes in water to cover for 10 minutes. Remove pits. Run prunes through food processor for 10–15 seconds. Add sugar and a little cooking water. Cook for 5 minutes until mixture is the consistency of a marmalade. Set aside to cool. Add lemon juice. Beat egg whites until stiff but not dry. Fold in cooling prune mixture. Pile lightly into buttered 9-inch Pyrex cake pan. Bake 25 minutes in 300° oven. Serve hot or cold with the soft custard poured over the top. If served immediately it will be as dramatic as any souffle. High and golden brown. It will deflate as it cools, but it is still delicious. Cold it's as chewy as a Fig Newton.

Dilly Beans or Okra
Pickled Asparagus
Pickled Peaches
Mustang Green Grape Preserves
Perfect Strawberry Preserves
Peach Preserves
Fig Conserve
Peach Mango Chutney
Agarita Jelly
Prickly Pear Jelly
Jalapeño Jelly
Easy Oven Red and Green Hamburger Relish
Tomato Catsup
Argyle Chile Sauce
Pear Relish
Chimichurri Sauce
Green Tomato Chow-Chow
Jalapeño Pepper Sauce

Every year when I get ready to put up jellies, pickles, and preserves, I do my best to imitate the harvest. I don't raise enough
garden vegetables to make canning worth the trouble, so I usually make one trip to the farmer's market, get the produce I want,
and put it all up at once.

This year I made an elaborate list, waited until the moment
when I thought the harvest should be peaking, then took $40 and
went to the Farmer's Market. It's the one place I know where you
can haggle over prices and feel successful. There is nothing like
the feeling of looking through an enormous barn and choosing
just the very peck of tomatoes you want, then arguing with the
seller about its worth.

Forty dollars bought a lot of produce, about 8 bushels. When I
got home, I immediately set big pots of water to boiling on the
stove, began sterilizing jars, washing fruits and vegetables. In
about a 3-day frenzy, I filled up an entire 6-foot wide shelf from
floor to ceiling with brilliant jars of food for the coming winter.

It's just the sort of job I like. I like getting my hands into food. I
like the smells. I like the feeling of urgency that comes from
knowing that if I don't get on with it, the last bushel will rot. But
best of all I like looking at all those gleaming jars on the shelf.

When General Foods freed us from the necessity of making
strawberry preserves and homemade chile sauce, they also
robbed us of a justified pride in a very real contribution to the
family. I don't even know if it saves much money to put up your
own pickles and preserves, but I don't really care. I just like that
once-a-year task that pays me back all year.

A lot of people my age and younger express a fear that they
will poison their families with home-canned foods. It can hap-
pen, but is unlikely in foods with high sugar or high acid content. I restrict myself to these sorts of recipes. I am careful to
thoroughly sterilize the jars—to see to it that a good seal occurs
when the hot product cools in the jar and makes that satisfying
"ping" as the flat lid is sucked down by the vacuum. I refrigerate
and use first any jar that doesn't seal. Home canning is not un-
safe if you use common sense and follow the directions.

Before you begin putting up food, make this equipment check.
1. Do you have enough jars? Are the rims free of any cracks or
   chips?
2. Do you need paraffin? Lids and rings?
3. Do you have tongs or a jar holder to handle hot jars of foods?
4. Do you need a kettle to boil jelly? How about a canner for a
   boiling water bath?

Once you have all the equipment, you'll need to sterilize everything by boiling 20 minutes; keep it sterile.

A friend of mine runs jars through the dishwasher, then puts
inverted jars into a 10-inch stainless steel skillet. Pour a couple

inches of water in skillet. Heat to boiling and keep hot until you're ready to fill.

You can sterilize lids separately in another pan of water, then keep them in just-below boiling water until ready to use. You will need tongs to fish them out of hot water.

If you're making jelly, always heat paraffin in a coffee can set in a water bath. Never over direct heat or it will flame up.

Place a piece of clean old sheet or a square of flannel in a very small saucepan. Cover with water and boil. Wipe the rims of jars with this sterile cloth to ensure a good seal before placing sterile lids on the tops.

When packing fruits or vegetables in jars always allow at least ½" head space. Cover completely with liquid. This head space is necessary for expansion.

You will know the jars have sealed when the lids pop and remain in a concave position. This means a vacuum has formed and the food is safe. Any jars that don't seal must be refrigerated and used first.

WHAT'S A BOILING WATER BATH?

To preserve acid fruits or brined or pickled vegetables, you will need to finish the procedure with a boiling water bath. Here's how.

Use a pot with rack that can be filled with water to a level at least 2 inches above the tallest jar. Have at hand a jar holder or tongs to lift jars out of boiling water.

Half fill the pot with water and heat water to almost boiling. Lower filled and closed jars into pot. Each jar must stand alone, so allow 2 inches between the jars. Jars should rest on the rack. Now add more very hot water to cover jars by 2 inches. Be careful not to pour this water directly onto the jars or they might crack. Bring water to a full, rolling boil, cover, and process according to recipe directions. When time is up, remove jars from boiling water using jar holder or tongs and place jars on a folded tea towel or a wooden surface.

Leave 2 inches between jars and let them cool. Avoid drafts of cold air which might cause the jars to crack.

If you are at a high elevation, such as the Panhandle, allow an extra minute cooking time for every 1,000 feet above sea level.

SLIPPING SKINS

Slipping skins from fruits and vegetables is one way to hasten peeling and to prevent an excess loss of the fruit. Here's how it works. Bring a large kettle of water to boiling. Then add tomatoes, or peaches, or pears, whatever it is from which you want the skins slipped and allow to stand in the boiling water for a minute or so. Remove with a slotted spoon. You can tell if you've let them stand long enough this way. Pinch up the skin and if it comes free like a blister, then you can just pop the fruit away from the skin and you've got it. If the skin still adheres to the meat, then put it back in the water for a few more seconds.

If you are slipping skins on a vegetable that you wish to use raw—like a tomato—you will want to transfer the vegetable from boiling water to ice water. If, however, you are slipping skins on a vegetable that will be further cooked, then simply lay the vegetable out to dry.

I only slip skins when I'm dealing with a large volume. It's fast and economical when you are preserving fruits and vegetables.

DILLY BEANS OR OKRA

2 quarts

Use small, tender green beans for this recipe. I like the Blue Lake variety. Wash the beans carefully, removing the remaining blossoms but not the stems.

2 lbs. beans

In each quart jar place:
2 cloves garlic
3 small heads of fresh dill
¼ tsp. dill seed

2 quarts apple cider vinegar
1 cup water
1 cup uniodized salt

Pack beans equally into 2 quart jars. In each quart jar place garlic cloves, fresh dill, and dill seed.

Combine vinegar, water, and salt and bring to a rolling boil. Pour pickling liquid over beans leaving ½ inch of head space. Seal jars and process 15 minutes in boiling water bath. Let stand 3 weeks before using. Serve chilled.

The better the water the better the finished product will be. If you have soft water or pure bottled water, use it in any recipe for canning and the product will be improved. Never use iodized salt in a recipe for canning unless you want to taste iodine. Actually, if you want to go to the trouble, you can find canning salt at some specialty stores. It has none of the anti-caking agent that—to the real purist—also contaminates the flavor.

You can make dilled okra by substituting tender, scrubbed, young okra pods for the beans. For okra, you should add 1 hot, red jap pepper to each jar. You'll probably want pint jars instead of quarts to better accommodate the size and shape of okra.

PICKLED ASPARAGUS
Peggy Karren

7 quarts

Asparagus is one of those vegetables which costs a lot in the store, but almost grows like a weed in Texas. My grandmother had a permanent patch out on the north side of the house. My cousin Charlie has bounded his entire Dallas backyard with asparagus and rotates the picking so that he has a nice feathery fern hedge as well as fresh asparagus to eat for many months of the year.

Here is a way to preserve asparagus that makes a beautiful jar as well as something good to eat. This would make a great Christmas gift. It is naturally red and green and dramatic looking. Choose thin stalks of asparagus.

10 lbs. fresh, thin asparagus	2 tbsp. salt
6 flat white onions, sliced thin	3 quarts cider vinegar
7 garlic cloves, peeled	⅔ cup sugar
6 red bell peppers, seeded and cut in julienne strips	½ cup mixed pickling spices
	1½ quarts water (best if distilled)

Wash asparagus in cold water and drain. Into each of the 7 sterilized quart jars, put sliced onion and 1 garlic clove. Now pack asparagus, cut end down, alternately with red bell pepper to give a striped effect to the filled jars.

Boil together remaining ingredients, then pour over asparagus. Seal and process in a boiling water bath for 20 minutes.

PICKLED PEACHES

3 quarts

Chances are you don't have a peach tree out in your backyard. So if you decide to put up peaches, you'll be buying them. You may as well get exactly what you want. Peaches for the market are graded by size—so many to the box. Just like shrimp. The larger the peach, the more they charge for the box on the theory that bigger is better. But you don't need the biggest peaches. In fact, they won't even fit through the top of a Mason jar; so you can go for a smaller, less expensive peach and get a box of uniform-sized peaches that will fit the jars and won't cost nearly as much as the big ones sold in the grocery store. Size 70 is the ideal size to buy. This means there are 70 peaches to the 30-pound box. And although this is strictly a matter of personal preference, I like white-meated peaches for pickling, because the juice from a white peach is a clear ruby color and the visual effect is wonderful. Ask for clingstone peaches. If you decide to pickle an entire 30-pound box of peaches, multiply this recipe times 6 and expect 18 quarts.

5 lbs. clingstone peaches	1 tsp. whole allspice
1 tsp. whole cloves plus 1 clove per peach	1½ cups apple cider vinegar (50 grain)
½ oz. stick cinnamon plus 1 stick per jar	½ cup water
	4 cups sugar

Slip skins from peaches. Insert a clove in each peach. Make a cloth bag to hold remaining spices and draw up with clean cotton string. Combine vinegar, water, and sugar. Bring to a boil. Add spice bag. Cook peaches in this juice, a few at a time until fork-tender (no more than 5 minutes usually). As soon as peaches are cooked, place them in hot sterilized jars. Once you've cooked all the peaches, reduce juice by half. Pour over peaches. Place 1 stick of cinnamon in each jar. Wipe rim with clean cloth. Seal. Process in boiling water bath 15 minutes.

MUSTANG GREEN GRAPE PRESERVES

8 pints

The best way I know to get a supply of wild grapes is to hire a boat in the spring and float down a Texas river until you see vines. Don't be choosy in the field. Take every grape you can get your hands on. When you get home you can sort them. For preserves, pick out the immature green grapes with soft seeds that are still grayish green with only a bluish hint. Wash them gently, being careful not to break the skins.

4 lbs. green Mustang grapes,   **5 lbs. sugar**
    washed and stemmed but not   **1 cup water**
    seeded

In a large jelly kettle, combine water and sugar, stirring until sugar is dissolved. Bring the syrup to a boil and cook until it reaches about 220°. Now add grapes, a few at a time, cooking and stirring over low heat until the syrup looks thick. Skim foam from top and discard. Pour into hot, sterilized pints and seal.

PERFECT STRAWBERRY PRESERVES
Mary Elizabeth Barnard

6 half pints

Be sure at least a fourth of the berries are underripe so that there will be enough pectin to make the preserves set. My Aunt Mary swears by this recipe, which produces clear, claret-colored preserves with whole berries suspended.

4 cups (2 pints) strawberries
1½ tbsp. cider vinegar
4 cups sugar

Gently wash, drain, and hull the berries. Place in a 4-quart heavy pan and add vinegar. Bring to a boil quickly and cook rapidly, exactly 3 minutes. (Hold a timer in your hand. No room for error here.) Shake the pan from time to time so berries don't stick to bottom. Add sugar, bring to a full rolling boil, and boil exactly 6 minutes (by the clock). While cooking, shake the pan frequently in a circular motion to plump berries. Don't mash them with a spoon. When 6 minutes have elapsed, remove from fire, cover, and allow to stand overnight. Next morning, sterilize 6 half-pint jars, heat the preserves to boiling, and then pack in hot sterilized jars. Seal with paraffin. Store in cool, dark place to preserve color and flavor. This is an old Texas recipe in use for 100 years.

PEACH PRESERVES

4 half pints

If you have a peach tree, or access to one, and want to make up some preserves in small quantity as the peaches ripen, this is a good foolproof recipe for that. And the smaller the volume, the quicker the fruit preserves. Use peaches that are just beginning to ripen. Still firm. It's okay to put in an occasional soft peach, but if the whole pan of peaches is soft and perfectly ready to eat, you are going to wind up with a good grade of pancake syrup instead of preserves. Pectin is present in fruit when it is green, and pectin is what makes the preserves set. Also remember to place the fruit in a pan at least 3 or 4 times larger than the ingredients because this will boil up and could make an awful mess on your stove.

3 cups peaches
2 cups sugar
1 tsp. Fruit Fresh

Slip skins from peaches, remove pits, and cut into good-sized chunks. Make layers in a large heavy stainless or porcelain pan. For every 3 cups of peaches, use 2 cups of sugar mixed with 1 teaspoonful of Fruit Fresh. Layer the peaches and sugar in the pan, making no more than 4 layers (I'd say a maximum of 12 cups of fruit before it gets risky), cover and allow to stand for several hours while the peaches draw their own juice.

When you turn on the fire, keep it low until the syrup looks clear, then raise it to high and, stirring frequently, boil it until the syrup looks thick. The more peaches you have in the pan, the longer this will take. But it is better to use a high temperature and do a lot of stirring and get the syrup reduced quickly. Allow to stand about 5 minutes before you begin putting the preserves into jars. Stir thoroughly. This will help prevent the fruit from floating to the top. Pour into hot sterilized jars and seal with paraffin.

FIG CONSERVE
Marion Orgain

3 pints

Oh, those ubiquitous figs. I hate them. They're so bland. So mushy. So plentiful. You almost have to add some acid to them. Here is one good version.

4 cups peeled figs	2 tbsp. chopped candied ginger
4 cups sugar	½ cup chopped pecans
2 limes, sliced thin	

Combine figs, sugar, lime slices, and ginger and cook over low heat until some liquid forms. Then turn heat up to medium and cook until thick, stirring occasionally. When thick, stir in nuts. Pour into hot sterile jars and seal with paraffin.

PEACH MANGO CHUTNEY

12 half pints

1 large green mango (about 1 lb.)	Grated rind and juice of 1 orange
¼ cup rock salt	2 cups brown sugar
3 lbs. slightly underripe peaches	2 cups cider vinegar
2 cups raisins	1½ tbsp. chile powder
2 lbs. white onions, cut fine	2 tbsp. whole mustard seeds
⅓ cup finely chopped fresh ginger root	1 tbsp. salt
1 clove garlic, minced	1 tsp. cayenne pepper
Grated rind and juice of 1 lemon	½ tsp. ground cinnamon

Peel and seed mango. Cut into bite-sized chunks. Place in a colander, cover with rock salt, and let stand while you are preparing the remainder of the ingredients. Slip skins from peaches; pit and cut them into bite-sized chunks. Combine peaches with remaining ingredients in large stainless steel or enameled kettle. Now rinse salt from mango and add mango to chutney. Cook slowly, stirring often, until thick. At least 1 hour. Pour into hot, sterilized half-pints. All chutneys improve with age. Allow to stand for a month or so and see how it has ripened into a splendid sauce. Seal. Process in boiling water bath 15 minutes.

AGARITA JELLY

3 pints

The same people who call the Pedernales River the Purr-Din-Alice call the lowly agarita berry an *algerita*—as if it came from Algeria. But whatever you call it, the agarita comes from a South Texas bush.

It takes a lot of nerve to gather the berries. First you need a broom. Second you need an old blanket. And third you need courage. The way it works is this. When the berries are ripe and the sun is blistering, you go forth into the field with your broom and blanket. You find a loaded agarita bush. Gingerly spread the blanket under the bush, then whack hell out of it. Berries will fall on the blanket. Pull it out, take the berries home, and make jelly. The place where the courage comes in is this: rattlesnakes love agarita bushes, too. If you stick your bare hand up under the bush, you might disturb one. So I think the best thing to do is stick the blanket up under the bush with the broom handle and have a second person standing by with a .22 so that—just in case—well, you know. You can always shoot the rattlesnake and eat him, too.

2 quarts agarita berries
6 cups water

¾ cup sugar for *each* cup berry juice that you extract

Wash berries thoroughly, then combine with water in a large jelly kettle and simmer until berries begin to burst (just like cranberries). Continue cooking until berries lose their color. Place an old sheet or a jelly bag inside a colander, wet it, and pour the berry juice through into another container. If you want your jelly perfectly clear, don't mash the berries. Now measure juice and add ¾ cup sugar to each cup of berry juice. Cook and stir to 222°. Skim off foam as you are cooking. Pour into hot sterile pints and seal with paraffin.

PRICKLY PEAR JELLY

How you are going to get those prickly pears without being punctured like a tire in a sea of tacks, I don't know. It's hard. First off, I'd suggest you put on gloves. Not some silly flowery gardener's gloves, but some rawhide gloves. Second, I'd suggest you carry a pair of kitchen tongs to pop the fruits from the cactus. And don't wear tennis shoes, 'cause sure as you reach for a good one way in the middle of the plant, a spine will get your toe. Don't mention the rattlesnakes. They love cactus. And how can you tell which fruit to pick? The ripe fruit of the prickly pear is a nice reddish purple. You should pick a few which still have yellow or green streaks. Add them for the pectin so you'll have real jelly and not soup. Fruit ripens in early summer and stays good well into August.

Prickly pear cactus fruit	**¾ cup sugar per cup of juice**
Water to cover	**1 tbsp. lemon juice per cup of juice**

When you get your gallon or so of prickly pears in the house, just keep your gloves on and, using the tongs, singe the spines off the fruit by holding them over the fire. You can do this with an electric range as well as you can a gas stove. It's the same principle Grandmother used in getting the pinfeathers off the chicken. But you must examine the pears carefully because some of the worst offenders look like tiny hairs, but they'll sure get you. Once you've singed the fruit evenly, rub it with a paper towel and examine in a good strong light. This really isn't hard. Sometimes I have stuck an ice pick in the fruit to twirl it over the fire. That seems to be quick.

Only after you're sure all the spines are off should you take off those leather gloves. Now wash the fruit carefully, cut in chunks, barely cover with water, and simmer until the fruit begins to go to mush (about 20 minutes). Now pour pears and juice through a colander lined with a wet jelly bag (or an old clean sheet) and catch the juice in a deep, heavy pot. Don't twist the cloth if you want really clear pretty jelly. Measure juice. Using no more than 3 cups of juice at a time, bring the juice rapidly to a boil and boil vigorously for 5 minutes. Skim foam off. Now add the sugar and lemon juice, and boil rapidly until a candy thermometer reads 222° and until the jelly sheets off a silver spoon (Grandmother's way of testing jelly). Skim off foam while jelly is cooking. What if the jelly reaches 222° but when you try to sheet it off the spoon, it just drips? That means you don't have enough natural pectin. If this happens you can always throw in a box of pectin at the last minute. If the jelly sheets nicely at 222°, simply pour into hot sterilized jars and seal immediately with paraffin. Although I personally think this jelly is sort of flat-tasting, the color almost makes it worthwhile. Hold a jar up to the light. Doesn't that look like the bloom on a baby's cheek? Beautiful.

JALAPEÑO JELLY

8 half pints

Jalapeño jelly is sold in every tourist trap in Texas. It is of varying quality, but uniformly expensive. In my opinion, the secret to successful jelly of this type is the vinegar. If you use an apple cider vinegar, 50 grain, it will produce a tasty, tart, and clear jelly. I also have a personal vendetta against food coloring and would love to smash an artificially greened bottle up against the cash register. The natural green of the Jalapeño and bell pepper combined with the clear amber color of the vinegar makes a jewel-like jelly that needs no cosmetic treatment.

¾ cup green bell peppers, seeded
½ cup fresh Jalapeño peppers, seeded
6 cups sugar

1½ cups apple cider vinegar, 50 grain
1 6-oz. bottle Certo

Chop fine both kinds of peppers, then combine with sugar and vinegar and bring to a rolling boil; boil hard for 1 minute. Remove from fire, add Certo, and mix well. Pour in hot sterilized half-pints and seal with paraffin.

All jellies boil up to about 3 times the original volume. Be sure and use a good-sized pot or jelly kettle. Otherwise you may have a boil-over and the most horrendous mess since a good-sized Texas tornado.

When you add the Certo, stir for 2 or 3 minutes before pouring into jelly glasses to insure that the pepper bits are evenly distributed throughout the jelly.

EASY OVEN RED AND GREEN HAMBURGER RELISH

4 pints

I like this recipe because it takes no watching, no stirring, and leaves the stovetop free for other cooking. It produces a tart, bright-flavored sauce.

1 gallon ripe tomatoes, skins slipped and chopped
2 cups onion, chopped fine
2 cups green bell peppers, chopped fine
2 cups red bell peppers, chopped fine

1 dried red Jap pepper, crushed
3 tbsp. salt
½ cup sugar
1 tsp. cinnamon, ground
1 tsp. allspice, ground
2½ cups cider vinegar

Combine all ingredients in a large enameled pot and place uncovered in a 300° oven and cook until thick (about 6 hours). Stir once in a while if you think of it. Pour in hot, sterile pints and seal. Process in boiling water bath 15 minutes.

TOMATO CATSUP

4 pints

Given a choice between catsup and chile sauce, I'll take chile sauce every time. Catsup, to me, is kid stuff and treated with such irreverence that I hesitate to go to the trouble. But for those of you who are gluttons for punishment, here is an old Texas catsup—adapted for some modern equipment.

10 lbs. totally ripe tomatoes
1 red bell pepper, seeded and
    chopped
4 large yellow onions, chopped
1½ cups apple cider vinegar, 50
    grain
2 garlic cloves, crushed
1 tbsp. black peppercorns
1 tsp. whole allspice

1 tsp. whole cloves
5 sticks cinnamon
1 tsp. celery seeds
½ tsp. dry mustard
¼ tsp. cayenne pepper
4 tbsp. brown sugar
3 tbsp. white sugar
1 tsp. salt

Cut tomatoes in quarters and puree them in processor along with pepper. Strain puree through a coarse sieve to remove skins and seeds. (You can dump the puree into a colander and work it through with your hands until there is nothing left in the colander but a dryish pulp of skins and seeds.) Now puree onions, combine with tomato and pepper puree, and pour into large stainless steel or enameled kettle. Cook and stir occasionally over low heat until it is reduced by about a third and is considerably thicker. Meanwhile put garlic, peppercorns, allspice, cloves, cinnamon, and celery seed into vinegar in a small pot and simmer covered for ½ hour to steep spices in the vinegar. Pour about half the spiced vinegar through a tea strainer into the thickened tomato mixture. Stir. Also add sugar, mustard, cayenne, and salt at this point. Here is where the tasting comes in. You can adjust any of these ingredients to suit you. You can add more spiced vinegar. Or a little plain vinegar. More or less sugar, mustard, cayenne. Just sort of tinker with it. Cook it some more, stirring often, until it looks like catsup should look. Taste and adjust again. You may notice that it looks slightly curdled. Not to worry. Hit it a lick in the food processor. Smooths right out. I like to store this catsup in bottles I have saved from store-bought catsup. Fools the kids. Pour into sterile jars leaving ⅛ inch of head space. Process in boiling water bath 15 minutes.

ARGYLE CHILE SAUCE

14 pints

This is an enormous old recipe from the *Argyle Cookbook* of 1942. It may look like a lifetime supply to you, but you'll find more uses for it than you might first imagine. Tomatoes for a sauce don't have to be picture perfect. If you don't have a garden, you can go to the farmer's market and buy the funny-looking tomatoes that the grocery stores and restaurants don't want. Usually these will be quite cheap. A box of tomatoes is 30 pounds, so you can split a box with a friend, or make both sauce and catsup. Now if you want a really perfect product you can slip the skins on the tomatoes, but when I faced 15 pounds of tomatoes, I decided to hell with it. I'll admit, the sauce would look better without skins, but weighed against time it wasn't worth it to me. I just cored and quartered the tomatoes, ran the onions and peppers through the fine slicer of the food processor, got in elbow-deep mixing it with my hands, and let 'er rip.

I also discovered that an old sock makes a good spice bag. Just cut the sock in half, put the spices down in the toe, tie it up with clean cotton string, and throw the whole thing away when you are finished.

Once I had all the vegetables cut up and ready to cook, I thought: this recipe is just too big, but in comparing it to other chile sauce recipes, it has such a wonderful undercarriage to it that I had to include it in the book. But I do warn you. It takes a large canning container to hold the ingredients and it cooks all day.

15 lbs. ripe tomatoes, cored and quartered	2 pints vinegar
12 large white onions, cut fine	4 cups sugar
12 large green and red peppers, cut fine	

Tie in a bag the following spices:

2 tbsp. celery seed	1 tbsp. mace
2 tbsp. whole cloves	4 tbsp. peppercorns
4 tbsp. whole allspice	2 dried red Jap peppers, crushed
2 large sticks cinnamon	½ cup salt

Cook slowly in uncovered kettle until thick. As it thickens, stir more often. Reduces in volume to about ¼ the original. Seal in hot, sterile jars. Process in boiling water bath 15 minutes.

Good for Thousand Island dressing or Swiss steak or stuffed bell peppers. Just any place you'd use tomato sauce and spices.

PEAR RELISH

12 pints

Here's a relish that tastes like bread and butter pickles. It is marvelous with a hot dog or knackwurst, beautiful on the shelf because the turmeric gives it that brilliant golden color, and ages well. It is much better 3 months after you put it up than it was the first week. Use Kieffer or old field pears, and choose pears that are full-sized but still hard.

12 good-sized hard pears, peeled and cut fine in processor or run through grinder	4 cups sweet red bell peppers, seeded and cut fine
4 cups onions, cut fine or ground	4 cups white sugar
4 cups green bell pepper, seeded and cut fine	6 tbsp. powdered mustard
	2 tbsp. powdered turmeric
½ cup jalapeño peppers, seeded and cut fine	5 tbsp. salt
	2 quarts apple cider vinegar
	Cayenne pepper to taste

Mix pears, onions, and peppers in a colander. Drain, but do not squeeze. Place in a deep enameled kettle. Add remaining ingredients except cayenne. Place over low heat and bring to a slow boil, stirring occasionally. Cook for 30 minutes, stirring from time to time. Remove from heat and add cayenne pepper to taste. Seal in hot sterile pints. Process in boiling water bath 15 minutes.

CHIMICHURRI SAUCE

1 cup

Here's a great meat sauce to serve with cold pork loin, venison, or lamb. It's a pungent yellow and green color and gives a Latin accent to roasts.

¼ cup fresh parsley	1 tsp. oregano
½ medium white onion	¼ tsp. cayenne pepper
1 garlic clove	1½ tsp. salt
1 tsp. coarsely ground black pepper	¼ cup wine vinegar
	½ cup mild olive oil

Combine all ingredients, one at a time and in order, in a food processor or blender. Store in refrigerator in covered jar. Let the sauce steep at least 1 hour before serving.

GREEN TOMATO CHOW-CHOW

8 quarts

First time I ever heard of chow-chow was at Aunt Zula's. We used to drive down to visit her farm near Dimmit. It was a long trip. (In retrospect I'd estimate 25 miles). Daddy would try to keep me still in the car by playing a game to see who would be the first to spot the tiny towns and hamlets along the way. Since the country is perfectly flat and treeless, it would seem easy enough. But big farms could fool you. Anyway, the first one to see the town would sing out:

"Ain't no town and it ain't no city. Just a little place called Diddie-wa-Diddie." Then you got to guess the name of the town. If you were right, the loser had to give you a yankee dime which anybody knows is a good sweet kiss.

Aunt Zula's farm dinners were staggering. There would be pork roast and apple sauce. Sweet potatoes and quart-sized glasses of sweet iced tea. I always ran the word chow-chow around in my head. Why that tart brilliant condiment had such a name I could never figure out. Once, when I asked Aunt Zula's husband, Uncle Clem, about the name he grabbed my arm and pretended to eat me up saying chow-chow, chow-chow. Everybody laughed. Everybody but me, that is.

When we would drive home, stuffed, sleepy and satisfied, Daddy would usually say, "Mother, my pants feel tighter than Dick's hatband." To which she replied, "Amen."

1 gallon green tomatoes	6 red bell peppers
½ gallon small white boiling onions	1 head cauliflower
12 green bell peppers	Water
6 jalapeños	2 cups salt

Cut vegetables into the largest container you can find (I use an enameled canner). Cover with water and salt and let stand overnight. Next morning, over medium heat, cook and stir until it reaches a boil (takes a while), then boil for 3 minutes. Remove from heat. Now clean out your kitchen sink thoroughly (this makes an enormous potful of stuff) and pour the vegetables into the perfectly clean sink. Rinse vegetables with hot water 5 times then drain thoroughly.

Meanwhile sterilize 8 quarts and begin making dressing.

2 quarts 50-grain apple cider vinegar	5 cups granulated sugar
5 tbsp. ground mustard	1 tbsp. celery seed
5 tbsp. turmeric	1 tbsp. mustard seed
6 tbsp. flour	2 cups water

Combine dressing ingredients until lump-free in a large stainless steel or enameled pot. Raise to a boil, then cook and stir until it is creamy. Remove from heat. Using a large slotted spoon, fill the hot sterile quarts with vegetables, leave ½ inch of head space, then fill with dressing. Seal immediately. Process in a boiling water bath for 15 minutes.

JALAPEÑO PEPPER SAUCE

4 pints

5 yellow onions, chopped	1 cup sugar
2 bell peppers, chopped	1 cup vinegar
12 dead-ripe tomatoes, peeled and chopped	½ cup mild oil
	1 cup water
6 garlic cloves, pressed	4 tbsp. salt
¾ cup Jalapeño peppers, seeded and chopped	4 tsp. coarsely ground black pepper

Combine all ingredients. Cook and stir occasionally over low heat in an uncovered stainless steel or enameled pot until thick, at least 3 hours. Skim any floating oil from top before pouring into jars. Pour into hot sterilized pints and seal. Process in boiling water bath 15 minutes.

INDEX

S